STEADY-STATE ECONOMICS

STEADY-STATE ECONOMICS

THE ECONOMICS OF BIOPHYSICAL EQUILIBRIUM AND MORAL GROWTH

HERMAN E. DALY
LOUISIANA STATE UNIVERSITY

W. H. FREEMAN AND COMPANY
San Francisco

I am grateful to the following journals for permission to use material from previously published articles: *American Journal of Agricultural Economics,* "In Defense of a Steady-State Economy," December 1972, 945–954; *Journal of the American Institute of Planners,* "Energy Demand Forecasting: Prediction or Planning?" January 1976, 4–15; *The Developing Economies,* "The Developing Economies and the Steady State," September 1975, 231–242; *Population Studies,* "A Marxian-Malthusian View of Poverty and Development," March 1971, 25–37; *Revista Interamericana/Review,* "Three Views of Current Brazilian Economic Development," Summer 1975, 250–257.

Library of Congress Cataloging in Publication Data

Daly, Herman E
    Steady-state economics.

    Includes index.
    1. Economic development.   2. Stagnation
(Economics)   I. Title.
HD82.D31415   338.9   77-8264
ISBN 0-7167-0186-3
ISBN 0-7167-0185-5 pbk.

Printed in the United States of America

1 2 3 4 5 6 7 8 9

To Marcia, Theresa, and Karen

CONTENTS

PREFACE

Part I of this volume is a positive, expository development of the idea of a steady-state economy. What is it? Why is it both necessary and desirable? Why is it efficient? How could it be attained starting from historically given initial conditions? Part I constructively sets forth the thesis as clearly as possible, without getting sidetracked by polemics.

The antithesis of the steady-state economy is the growth economy, which is still defended by a large majority of economists and politicians. Part II enters the polemics of the growth debate, seeking to clear the road to the steady state of the detritus of obfuscations, non sequiturs, and assorted other fallacies, and to defend the steady-state view from the loud but badly aimed cannonades of the partisans of the current growth economy. The aim of Part II is enlightenment through controversy. Controversy is most enlightening when dealing with the specific views of specific people. Hence I have named names and cited works, rather than argued against an unspecified aggregate "progrowth critic," who could easily turn into a straw man. It would be easy to lump divergent progrowth arguments into one conglomerate and then expose this composite position to criticism and to ridicule the inconsistencies that naturally result when different positions are merged and treated as if the merger had been the product of a single mind. Leaving individuals anonymous usually passes as scholarly abhorrence of polemics. More often, the merciful anonymity granted toward one's soon-to-be-vanquished adversary is nothing but a lazy preference for debating mute straw men rather than real people. Therefore, I hope that my disagreements with specific spokesmen of economic orthodoxy will not be thought of as *ad hominem* attacks or as implying any disrespect for the specific individuals cited as representatives of standard economics.

It is not enough simply to attack the progrowth orthodoxy; we must have an alternative vision. But neither is it sufficient to have an alternate vision; we must expose the errors of the prevailing view. Hence the division between Parts I and II.

It is hardly necessary to add that this endeavor did not begin with me, nor will it end with me. In a previous volume, *Toward a Steady-State Economy,* I collected a number of articles by various writers of diverse backgrounds that seemed to me to cohere into a case for a steady-state economy. The present volume seeks to treat the same theme more succinctly and systematically than could be done in a collection and perhaps also more from within the tradition of political economy, broadly conceived.

To hundreds of colleagues, students, and fellow environmentalists I owe a general intellectual debt of enormous magnitude. To the extent that I am aware of my special intellectual debts I have tried to acknowledge them. From the generation of my teachers I have learned most from Nicholas Georgescu-Roegen and Kenneth Boulding. From the generation of my teachers' teachers I have learned much from Irving Fisher. All economists, of course, are indebted to the classical economists, among whom Thomas Robert Malthus and John Stuart Mill are the most closely connected with the ideas here developed. I claim no originality, not even for those few ideas which seem to me to be my own. Too many times I have rediscovered "my most original ideas" in pages of books that I had read five or ten years ago, underlined, with my enthusiastic, but forgotten, comments in the margin. In any event, originality is a false god. We should be concerned with whether facts are true or false, whether arguments are valid or invalid, and whether underlying values are good or evil. The true, the valid, and the good are less likely to be original than the false, the invalid and the evil. Broad is the path that leads to destruction.

Herman E. Daly
Baton Rouge, La.
February 1977

STEADY-STATE ECONOMICS

I
THE
STEADY-STATE
ECONOMY

1

AN OVERVIEW OF THE ISSUES

> Society must cease to look upon "progress" as some-
> thing desirable. "Eternal Progress" is a nonsensical
> myth. What must be implemented is not a "steadily
> expanding economy," but a *zero growth economy,* a
> stable economy. *Economic growth is not only unneces-
> sary but ruinous.*
>
> Aleksandr I. Solzhenitsyn (1974)

The theme of this book is that a steady-state economy is a necessary and desirable future state of affairs and that its attainment requires quite major changes in values, as well as radical, but nonrevolutionary, institutional reforms. Once we have replaced the basic premise of "more is better" with the much sounder axiom that "enough is best," the social and technical problems of moving to a steady state become solvable, perhaps even trivial. But *unless* the underlying growth paradigm and its supporting values are altered, all the technical prowess and manipulative cleverness in the world will not solve our problems and, in fact, will make them worse.

The recognition that there are problems of political economy that have no technical solution but do have a moral solution goes very much against the grain of modern economic theory. Yet economics began as a branch of moral philosophy, and the ethical content was at least as important as the analytic content up through the writings of Alfred Marshall.* From then on, the structure of economic theory became more and more top-heavy with analysis. Layer upon layer of abstruse mathematical models were erected higher and higher above the shallow concrete foundation of fact. The behavior of a peasant selling a cow was analyzed in terms of the calculus of variations and Lagrangian multipliers. From the angelic perspective of hyperplanes cavorting in n-space, economists overlooked some critical biophysical and moral facts. The biophysical facts have asserted themselves in the form of increasing ecological scarcity: depletion, pollution, and ecological disruption. The moral facts are asserting themselves in the form of increasing existential scarcity: anomie, injustice, stress, alienation, apathy, and crime. The second chapter will analyze these omissions further in terms of the ends-means spectrum.

In the face of these now undeniable facts, modern economic thought cuts its losses in two ways: (1) It argues that the newly revealed dimension of ecological scarcity simply requires more clever technology and more growth, albeit growth of a slightly different kind. (2) It argues that existential scarcity (resulting from a shortage of whatever does in fact make people whole, well, and happy) is simply not real. This point has been well discussed by Walter Weisskopf (1971). Whatever the public chooses is assumed to be in the public interest, and there is no distinction between what people of the present age of advertising *think* will make them whole and happy and what would *in fact* make them so.

It is not easy (beyond the level of basic necessities) to make factual statements about what is good for people, but it is rash to assume that no such statements are possible—that all of ethics can be reduced to the level of personal tastes and that the community is nothing but an aggregate of isolated individuals.

The attraction of these simple, and I believe quite erroneous, assumptions is that by emasculating the concepts of ecological and existential scarcity, the orthodox economic growth paradigm covers up the weaknesses in its factual foundations and can thus continue building its analytical tower of babel up to a theoretical bliss point.

Only by returning to its moral and biophysical foundations and shoring them up, will economic thinking be able to avoid a permanent commitment to misplaced concreteness and crackpot rigor. Scientistic pretention

---

*For example, in the first textbook of political economy (T. R. Malthus' *Principles of Political Economy*) we find the following statement: "It has been said, and perhaps with truth that the conclusions of Political Economy partake more of the stricter sciences than those of most of the other branches of human knowledge. . . . There are indeed in Political Economy great general principles . . . [but] we shall be compelled to acknowledge that the science of Political Economy bears a nearer resemblance to the science of morals and politics than to that of mathematics" (Malthus, 1820, p. 1).

and blind aping of the mechanistic methods of physics, even after physics has abandoned the mechanistic philosophy (Georgescu-Roegen, 1971), should be replaced by value-based thinking in the mode of classical political economy. Separation of "is" from "ought" is an elementary rule of clear thinking. But this separation belongs within the mind of the individual thinker. It should never have become the basis for division of labor between people and professions, much less an excuse for "running to hide in thickets of Algebra, while abandoning the really tough questions to journalists and politicians" (Robinson, 1962). Of all fields of study, economics is the last one that should seek to be "value-free," lest it deserve Oscar Wilde's remark that an economist is a man who knows the price of everything and the value of nothing.

Not all physical scientists have been flattered by the economists' emulation. For example, Norbert Wiener observed:

> The success of mathematical physics led the social scientists to be jealous of its power without quite understanding the intellectual attitudes that had contributed to this power. The use of mathematical formulae had accompanied the development of the natural sciences and become the mode in the social sciences. Just as primitive peoples adopt the Western modes of denationalized clothing and of parliamentarism out of a vague feeling that these magic rites and vestments will at once put them abreast of modern culture and technique, so the economists have developed the habit of dressing up their rather imprecise ideas in the language of the infinitesimal calculus. . . . To assign what purports to be precise values to such essentially vague quantities is neither useful nor honest, and any pretense of applying precise formulae to these loosely defined quantities is a sham and a waste of time [Wiener, 1964, p. 89].

The challenge is to develop a political economics that recognizes both ecological and existential scarcity and develops its propositions at a low to intermediate level of abstraction, understandable by the layman or average citizen, rather than dictated by a priesthood of "technically competent" obscurantists. If economic reality is actually so complex that it can only be described by complicated mathematical models that add epicycles to epicycles and externalities to externalities, then the reality should be simplified. Human institutions should not be allowed to grow beyond the human scale in size and complexity (Schumacher, 1973). Otherwise, the economic machine becomes too heavy a burden on the shoulders of the citizen, who must continually grind and regrind himself to fit the imperatives of the overall system, and who becomes ever more vulnerable to the failure of other interdependent pieces that are beyond his control and even beyond awareness (Vacca, 1974). Lack of control by the individual over institutions and technologies that not only affect his life but determine his livelihood is hardly democratic and is, in fact, an excellent training in the acceptance of totalitarianism.

That man is fully expected to make whatever adaptations are technologically required is part of the Faustian covenant that we have made with Big Science and High Technology. The guidebook to the 1933 Chicago World's Fair on science and industry proclaimed or reaffirmed the covenant: "Science discovers, industry applies, and man adapts himself to or is molded by new things. . . . Individuals, groups, entire races of men, fall into step with Science and Industry" (quoted in Dubos, 1974–1975, p. 8). Man receives wealth but accepts the obligation to adapt to, be molded by, and fall into step with Big Science and High Technology.

But have we not outgrown the naive 1933 faith in Science as the benevolent master? Some have, but in others the faith has taken on a more sophisticated and dangerous form. A famous social scientist ends an article on "sociological aspects of genetic control" with the following words:

> Deliberate control, once begun, would soon benefit science and technology, which in turn would facilitate further hereditary improvement, which again would extend science, and so on in a self-reinforcing spiral without limit. In other words, when man has conquered his own biological evolution he will have laid the basis for conquering everything else. The universe will be his, at last. [Davis, 1972, p. 379].

We might ask precisely *who*, finally, will be master of the universe, since when man has conquered his own biological evolution then victor and vanquished are one and the same, and the statement is self-contradictory (Lewis, 1947). What is probably meant is that some men will have conquered the biological evolution of other men. But I mention that problem only in passing. The point of Davis' statement is that we will not only conform ourselves socially to the dictates of High Technology, but we will reprogram our very genetic inheritance in its service! In return for this total subservience we are offered progress in the form of a "self-reinforcing spiral without limit." The principle ideological manifestation of this "progress" is the doctrine of unlimited economic growth, which requires, among other things, a lot of energy, though not so much as the energy companies think. Dr. Alvin Weinberg tells us that to get the energy:

> We nuclear people have made a Faustian bargain with society. On the one hand, we offer—in the catalytic burner—an inexhaustible source of energy. . . . But the price that we demand of society for this magical energy source is both a vigilance and a longevity of our social institutions that we are quite unaccustomed to [Weinberg, 1972, p. 33].

If we believe in "self-reinforcing spirals without limit" and "magical energy sources," consider enforced human adaptation an honor rather than a cost, and believe that the whole universe could be "ours" at last, then we surely will dismiss as a "failure of nerve" any talk about the necessity and desirability of a steady-state economy. The no-limits attitude is not often as explicit as in the expressions I have quoted, but a little scratching often reveals it to be just below the surface, as will be seen in Chapter 5, when we consider the specific views of several representative economists.

In paradoxical conflict with this Faustian view of the power of technology stands the fact that the most basic laws of science are statements of impossibility: it is impossible to create or destroy matter-energy; it is impossible to travel faster than the speed of light; it is impossible to have perpetual motion; it is impossible for an organism to live in a medium consisting only of its own waste products; it is impossible to measure anything without altering the thing measured; and so on. Mathematicians, before they invest much time in trying to solve a problem, first attempt to prove the existence or nonexistence of a solution. If it can be shown that a solution does not exist, then they save an infinite amount of futile effort by not looking for it. Perhaps the success of science is due to its refusal to attempt the impossible; this success has paradoxically fostered the popular belief that nothing is impossible. It is economically very valuable to know what is impossible, and economic theory also contains some impossibility theorems: the impossibility of deriving social preferences from individual preferences, for example, or the impossibility of having more than one equilibrium price for a given commodity in a purely competitive market.

We need to recognize another impossibility theorem in political economy: specifically, that a U.S.-style high-mass consumption, growth-dominated economy for a world of 4 billion people is impossible. Even more impossible is the prospect of an ever growing standard of per-capita consumption for an ever growing world population. The minerals in concentrated deposits in the earth's crust, and the capacity of ecosystems to absorb large quantities or exotic qualities of waste materials and heat set a limit on the number of person-years that can be lived in the "developed" state, as that term is understood today in the United States. How the limited number of person-years of "developed" living will be apportioned among nations, among social classes, and over generations will be the dominant economic and political issue for the future (Keyfitz, 1972).

The steady-state economy respects impossibilities and does not foolishly squander resources in vain efforts to overcome them. Our present institutions allow technology to be autonomous and force man to play the accommodating role. The steady-state economy seeks to change institutions in such a way that people become autonomous and technology is not abandoned, but is demoted to its proper accommodating role. Growth economics gave technology free rein. Steady-state economics channels technical progress in the socially benign directions of small scale, decentralization, increased durability of products, and increased long-run efficiency in the use of scarce resources. Institutions for redirecting technical evolution are discussed in Chapter 3.

Probably the major disservice that experts provide in confronting the problems of mankind is dividing the problems in little pieces and parceling them out to specialists. Food problems belong to agriculture and energy problems to engineering or physics; employment and inflation belong to economics; adaptation belongs to psychologists and genetic engineers; and the "environment" is currently up for grabs by disciplinary imperialists. Although it is undeniable that each specialty has much of importance to say, it is very doubtful that the sum of all these specialized utterances will ever add up to a coherent solution, because the problems are not independent and sequential but highly interrelated and simultaneous. Someone has to look at the whole, even if it means foregoing full knowledge of all of the parts. Since "economics" as well as "ecology" come from the same Greek root *(oikos)*, meaning "management of the household," and since man's household has extended to include not only nations but also the planet as a whole, economics is probably the discipline that has least justification for taking a narrow view. Let us take a minute to consider the economy, environmental quality, food, energy, and adaptation as interrelated subtopics within the framework of economics viewed as management of the household of man.

The economy, or household of mankind, consists of two things: the members of the family and their furniture and possessions, or, in purely physical terms, human bodies and physical commodities or artifacts. For the last century or more, the most salient characteristic of the human household has been its enormous quantitative growth. Population has grown at rates vastly in excess of any that have ever prevailed in the entire history of the species. This unprecedented population growth has been accompanied by, and in part made possible by, an even greater rate of increase in the production of artifacts. World population has grown at around 2 percent annually, doubling every thirty-five years, and world consumption has grown at about 4 percent annually, doubling every seventeen or eighteen years. But production and consumption are not the precise words, since man can neither produce nor destroy matter and energy but only transform them from one state to another. Man transforms raw materials into commodities and commodities into garbage. In the process of maintaining ever larger populations of both people and artifacts, the volume of raw materials transformed into commodities and ultimately into garbage has increased greatly. In the United States in 1972, about 43,000 pounds of basic nonfood raw materials were used per person to produce commodities and will eventually end up as waste (National Commission on Materials Policy, 1973, p. 2:6).

Furthermore, man cannot convert waste back into raw materials except by expending energy that inevitably degrades into waste heat, which cannot be recycled. Man can let nature recycle some wastes if he is not too impatient and refrains from overloading natural cycles. Recycling is a good idea, but it has limits provided by the second law of thermodynamics, which, in effect, says that energy cannot be recycled and that matter can only be recycled at something less than 100 percent.

Why has the human household grown so rapidly? Basically, because we made it grow. Since procreating is a more popular activity than dying, and is likely to remain so, we eagerly reduce death rates and only half-heartedly talk about reducing birth rates. Even though we have reached replacement fertility in the United States (each new family has on the average only 2.1 children), our population will continue to grow because such a large proportion of the population (the baby boom of the 1940s) is now moving into the high fertility age brackets, and it will be 50 years before these people enter the high mortality age brackets. In fact, our population would grow by about 70 million before it levels off at about 280 million around the year 2050, assuming replacement fertility is maintained (Frejka, 1973, p. 165). In a young population, the net popularity of procreating over dying is even greater than it is in an older population. At the world level, even on the optimistic assumption that the net reproductive rate (NRR) falls to unity by the year 2000, the present 4 billion will have reached 6 billion by the end of the century (Frejka, 1973, p. 55). Of course, famine may well prevent this figure from being reached. Even though many, but not all, governments have decided that further population growth is not desirable, it is likely to occur whether they want it or not, especially in the underdeveloped countries, for at least the remainder of the century.

Although many question whether further population growth is desirable, very few people question the desirability or possibility of further economic growth. Indeed, economic growth is the most universally accepted goal in the world. Capitalists, communists, fascists, and socialists all want economic growth and strive to maximize it. The system that grows fastest is considered best. The appeals of growth are that it is the basis of national power and that it is an alternative to sharing as a means of combating poverty. It offers the prospect of more for all with sacrifice by none—a prospect that is in conflict with the "impossibility theorem" discussed above. If we are serious about helping the poor, we shall have to face up to the moral issue of redistribution and stop sweeping it under the rug of aggregate growth.

What are the implications of this growth-dominated, imperialistic style of managing the human household for the specific issues of environmental quality, food, energy, and adaptation?

While the human household has been rapidly growing, the environment of which it is a part has steadfastly remained constant in its quantitative dimensions. Its size has not increased, nor have the natural rates of circulation of the basic biogeochemical cycles that man exploits. As more people transform more raw materials per person into commodities, we experience higher rates of depletion; as more people transform more commodities into waste, we experience higher rates of pollution. We devote more effort and resources to mining poorer mineral deposits and to cleaning up increased pollution, and we then count many of these extra expenses as an increase in GNP and congratulate ourselves on the extra growth! The problem with GNP is that it counts consumption of geological capital as current income (Schumacher, 1973). Better concepts for social accounting will be suggested in Chapter 2.

While the growth-induced increases in depletion and pollution have adverse direct effects on the human household that are bad enough (e.g., lead and mercury poisoning, congestion, air and water pollution), they also have indirect effects that are likely to be worse. The indirect effects occur through interferences with natural ecosystems that inhibit their ability to perform the free life-support services that we take for granted (Daly, 1968). For example, the most important service of all, photosynthesis, may be interfered with by changing the acidity of the soil that supports plant life, a change resulting from acid rains induced by air pollution caused by burning fossil fuels. In addition, the heat balance and temperature gradients of the earth can be changed by air pollution and by intensive local use of energy, with unpredictable effects on climate, rainfall, and agriculture. Deforestation results in the loss of water purification and flood and erosion control services formerly provided gratis by the forests, as well as the loss of wildlife habitats and of a potentially perennial source of timber. Ecologists have convincingly argued that the natural services provided by Louisiana marshlands (a spawning ground for much marine life of the Gulf of Mexico, a natural tertiary sewage treatment plant, a buffer zone for hurricane protection, and a recreation area) are probably much more valuable than the so-called development uses of new residential areas and shopping centers or even oil wells, at least beyond a limited number (Gosselink et al., 1973).

As the economy grows, man's impact on the environment increases by a rate of 5 percent per year (doubling every fourteen years), according to the SCEP (1971) estimate. The impact is usually of a random, unforseen nature and therefore overwhelmingly likely to be harmful, like a random mutation or the blind poke of a screwdriver in the back of a TV set. The relationship of fitness to the environment is reciprocal and can be destroyed by a random change in the environment as well as by a random change in the organism. As man experiences these limitations to the growth and maintenance of his household, he realizes that he is not as wealthy as he thought. Unfortunately, the typical reaction to this heightened perception of scarcity is to call for still more economic growth —leading too often to still more depletion, pollution, and further interferences with the essential services of ecosystems. This process can be illustrated specifically with reference to food and energy.

Food is the source of energy required to run human bodies and is closely related to more general energy questions. World per-capita food production has remained remarkably constant for the past twenty years, actually declining slightly between 1969 and 1970. The world's 1 to 2 billion hungry are still just as hungry as they were 20 years ago. Food prices, especially for protein, have been rising dramatically. In 1969 the total catch of world fisheries of 63 million metric tons represented a 2-percent decline from the previous year (Ehrlich and Ehrlich, 1972, pp. 102–138). This decline occurred in spite of increased efforts, and it indicates that the oceans are being overfished. Overexploitation and coastal pollution may well have already reduced the productivity of the seas. World grain stocks have declined from the equivalent of 105 days' consumption in 1961 to the equivalent of 31 days' consumption in 1976 (Brown, 1975, p. 8). Moreover, practically all the world's net exports of grain come from one geographic and climatic region, North America. In 1973 the rising trend of grain yield per hectare reversed itself and began falling. Throughout the Third World, pressure on the land has increased as rising petroleum prices have forced increased use of firewood and dung as fuel. The result has been an increased rate of deforestation, flooding, and erosion, as well as impoverishment of cultivated land as animal dung is increasingly burned for fuel rather than returned to the soil as fertilizer (Eckholm, 1975).

Food, unlike coal or petroleum, is a renewable resource—a means of capturing the continual flow of solar energy. But the necessity to feed a large and growing population at an increasing level of per-capita consumption in rich countries like the United States has made agriculture dependent on a continuous subsidy of nonrenewable fossil fuels, chemicals, and mineral fertilizers. For each calorie of food produced in the United States in 1970, about seven calories of nonfood fuels were consumed by agriculture and related activities (Steinhart and Steinhart, 1974, p. 80). As Howard Odum says, industrial man no longer eats potatoes made from solar energy; he now eats potatoes made partly of oil (Odum, 1971). As the fossil fuel subsidy becomes scarcer and more expensive, agriculture will have to rely more on solar energy and human labor. It may be that (as is already happening in Brazil) more cropland will be devoted to sugarcane in order to make alcohol to mix with gasoline for fuel—just the reverse of the process of turning petroleum into food that was attracting attention a few years ago! Agriculture will have to start maximizing productivity per ton of fertilizer or per Btu of fossil-fuel input, and worry less about productivity per acre or per man.

The drive to increase agricultural productivity leads to the replacement of low-yield species by newly developed high-yield species, which results in greater homogeneity of crops, that is, in a reduction in the diversity of the genetic stock and consequently a greater vulnerability to future pest and disease mutants. The increased vulnerability of the monoculture calls for even more protection by pesticides. In addition, more inputs of fertilizer and fresh-water irrigation are required by "green revolutions," with resulting problems of water pollution and shortage.

In the words of agriculture expert Lester R. Brown, the question is not can we produce more food, but what are the ecological consequences of doing so? A similar point was made long ago by Malthus, who observed that "It is not easy to conceive a more disastrous present, one more likely to plunge the human race in irrecoverable misery, than an unlimited facility for producing food in a limited space" (Malthus, 1820, p. 227). Unlimited food would simply allow a larger population to run into the harsher limits of air and water scarcity. With limits on population and economic growth (i.e., within a steady-state economy), free food, and free energy as well, would be a blessing. But in the current growth context they would be a curse; free energy would simply make it easier for a growth society to destroy the ecosystem. This consideration itself is a powerful argument against growthmania—any context that converts free energy and free food from a boon to a bane must embody some serious irrationalities. Although anyone who discovers how economically to control fusion will no doubt receive the Nobel prize and be hailed as a benefactor of mankind, several perceptive physicists have privately expressed the hope that such a discovery may be delayed until such time as we have learned to limit our energy use. But no Nobel prizes are likely to be given to the proponents of low energy use!

The Malthusian question is thus relevant for energy: not can we produce more energy, but what are the ecological consequences of doing so? And are the benefits worth the extra costs? And what source of energy will best serve man's total needs? Unfortunately, these questions not only are unanswered but remain largely unasked. Instead, we have asked such very short-sighted questions as "How can we most quickly convert fission power from military to civilian uses?" The goal seems to be to maintain the historical 7-percent annual rate of growth of electric power, which everyone should know is simply not maintainable for very long. The utility companies have finally realized this and revised their demand estimates downward, but they are still committed to continuous growth at a slower rate. Fission has received top priority in governmental research and development, with fusion a poor second and solar energy a very poor third. Yet solar energy is by far the superior source in that it is nondepletable and nonpolluting. Everything in the biosphere is preadapted to solar energy by millions of years of evolution. Since plutonium did not exist until very recently, everything in the biosphere is totally unadapted to it; it is the most toxic and dangerous substance known, yet it is basic material in the fuel cycle of the fast breeder reactors, upon which the whole fission program depends.

We will have more to say on fission power in Chapter 6, but for now it will suffice to note four facts: (1) There are viable energy alternatives that have been largely ignored (especially solar). (2) There are extreme dangers involved in using plutonium, some of which require a level of social discipline and control far beyond what is possible or desirable. (3) No matter what technology is used, we cannot for long increase electric energy output at 7 percent, and in any event production will have to stabilize at some level. (4) Stabilizing at current levels would not be so terrible, in view of the fact that the per-capita energy consumption of Sweden and West Germany is one-half that of the United States and that of Switzerland is only one-third, yet all three countries have very high standards of living. By stabilizing energy consumption now and making careful use of petroleum and coal, we would have plenty of time to develop solar-energy technology. If we waste our fossil-fuel capital on trivia, then we will not be able to construct either a solar- or a nuclear-based economy. Fission energy is probably the biggest mistake we could make, and we seem determined to make it. This is the *real* energy crisis, not the short-run manipulation of gasoline supplies by a few Arab sheiks and a few big oil companies.

Growth of the human household within a finite physical environment is eventually bound to result in both a food crisis and an energy crisis and in increasingly severe problems of depletion and pollution. Within the context of overall growth, these problems are fundamentally insoluble, although technological stopgaps and palliatives are possible. Technological adaptation has been the dominant reaction, aided by the information and incentives provided by market prices. We need, however, to shift the emphasis toward ecological adaptation, that is, to accept natural limits to the size and dominion of the human household, to concentrate on moral growth and qualitative improvement rather than on the quantitative imperialist expansion of man's dominion. The human adaptation needed is primarily a change of heart, followed by a shift to an economy that does not depend so much on continuous growth. As Arnold Toynbee (1972) put it:

> More and more people are coming to realize that the growth of material wealth which the British industrial revolution set going, and which the modern British-made ideology has presented as being mankind's proper paramount objective, cannot in truth be the wave of the future. Nature is going to compel posterity to revert to a stable state on the material plane and to turn to the realm of the spirit for satisfying man's hunger for infinity.

REFERENCES

Brown, Lester R. *The Politics and Responsibility of the North American Bread-basket*. Washington, D.C.: Worldwatch Institute, 1975.

Daly, Herman E. "On Economics as a Life Science," *Journal of Political Economy,* May/June 1968.

Davis, Kingsley. "Sociological Aspects of Genetic Control," in William Petersen, ed., *Readings in Population*. New York: Macmillan, 1972.

Dubos, René. "The Despairing Optimist," *The American Scholar,* Winter 1974–1975.

Eckholm, Erik P. *The Other Energy Crisis: Firewood*. Washington, D.C.: Worldwatch Institute, 1975.

Ehrlich, Paul, and Anne Ehrlich. *Population, Resources, Environment*. San Francisco: W. H. Freeman, 1972.

Frejka, Tomas. *The Future of Population: Alternative Paths to Equilibrium*. New York: Wiley, 1973.

Georgescu-Roegen, Nicholas. *The Entropy Law and the Economic Process*. Cambridge, Mass.: Harvard University Press, 1971.

Gosselink, James, Eugene Odum, and R. M. Pope, "The Value of the Tidal Marsh," Work Paper #3. Gainesville, Florida: Urban and Regional Development Center, University of Florida, 1973.

Keyfitz, Nathan. "Population Theory and Doctrine: A Historical Survey," in William Petersen, ed., *Readings in Population*. New York: Macmillan, 1972.

Lewis, C. S. *The Abolition of Man*. London: Macmillan, 1947. Reprinted in Herman E. Daly, ed., *Toward a Steady-State Economy*. San Francisco: W. H. Freeman, 1973.

Malthus, T. R. *Principles of Political Economy*. London: Kelley, 1836.

National Commission on Materials Policy. *Material Needs and the Environment Today and Tomorrow*. Washington, D.C.: U.S. Government Printing Office, 1973.

Odum, Howard T. *Environment, Power, and Society*. New York: Wiley, 1971.

Robinson, Joan. *Economic Philosophy*. London: C. A. Watts, 1962.

SCEP (Study of Critical Environmental Problems). *Man's Impact on the Global Environment*. Cambridge, Mass.: M.I.T. Press, 1971.

Schumacher, E. F. *Small Is Beautiful: Economics as If People Mattered*. New York: Harper & Row, 1973.

Solzhenitsyn, Aleksandr I. *Letter to the Soviet Leaders*. Harper & Row, New York: 1974.

Steinhart, Carol, and John Steinhart. *Energy: Sources, Uses, and Role in Human Affairs*. Belmont, Caif.: Duxbury Press, 1974.

Toynbee, Arnold. *The Observer,* June 11, 1972.

Vacca, Roberto. *The Coming Dark Age*, trans. by J. S. Whale. Garden City, New York: Doubleday, 1974.

Weinberg, Alvin. "Social Institutions and Nuclear Energy," *Science,* July 7, 1972, 32–34.

Weisskopf, Walter A. *Alienation and Economics*. New York: Dutton, 1971.

Wiener, Norbert. *God and Golem, Inc*. Cambridge, Mass.: M.I.T. Press, 1964.

2

THE CONCEPT OF
A STEADY-STATE ECONOMY

I cannot . . . regard the stationary state of capital and
wealth with the unaffected aversion so generally manifested towards it by political economists of the old
school. I am inclined to believe that it would be, on the
whole, a very considerable improvement on our present
condition.

John Stuart Mill (1857)

What Is a Steady-State Economy?

Economic analysis, or any analytic thought for that matter, must begin
with what Joseph Schumpeter (1954) calls a "preanalytic vision" or what
Thomas Kuhn (1962) calls a basic "paradigm." Analytic thought carves
up this vision into parts and shows the relationship among the parts. If
the analytic knife is wielded skillfully, the pieces will be cut cleanly
along natural seams rather than torn raggedly, and the relations among
the parts will be simple and basic rather than contrived and complex. But
prior to analytic thought there must be a basic vision of the shape
and nature of the total reality to be analyzed and some feeling for
where natural joints and seams lie, and for the way in which the whole
to be analyzed fits into the totality of things. Our basic definitions arise
out of this preanalytic vision, which limits the style and direction of our
thinking.

The vision of the economy from which the steady-state concept arises is that of two physical populations—people and artifacts—existing as elements of a larger natural system. These physical populations have two important aspects. On the one hand, they yield services—artifacts (physical capital) serve human needs, and so do other human beings. The body of a skilled worker or doctor is a physical asset that yields services both to the immediate owner of the body and to others. On the other hand, these populations require maintenance and replacement. People continually get hungry, cold, and wet, and eventually they die. Artifacts wear out and must be replaced. These two populations may be thought of as a fund, like a lake, with an outflow necessitated by death and depreciation, which can be reduced but never eliminated. The outflow is offset by an inflow of births and production which may exceed, fall short of, or equal the outflow. Consequently the fund or lake may grow, decline, or remain constant.

From the physical nature of these populations, several things are apparent. Since, from the first law of thermodynamics, we know that matter-energy can be neither created nor destroyed, it is apparent that the fund of physical and human capital has some important relations with the rest of the world. The rest of the world is a source for its inputs of matter-energy and a sink for its outputs. Everything has to come from somewhere and go somewhere. "Somewhere" is in both cases the natural environment. The larger the lake, the larger must be the outflow, because death and depreciation cannot be reduced beyond some lower limit, and consequently the larger must be the offsetting inflow. If there were no death or depreciation, then our "lake of capital" (to use A. C. Pigou's phrase) would be a closed system rather than an open system and would be limited in its size only by the total amount of water, not by the conditions governing the flow of water through the total natural system. The second law of thermodynamics tells us that death and depreciation cannot be eliminated, so it is clear that our lake must remain an open system if it is to maintain a constant level. If inflow is less than outflow, the lake will eventually disappear; if inflow is greater than outflow, it will eventually contain all the water there is and will not be able to have any more inflow. But the outflow will continue and bring the lake down to some smaller equilibrium size which can be maintained by the natural hydrologic flows.

However, the lake analogy fails in several important aspects. First, the fund of water in the lake is homogeneous, whereas the fund of people and artifacts is highly varied and complex. Second, the water entering the lake is both quantitatively and qualitatively equal to the water flowing out, assuming an equilibrium lake. But while the equilibrium lake of people and artifacts is maintained by an inflow of matter-energy equal in *quantity* to the outflow, the two are very different in *quality*. The matter-energy going in is useful raw material, while that coming out is useless waste. The flowthrough, or throughput of matter-energy that maintains the fund of artifacts and people, is entropic in nature. Low-entropy inputs are imported and high-entropy outputs are exported. The high-entropy output cannot be directly used again as an input for the same reason that organisms cannot eat their own excrement. Although it would appear that the real lake's outflow is qualitatively the same as the inflow, this is not strictly true. The outflow water could not return to the inflow stream without being pumped or without being evaporated and lifted again by the hydrologic cycle powered by the sun. So even the throughput of water that maintains a lake is an entropic flow, although this is obscured by the fact that the water looks the same going in as it does coming out. The matter-energy throughput that maintains the fund of people and artifacts does not even look the same. Anyone can tell the difference between equal quantities of raw materials and waste.

In sum, the vision is that of a physical open system, a fund of service-yielding assets maintained by a throughput that begins with depletion of nature's sources of useful low entropy and ends with the pollution of nature's sinks with high-entropy waste. There are two physical magnitudes, a *stock* of capital (people and artifacts) and a *flow* of throughput. There is one psychic magnitude of service or want satisfaction that is rendered by the stocks and is, of course, their reason to be. Whatever value we attribute to the satisfaction of our wants and needs is imputed to the stocks that satisfy those needs and, in turn, is imputed to the throughput that maintains the stocks.

The important role of the laws of thermodynamics in this vision will be developed later, but for now it is enough to recognize that the entropy law is the basic physical coordinate of scarcity. Were it not for the entropy law, nothing would ever wear out; we could burn the same gallon of gasoline over and over, and our economic system could be closed with respect to the rest of the natural world.

From this general vision we must now distill a precise definition of a steady-state economy. What is it precisely that is not growing, or held in a steady state? Two basic physical magnitudes are to be held constant: the population of human bodies and the population of artifacts (stock of physical wealth). Since artifacts are, in a very real sense, extensions of the human body, the steady-state economy may be thought of as a logical continuation of the demographer's notion of a stationary population to include not only human bodies but also their multifarious physical extensions. What is held constant is capital stock in the broadest physical sense of the term, including capital goods, the total inventory of consumer goods, and the population of human bodies.

Of equal importance is what is *not* held constant. The culture, genetic inheritance, knowledge, goodness, ethical codes, and so forth embodied in human beings are not held constant. Likewise, the embodied technology, the design, and the product mix of the aggregate total stock of artifacts are not held constant. Nor is the current distribution of artifacts among the population taken as constant. Not only is quality free to evolve, but its development is positively encouraged in certain directions. If we use "growth" to mean quantitative change, and "development" to refer to qualitative change, then we may say that a steady-state economy develops but does not grow, just as the planet earth, of which the human economy is a subsystem, develops but does not grow.*

The maintenance of constant physical populations of people and artifacts requires births to offset inevitable deaths and new production to offset inevitable physical depreciation. Births should be equal to deaths at low rather than high levels so that life expectancy is long rather than short. Similarly, new production of artifacts should equal depreciation at low levels so that the durability or "longevity" of artifacts is high. New production implies increasing depletion of resources. Depreciation implies the creation of physical waste, which, when returned to the environment, becomes pollution. Depletion and pollution are costs, and naturally they should be minimized for any given level of stocks to be maintained.

Thus we may succinctly define a *steady-state economy* (hereafter abbreviated SSE) as *an economy with constant stocks of people and artifacts, maintained at some desired, sufficient levels by low rates of maintenance "throughput"*, that is, by the lowest feasible flows of matter and energy from the first stage of production (depletion of low-entropy materials from the environment) to the last stage of consumption (pollution of the environment with high-entropy wastes and exotic materials). It should be continually remembered that the SSE is a *physical* concept. If something is nonphysical, then perhaps it can grow forever. If something can grow forever, then certainly it is nonphysical.

How does this physical concept of growth relate to economic growth? As currently measured by real GNP, which is a value *index* of a *physical* flow, economic growth is strictly tied to physical quantities. Even services are always measured as the use of some*thing* or some*body* for a

---

*The capital stock is an aggregate of unlike things, and to speak of it as constant in the aggregate, yet variable in composition, implies some coefficients of equivalence among the various unlike things. This problem haunts standard economics as well. However, as will be seen later, we do not really need an operational measure of the aggregate stock. We can control throughput and let the stock grow to whatever maximum size can be supported by the limited throughput. Control over aggregate throughput will result from controls (depletion quotas) on particular resources. If, thanks to technological progress, it becomes possible to support a larger stock with the same throughput, that is all to the good and should be allowed to happen. Eventually diminishing returns requires that the mix of artifacts will shift more towards producer's capital and away from consumer's capital, and a given gross throughput will contain an ever smaller net amount of usable matter-energy.

period of time, and these things and persons require physical maintenance; more of them require more physical maintenance. In calculating
real GNP, efforts are made to correct for changes in price levels, in
relative prices, and in product mix, so as to measure only real change in
physical quantities produced. However, the SSE is defined in terms of
constant *stocks* (a quantity measured at a point in time, like an inventory), not *flows* (a quantity measured over an interval in time, like annual sales). GNP is a flow and is logically irrelevant to the definition
of an SSE. Nevertheless, to the considerable extent that GNP reflects
throughput, then a policy of maximizing GNP growth would imply maximizing a cost. The steady-state perspective seeks to maintain a desired level of stocks with a minimum throughput, and if minimizing the
throughput implies a reduction in GNP, that is totally acceptable. The
steady-state paradigm assumes some *sufficient* level of stocks, an assumption that is absent from the growth paradigm. This idea will be further
discussed later in this chapter.

Although the idea of a SSE may seem strange to us who have always
lived in a growth economy, neither the concept nor the reality is at all
novel. John Stuart Mill discussed the notion with compelling clarity over
a century ago. And it is instructive to remember that mankind has, for
over 99 percent of its tenure on earth, existed in conditions closely
approximating a SSE. Only in the last 200 years has growth been suffi-
ciently rapid to be felt within the span of a single lifetime, and only in
the last forty years has it assumed top priority and become truly explosive. In the long run, stability is the norm and growth the aberration. It
could not be otherwise.

Why Is a Steady-State Economy
Both Necessary and Desirable?

Economics has to do with ends and means. The standard textbook definition somewhat ponderously states that economics is the study of the
allocation of scarce means among competing ends, where the object of
the allocation is the maximization of the attainment of those ends. In
other words, how to do the best with what you've got. But the *entire*
ends-means spectrum is not considered—economists do not speak of the
Ultimate End, nor of the ultimate means. Economists' attention is entirely focused on the middle range of the ends-means spectrum—on allocating given intermediate means (artifacts, labor power) in the service
of given intermediate ends (food, comfort, education, etc.). This limited
focus, it will be shown, has been the source of most of the confusions
about economic growth.

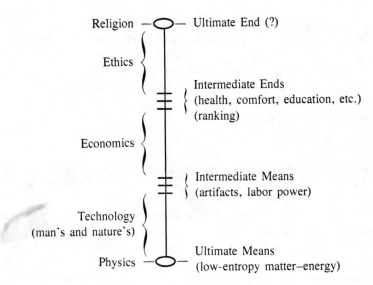

Figure 1

Consider Figure 1, which represents the entire ends-means continuum. The labels on the right indicate position in the ends-means continuum; the labels on the left indicate the discipline traditionally most concerned with each part of the spectrum. Each intermediate category in the spectrum is an end with respect to lower categories and a means with respect to higher categories. Thus intermediate ends may be thought of as means in the service of the Ultimate End, and intermediate means may be thought of as ends that are served by ultimate means. Only at the extremes do we have that which is pure end or pure means. The Ultimate End is that which is intrinsically good in and of itself and does not derive its value from being instrumental in achieving some other end. Ultimate means is that which is useful for serving human ends, but cannot be created by human beings, and hence cannot be the end of any human activity.

In looking only at the middle range of the ends-means spectrum, economics naturally has not dealt with ultimates or absolutes, found only at the extremes, and has falsely assumed that the middle range pluralities, relativities, and substitutabilities among competing ends and scarce means were representative of the whole spectrum. Absolute limits are absent from the economists' paradigm because we encounter absolute limits only in confrontation with ultimates, which have been excluded from our tunnel vision. The lack of attention by economists to the ultimate extremes has been insulated by a relative lack of attention to ethics and to technics.

The very definition of economics tells us that ends compete for scarce means and implies that there must be some priorities or ethical ranking of ends. Ranking or ordering of ends implies some ordering principle or Ultimate End, with reference to which the intermediate ends are ranked. Nothing could be clearer. Logically, we cannot even pronounce the word "priorities" without implicitly postulating a first position, an ordering principle, an Ultimate End.

But the temper of the modern age resists any discussion of the Ultimate End. Teleology and purpose, the dominant concepts of an earlier age, were banished from the mechanistic, reductionistic, positivistic mode of thought that came to be identified with a certain phase of the evolution of science. Economics followed suit by reducing ethics to the level of personal tastes: individuals set their own priorities, and economics is simply the "mechanics of utility and self-interest" (Jevons, 1924, p. 21), with no questions asked about whether individual priorities are right or wrong or even about how they are formed. Our refusal to reason about the Ultimate End merely assures the incoherence of our priorities, at both an individual and a social level. It leads to the tragedy of Captain Ahab, whose means were all rational, but whose purpose was insane. We cannot lend rationality to the pursuit of a white whale across the oceans merely by employing the most advanced techniques of whaling. To do more efficiently that which should not be done in the first place is no cause for rejoicing.

The logical demands of the ultimate are also ignored at the lower extreme of the spectrum. There is no recognition in modern economics of any limit on the total amount of ultimate means or on the rate of their use. Technology is assumed to be able to turn ultimate physical means into intermediate means (stocks of artifacts) without limit, or subject only to the limits of technological inventiveness and not to any limits imposed by the absolute scarcity of ultimate means. To quote a classic modern treatise on the subject:

> Advances in fundamental science have made it possible to take advantage of the uniformity of energy/matter—a uniformity that makes it feasible without preassignable limit, to escape the quantitative constraints imposed by the character of the earth's crust. . . . Nature imposes particular scarcities, not an inescapable general scarcity [Barnett and Morse, 1963, p. 11].

This view is not easy to reconcile with the laws of thermodynamics. It is not the uniformity of matter-energy that makes anything feasible, but precisely the opposite. It is nonuniformity, differences in concentration and temperature, that make for usefulness. If all materials and energy were uniformly distributed in thermodynamic equilibrium, the result would be the complete absence of potential for any process, including life. Just below the surface of the quoted statement lies the old alchemists' dream of converting lead into gold. It may be possible to convert lead into gold, but that does not remove general scarcity, because the *potential for making such conversions* is itself scarce.

We can define economic growth in this context as the conversion of ever more ultimate means into ever more intermediate means (stocks of artifacts) for the purpose of satisfying ever more intermediate ends, whatever they may be. The process is thought to be an endless one. Though it is admitted by orthodox economics that any given want can be satisfied, it is held that all wants in the aggregate are infinite and therefore can never be satisfied. Therefore, if ends are unlimited and means are unlimited, the process of growth can go on forever. This is the view that emerges from looking only at the middle of the spectrum, and only at the last 200 years of history.

Looking at the ultimate extremes of the spectrum, however, forces two sets of questions upon us. First, may we not eventually run out of worthwhile ends or, more specifically, worthwhile ends whose satisfaction depends on further conversion of ultimate into intermediate means? Is the nature of the Ultimate End such that, beyond some point, further accumulation of physical artifacts is useless or even harmful? Are some of the intermediate ends now being served, and those newly proposed, really undesirable, or less than worthwhile, in the light of the Ultimate End? Could it be that one of our wants is to be free of the tyranny of infinite wants? Second, will we not at some point run out of ultimate means or reach limits to the *rate* at which ultimate means can be used? Are ultimate means limited in ways that cannot be offset by technology? It will be argued that the answer to both sets of questions is "yes." The nature of the Ultimate End does in fact limit the *desirability* of continual economic growth, and the nature of the ultimate means does in fact limit the *possibility* of continual growth. Since the latter condition is easier to demonstrate, we will deal with it first.

From a basic branch of physics, thermodynamics, we learn that for man's purposes the ultimate usable stuff of the universe is low-entropy matter-energy.* Low entropy is the ultimate means, and it exists in two forms: a terrestrial stock and a solar flow. The terrestrial stock consists of two kinds of resources: those renewable on a human time scale and those renewable only over geologic time and which, for human purposes, must be treated as nonrenewable. Terrestrial low-entropy stocks may also be classified into energy and material. Both sources, the terrestrial and the solar, are limited. Terrestrial nonrenewables are limited in total amount available. Terrestrial renewables are also limited in total amount available and, if exploited to exhaustion, become just like nonrenewables.

---

*The following paragraphs draw heavily on the pioneering work of Nicholas Georgescu-Roegen (1971), and on a seminal work by Frederick Soddy (1922).

If exploited on a sustained-yield basis, then they are limited in rate of use, though practically unlimited in terms of the total amount eventually harvestable over time. Likewise, the solar source is practically unlimited in total amount but strictly limited in its rate and pattern of arrival to earth. Thus both sources of low entropy are limited. Ultimate means are limited. Resources can be substituted and new resources developed, but all of this occurs within the strictly limited total of low-entropy sources, and no rearrangement or substitution within the limited total will increase the total. Substitution will increase the efficiency with which the total terrestrial stock of ultimate means is used but not the size of the total stock.

That low entropy is the common denominator of all useful things is evident from the second law of thermodynamics. All states of matter and all forms of energy do not have equal potential for use. Though we neither create nor destroy matter-energy in production and consumption, we do transform it. Specifically, we transform matter from organized, structured, concentrated, low-entropy states (raw materials) into still more highly structured commodities, and then through use into dispersed, randomized, high-entropy states (waste). In the production of commodities, energy is transformed from high-temperature energy with a potential to do work into a low-temperature energy whose capacity to do work is lost when the temperature reaches equilibrium with the general environment. All life processes and all technological processes work on an entropy gradient. In all physical processes the matter-energy inputs in their totality are always of lower entropy than the matter-energy outputs in their totality. Organisms cannot survive in a medium consisting of their own final outputs. Neither can economies. Like nature's technology, man's technology is strictly confined within the laws of thermodynamics.

The solar source of low entropy is more abundant than the terrestrial source. If all of the world's fossil fuels were burned, they would provide only the equivalent of a few weeks of sunlight. The sun is expected to last for another 5 or 6 billion years. In addition to being nondepletable, the sun is also a nonpolluting source of energy. It would seem prudent, therefore, to make our technology run on solar low entropy to the greatest possible extent. The scarce nonrenewable terrestrial sources should be invested in structures to increase our ability to capture solar energy and should not be frivolously consumed. The biosphere runs on solar energy, and man has lived on solar energy for the vast majority of his history. Only in the last 200 years have we become dependent on nonrenewable minerals. Modern industry runs on the scarcest of the available forms of low entropy. Traditional technology (windmills, waterwheels, etc.) runs on the more abundant solar source. How ironic, therefore, to be told by technological optimists that modern technology is freeing man from dependence on resources (Barnett and Morse, 1963, p. 11). The very opposite is true.

The failure to pay attention to ultimate means has led to an enormous and elementary economic mistake: becoming dependent on the scarce source rather than the abundant source of ultimate means. The seductive advantage of terrestrial stocks is that they can be used at a rate of man's own choosing (i.e., rapidly), while the rate of solar flow is limited and interrupted by seasonal and diurnal variations. Rapid growth is easier when fueled with terrestrial stocks, because these stocks can, for a while at least, be depleted as rapidly as we wish. Also, of course, the concentration of terrestrial deposits permits concentrated, high-energy uses, whereas dispersed solar energy favors decentralized, low-energy patterns. On the one hand, the dispersed nature of solar energy is a disadvantage in that it requires concentration; on the other hand, it is an advantage in that it does not require a distribution system from a central source. The other side of the coin of rapid depletion of terrestrial stocks is abundant short-run supplies, low prices, and lavish use.

The rapid growth of the last 200 years has occurred because man broke the budget constraint of living on solar income and began to live on geological capital. The geological capital will run out. But an even greater problem exists. The entire evolution of the biosphere has occurred around a fixed point—the constant solar-energy budget. Modern man is the only species to have broken the solar-income budget constraint, and this has thrown him out of ecological equilibrium with the rest of the biosphere. Natural cycles have become overloaded, and new materials have been produced for which no natural cycles exist. Not only is geological capital being depleted but the basic life-support services of nature are impaired in their functioning by too large a throughput from the human sector.

Ecologist George M. Woodwell (1974) estimates that "30 to 50 percent of net primary production of the earth is being diverted to direct use by man for support of the current population." This estimate does not include the "public-service" functions of nature such as air and water purification. Woodwell notes that the use of nonrenewable energy sources often is allowed to destroy renewable resources. For example, if acid rains resulting from burning fossil fuel continue in New England for another decade, a net reduction of 10 percent in the primary productivity of New England forests and agriculture is likely, due to the rising pH of the soil. This would represent a loss of energy to the region "equivalent to the power produced by fifteen 1,000-megawatt reactors." From these and other considerations, Woodwell concludes:

> We have reached a point in the development of our current civilization where further increase in flows of energy through technology will cause significant reduction in the capacity of the earth to support mankind. The world cannot use more energy safely. . . . The world is overpopulated and overdeveloped; the important problem now is ecology, not energy and not economics [Woodwell, 1974].

But have we not given insufficient credit to the marvelous power of technology in our discussion of ultimate means? Is not technology itself an infinite resource? No, it is not. Improved technology means using the entropic flow more efficiently not reversing the direction of the flow. Efficiency is subject to thermodynamic limits. All existing and currently conceivable technologies function on an entropy gradient, converting low entropy into high entropy, in net terms. It is imaginable that someday we will discover how to create materials from nothing, how to achieve perpetual motion, how to reverse time's arrow, and so on. But to take such science-fiction miracles as a basis for economic policy would be absurd. Einstein considered the laws of thermodynamics to be the least likely ever to be overthrown:

A theory is more impressive the greater the simplicity of its premises is, the more different kinds of things it relates and the more extended is its area of applicability. Therefore the deep impression which classical thermodynamics made upon me. It is the only physical theory of universal content concerning which I am convinced that, within the framework of the applicability of its basic concepts, it will never be overthrown [Quoted in Schlipp, 1959, p. 33].

An even more emphatic statement to the same effect came from Sir Arthur Eddington:

The law that entropy increases—the Second Law of Thermodynamics— holds, I think, the supreme position among laws of nature. If someone points out to you that your pet theory of the universe is in disagreement with Maxwell's equations—then so much the worse for Maxwell's equations. If it is found to be contradicted by observation—well, these experimentalists do bungle things sometimes. But if your theory is found to be against the Second Law of Thermodynamics, I can give you no hope; there is nothing for it but to collapse in deepest humiliation [Eddington, 1953, p. 74].

The laws of thermodynamics restrict all technologies, man's as well as nature's, and apply to all economic systems whether capitalist, communist, socialist, or fascist. We do not create or destroy (produce or consume) anything in a physical sense—we merely transform or rearrange. And the inevitable cost of arranging greater order in one part of the system (the human economy) is creating a more than offsetting amount of disorder elsewhere (the natural environment). If "elsewhere" happens to be the sun, as it ultimately is for all of nature's technologies, then we need not worry. There is nothing we can do about it in any case. But if "elsewhere" is somewhere else on earth, as it is for all terrestrial sources of low entropy, then we must be very careful. There is a limit to how much disorder can be produced in the rest of the biosphere without inhibiting its ability to support the human subsystem. We must stop talking about free and inexhaustible gifts of nature and start talking about the throughput, the entropic flow of matter-energy that is the ultimate cost of maintaining life and wealth.

In sum, by focusing only on plural, intermediate means and substitutabilities among them, and on the ability of new technologies to tap new resources, economists fell into the trap of ignoring the ultimate finitude of the common denominator of all useful things, low-entropy matter-energy, which is scarce in an absolute sense. Even less did such economists notice the crucial asymmetry between the solar and terrestrial sources of low entropy (Georgescu-Roegen, 1971).

The base of the ends-means spectrum thus provides us with a concept of "real cost"—low entropy that is irrevocably spent in satisfying ends. Since low entropy spent for one purpose cannot be spent for another purpose, the cost of the particular amount of low entropy used must be evaluated according to the worth of the best alternative sacrificed. The notion of low entropy as a real cost is not at all inconsistent with the principle of opportunity cost for determining the *value* of the physical real cost. Low entropy is the physical coordinate of value—the ultimate supply limit. A hierarchy of ends is the psychic coordinate of value, the ultimate demand limit, a concept which will be considered further below.

Before leaving the subject of ultimate means, however, we should acknowledge and resist a very strong temptation to proclaim an "entropy theory of value." Although low entropy is a necessary condition for something to have any value at all, it is not a sufficient explanation of the value of one commodity relative to another. For one thing, entropy is entirely on the supply or cost side. There is still demand to consider. Hemlock may have lower entropy than orange juice. Bathwater heated to 211°F has lower entropy than 110°F bathwater but is not more valuable. But even on the supply side, all low entropy cannot be treated alike. Terrestrial low entropy cannot be valued equally with solar low entropy, since they are not always convertible and are not equally abundant. Furthermore, terrestrial low entropy takes two forms: material and energy. Although we can turn matter into energy, we have no means for turning energy into matter on a significant scale, so material low entropy is not reducible to energy terms for earthly purposes (Georgescu-Roegen, 1976). In addition, expenditure of human energy must be kept separate from other low-entropy sources, because man is an end as well as a means, and some expenditure of human energy is irksome and some is pleasurable, even though the same number of calories may be involved. The same amounts of usable energy in the forms of food, feed, and fuel are not necessarily of equal value unless animals are equal to people, and machines, in turn, are equal to animals. Supply and demand determine relative values, not entropy. Low entropy is the ultimate supply limit, the source of absolute scarcity. But within the category of absolutely scarce low entropy, there are various forms that are differentially scarce, and of differing utility, so that an entropy theory of value would be no more satisfactory than a labor theory of value. On the other hand, a theory of value that ignores entropy is no more satisfactory than one that ignores labor.

Just as we defined costs as "spent means," so we may define benefits at the other end of the spectrum as "accomplished or satisfied ends." The ultimate benefit or Ultimate End is less definable than the ultimate means. Perhaps, as a *minimum* definition, it could be considered as the survival and continuation of the evolving life process through which God has bestowed upon us the gift of conscious life. I hasten to add that this minimum definition begs some important questions. Evolution of life along what path, in what direction? To what degree should this evolution be spontaneous, and to what degree consciously directed? Survival of the process—especially, but not exclusively, the highest product of that process, mankind—must be considered as a precondition for the realization of all other values. Survival of the entire evolutionary process is different from personal survival. Personal survival may be sacrificed to higher goals; sacrificing the remaining years of one's expected lifetime to a higher cause can be a noble thing. Sacrificing all of creation for some "higher" cause is surely fanaticism. Is man basically a fallible creature whose salvation lies with his Creator rather than with his own creations? Or is man potentially the infallible creator himself, whose salvation lies in his own creations? The first view of man as fallible creature, ultimately dependent on his Creator, is the view that underlies the SSE. It is the traditional wisdom of the ages, taught by the great religions. The second view, man as potentially infallible creator seeking salvation in the perfection of his creations, leads to cosmic vandalism. It is the view not of great scientists but of the third-rate devotees of modern scientism, whose numbers are legion.

It is difficult to think of any philosophy or religion that holds that continual growth in population and per-capita resource use is the Ultimate End. At a time when the survival of the species was threatened by disease and starvation, maximizing birth rates and production rates was necessary for survival. But the final end was survival, and growth was a means (or intermediate end). Now we are threatened by overpopulation and overuse of resources. The end is still survival, but the means should now be to restrain growth. Yet we cling to old priorities and keep growth in first place.

Even though it is difficult to give a satisfactory definition of the Ultimate End, we are forced to choose among competing intermediate ends. The ranking of intermediate ends into a list of priorities logically implies some ordering principle, some concept, however vague, of the Ultimate End, with reference to which intermediate ends are ordered. Some of these ends cannot be served by aggregate growth. In fact, production and consumption often just get in the way. Leisure, silence, contemplation, even conversation, are made more difficult by the production-consumption drive. E. J. Mishan has forcefully made the point that aggregate growth is worthless for satisfying the relative wants of status:

> In an affluent society, people's satisfactions, as Thorstein Veblen observed, depend not only on the innate or perceived utility of the goods they buy, but also on the status value of such goods. Thus to a person in a high income society, it is not only his absolute income that counts but also his relative income, his position in the structure of incomes. In its extreme form—and as affluence rises we draw closer to it—only relative income matters. A man would then prefer a 5 percent reduction in his own income accompanied by a 10 percent reduction in the incomes of others to a 25 percent increase in both his income and the incomes of others.
>
> The more this attitude prevails—and the ethos of our society actively promotes it—the more futile is the objective of economic growth for society as a whole. For it is obvious that over time everyone cannot become relatively better off [Mishan, 1973, p. 30].

Aggregate growth can no more satisfy the relative wants of distinction than the arms race can increase security. The only way this self-cancelling effect and its resulting futility can be avoided is if growth is allowed to make the relatively well-off become relatively better-off. But then the price of continuing growth would be ever increasing inequality, and all the pious talk about growth for the poor would be seen as the evasion that it really is.

The dominance of the relative dimension of pecuniary wealth was clearly stated by John Ruskin in 1860:

> Primarily, which is very notable and curious, I observe that men of business rarely know the meaning of the word "rich." At least, if they know, they do not in their reasonings allow for the fact, that it is a relative word, implying its opposite "poor" as positively as the word "north" implies its opposite "south." Men nearly always speak and write as if riches were absolute, and it were possible, by following certain scientific precepts, for everybody to be rich. Whereas, riches are a power like that of electricity, acting only through inequalities or negations of itself. The force of the guinea you have in your pocket depends wholly on the default of a guinea in your neighbor's pocket. If he did not want it, it would be of no use to you; the degree of power it possesses depends accurately upon the need or desire he has for it,—and the art of making yourself rich, in the ordinary mercantile economist's sense, is therefore equally and necessarily the art of keeping your neighbor poor [Ruskin, 1967, p. 30].

So far we have discussed limits arising from the nature of ultimate means and from the nature of the Ultimate End. But the *effective* limit to economic growth lies not in having satisfied all worthwhile ends whose

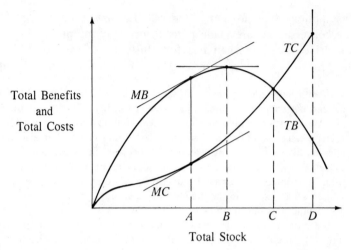

Figure 2

satisfaction depends on growth, nor in having used up all ultimate means. It is not necessary that marginal benefits fall all the way to zero nor that marginal costs rise to infinity but only that the two should become equal. The limit that results from their intersection, from the interaction of desirability and possibility, is the *economic* limit to growth. We do not satisfy ends in any arbitrary sequence but seek rationally to satisfy our most pressing needs first. Likewise, we do not use up means in any order but first exploit the most accessible means known to us. The former fact gives rise to the law of diminishing marginal benefits, the latter to the law of increasing marginal costs. The marginal cost curve rises, the marginal benefits curve declines. At some point they intersect.

Here we are at the intermediate range of the ends-means spectrum, where the economist's concepts are applicable. The activity in question, growth, should be carried only to the point at which marginal costs equal marginal benefits.

Consider Figure 2. *TB* is a curve that shows the relation of total benefits to total stock (diminishing marginal benefits); *TC* shows the relation of total cost to total stock (increasing marginal costs). The slopes of the total cost and benefit curves measure, respectively, marginal costs and benefits. The vertical difference between the two curves measures *net* benefits (*TB* minus *TC*), which is a maximum at *A*, where marginal cost equals marginal benefit (the slopes of the tangents to the two curves are equal at *A*). Growth in stocks should cease at point *A*, which is the *economic* limit. At *B* the marginal benefit falls to zero (horizontal slope), so there would be no point in growing beyond *B* even if costs were zero. At point *D* the marginal costs of growth become infinite (vertical slope), so even if the benefits were very great growth in stocks would have to cease. *C* represents a kind of break-even point, at which the total benefits of past growth are exactly offset by the total costs. Between *A* and *C* the total benefits of past growth outweigh the total costs. Contrary to popular argument, the fact that, on the whole or on the average, the benefits of past growth still outweigh the costs is no reason for advocating more growth. We must be governed by current marginal costs and benefits, not past averages. Note, however, that the various limits need not occur in the order shown. Specifically, *TC* might become discontinuously vertical *before* reaching point *A*, in which case the optimizing rule of marginal cost equal to marginal benefit is not adequate.

But this analysis is too static, say the critics, and rightly so. Technical progress shifts the position of the cost curve, and changing wants shift the position of the benefits curve. Therefore, point *A* could move continually to the right, and we must chase it by growing. There are two replies to this argument. First, even though the curves shift apart, point *A* need not move to the right; it could stay the same or move to the left. It all depends on *how* the curves shift apart, because the location of point *A* is determined by the slopes of the curves, not by their positions. Growth advocates do not explain why they always assume that dynamic change in technology and wants will not merely shift the curves apart but also change their relative slopes so that point *A* will move to the right. This seems to be overspecifying the kinds of dynamic change permitted.

The second reply is that, even assuming the particular kind of shift needed, there are limits to how far the curves can be shifted. While it is true that technical progress can shift the cost curve down, it cannot do so without limit. Our analysis of ultimate means and the second law assures us that there are limits to the efficiency increase represented by a downward shift in cost curves. Similarly, our discussion of the Ultimate End leads us to expect a limit to the increase in benefits arising from material production beyond some point. In our current economy billions are spent to artificially push up the benefits curve by stimulating new wants through noninformative advertising. The net result of all this expense may be actually to lower the true benefits curve, since the stimulated wants are often meretricious. Likewise, billions are spent on research and development efforts to lower costs. The net result of these expenditures may often be to increase real costs by engaging in irresponsible technological razzle-dazzle (e.g., nuclear power). Did the automobile reduce the costs of transport? Low resource prices resulting from rapid depletion will bias technology toward intensive use of the scarcest factor. This has been the most common form of shifting the cost curve down, and it has purchased short-run efficiency at the price of sacrificing long-run efficiency. Chapter 4 will look more closely at the concept of efficiency.

This is not to deny that the cost and benefit curves do shift, and that point *A* can move to the right. But the scarcity of ultimate means limits the downward shift of the cost curve, and the nature of the Ultimate End limits the upward shift of the benefits curve. There are limits to how far apart the curves can shift. The slopes of the two curves and the location of point A depend on the laws of diminishing marginal utility and increasing marginal cost.

However, such diagrams are of heuristic value only. We have no national accounting measures of either the cost or the benefits of growth, although we often treat GNP as a measure of benefits. The problem with GNP is that it adds together three very unlike categories: throughput, additions to capital stock, and services rendered by the capital stock. Throughput (the entropic depletion-pollution flow) is the ultimate physical cost. Services rendered by physical and human capital represent a value estimate of the final benefit, or true psychic income, resulting from economic activity. Additions to capital stock represent an increased capacity for future service, the net cost of which (throughput) has been incurred in the present, but the net benefits of which accrue only in the future. These three distinct concepts should be kept in separate accounts. It makes no sense to add together costs, benefits, and changes in capital stock. It is as if a firm were to add up its receipts, its expenditures, and its change in net worth. What sense could any accountant make of such a sum?

By virtue of prices and the common denominator of value, it may be possible to add together a physical flow of throughput, a psychic flux* of service, and a change in physical stocks, but such an agglomeration of diverse dimensionality obscures more than illuminates. We should have one value index of throughput and count it as cost—the cost of maintaining or adding to the existing stock. In a separate account we should measure the value of services yielded over the year by the total stock of human and physical capital. Although service, or psychic income, is unmeasurable (there are no units in which to measure satisfaction or utility), we cannot do without the concept because it provides the whole raison d'être of economic activity.

Although service cannot be directly measured, it is possible to get a measure of the value of psychic income from market prices. For example, the service rendered during one year by a car could be estimated by the rental value of a car for one year (not by the total price of the car, which is the value of an addition to capital stock). The services of stocks that last less than one year could be valued at the market price of the item. Human beings are rented rather than bought, so wages and professional fees should measure the value of services rendered by the stock of human capital. Of course, the service account would include the rental value of all existing members of the capital stock, not just those newly added. All assets would be treated in the same way that we treat owner-occupied houses in current GNP accounting—the services to the owner are estimated at an imputed equivalent rental value. Lack of rental mar-

---

*A flux may be thought of as a flow that cannot be accumulated.

kets for some assets makes the task difficult, but perhaps no more so than many current practices. The benefits of additions to the stock of capital would be counted in future years as they are actually realized, just as the costs would be counted in the present, when they are actually borne.

Some readers may have noted a similarity to the concepts of Irving Fisher (1906), and that is certainly the case. In fact, I would argue that if economists had accepted and built upon Fisher's definitions of capital and income, the major confusions of growthmania might have been avoided; the idea of a steady-state economy would have grown quite naturally out of Fisher's concepts of capital and income. Such an argument is offered below.

Capital, Income, and the SSE

Capital and income are basic concepts in economics, concepts whose definitions form the foundation supporting such an enormous superstructure of analysis that we have become very reluctant to rethink them lest we should have to rebuild the whole superstructure. Yet it is only as the building grows taller that we recognize the importance of being slightly out of plumb at the foundation level. What was hardly noticeable initially becomes, when projected ten stories, an unmistakable tendency to fall.

The analytically clearest and theoretically most satisfying concepts of capital and income are those of Fisher. Fisher's definitions have been sacrificed in order to attain somewhat more measurable definitions, presumably closer to common business usage. As Pigou put it:

> This [Fisher's] way of looking at the matter is obviously very attractive from a mathematical point of view. But the wide departure that it makes from the ordinary use of language involves disadvantages which seem to outweigh the gain in logical clarity. It is easy to fall into inconsistencies if we refuse to follow Professor Fisher's way; but it is not necessary to do so. So long as we do not do so, the choice of definitions is a matter, not of principle, but of convenience [Pigou, 1932, p. 35].

While it may be true that definitions, in the sense of names, are more a matter of convenience than principle, it is not true that concepts are mere matters of convenience. Misspecified concepts make analysis too complicated and too artificially contrived. The question here is not "What name shall we give the agreed upon concept?" but rather "What *concept* shall we denote by the agreed upon names of capital and income?"

Fisher claimed that his definitions were in accord with business usage, at least the customary usage before the terms were redefined in so many contradictory ways by economists, and more importantly that his definitions reflect the all-important distinctions between stocks and flows and between physical and psychic magnitudes. For Fisher, capital or wealth is the stock of material objects owned by human beings at an instant of time. Income is the flow of service through a period of time that is yielded by capital. Capital includes the inventory of all consumer goods and human bodies, as well as producer goods. Income is ultimately psychic income, subjective satisfactions that come through the want-satisfying services rendered by the human body and all of its material extensions, which together constitute the stock of capital.

Although Fisher did insist on including human bodies as part of capital, he did not emphasize the view later expressed by A. J. Lotka (1956) that all capital can be viewed as material extensions of the human organism, or as "exosomatic organs," to use Lotka's term. Clothes and houses extend our skin; stoves, cooking utensils, and sewers extend the digestive tract; libraries and computers extend the brain, and so on. Conversely, the organs of the body might be considered endosomatic capital, our within-skin capital equipment as opposed to outside-skin capital equipment. It is interesting to note that if we view capital as material extensions of the body, and we accept the fact that there are limits to the total number of human bodies supportable, then by the same logic we should recognize that the stock of extensions of human bodies is also limited and thus be led naturally to a steady-state perspective on the economy.

But this is getting away from Fisher. Fisher argued that a proper accounting of income must reflect only the flow of services of capital enjoyed in the subjective stream of consciousness by people, during the relevant time period. Thus a piano purchased this year is not a part of this year's income, but an addition to capital. Only the service rendered in producing music during the year is a part of this year's income. Shorter-lived components of the stock of capital, such as clothing or even food, should be considered analogously if their lifetimes should happen to overlap accounting periods.

All intermediate transactions involving exchange and transformation of physical goods will, when summed up in value terms over the whole community, exactly cancel out, leaving only what Fisher called the "uncancelled fringe" of psychic income enjoyed by the final consumer. Every intermediate transaction involves both a receipt and an expenditure of equal magnitude, which cancel out in arriving at total social income. There is no further exchange once a final consumer has obtained the serviceable good. The satisfaction yielded to the final consumer by this capital asset is the uncancelled fringe, or net result, of all the gross transformations and transactions that went before. Even this uncancelled magnitude must be somewhat diminished by the psychic disservices incurred in labor, and this gives us the final uncancelled fringe of *net psychic income*. Thus for Fisher net psychic income is the final net benefit of economic activity.

It is highly interesting that Fisher did not identify any ultimate or uncancelled cost other than the psychic disservices of some kinds of labor that were simply netted out against psychic income to obtain net psychic income. But there is for Fisher no ultimate real cost against which the ultimate value of net psychic income should be balanced.

At this point we must supplement Fisher's vision with the more recent visions and analyses of Kenneth Boulding and Nicholas Georgescu-Roegen concerning the physical basis of real cost. As everyone recognizes, the stock of capital wears out and must be replaced. This continual maintenance and replacement activity is an unavoidable cost. Fisher treated it as cancelling out in the aggregate: house repair was income to the account of the carpenter and his tools and an equal outgo to the account of the house. But Fisher did not trace the series of cancelling accounts backward to any "uncancelled fringe" at the beginning, which would be the ultimate uncancelled cost, just as his net psychic income was the ultimate uncancelled benefit. If we do this we come to the unpaid inputs from nature. Useful matter and energy taken from nature have no cost of production, only a cost of collection or extraction, which is paid and which enters the cancelling stream of accounts. But we do not pump money into a well as we pump oil out. The *net* energy yielded by an oil well is an uncancelled fringe, a one-way transfer, a grant from nature to man, a "natural subsidy" (Cook, 1976, p. 110).

It is true that in a capitalist economy differential rents are paid to resource owners, and this represents a kind of payment to nature. The amount of the payment, however, bears no relation to any cost of production of the resource *in the ground*. Differential rent is determined solely by differential costs of extraction. Supply and demand determine the price of resources *in situ*. But underlying the supply curve are cost curves, which require a definition of cost. If we adopt a historical cost convention then the price of resources *in situ* is zero. If we adopt a replacement cost definition then the price is high. Similarly the market demand curve is the sum of individual demand curves. What is the population of individuals whose demands are summed? The present only? The next ten generations? If we include the demands of many future generations the price will be high. Two arbitrary choices exist. On the supply side the competitive market selects for the lowest cost or historical cost of the production (zero), and on the demand side it counts only the present generation. It is apparent that resource prices are to a large extent arbitrary—a fact that is seldom recognized. In the next chapter we will examine a plan for auctioning depletion rights, which in effect gives a positive value to resources in the ground in the form of a pure scarcity rent. It requires a payment for natural subsidies, but the money goes to the government rather than to the landlord or down the well.

If nature had an unlimited bounty out of which to make grants of useful matter-energy to mankind, such transfers could not really be considered as costs, since they would involve no sacrificed alternatives. But all usable matter-energy has the common property of low entropy, and low entropy is scarce. Terrestrial sources of minerals and fossil fuels are limited in total amount and relative accessibility. The solar source of radiant energy is limited in its rate of arrival to earth. As long as the scale of population and per-capita consumption did not make demands that were beyond the budget of solar energy and renewable resources to supply on a sustained basis, then there were, in effect, no alternatives sacrificed and the flow from nature was still not a cost. But with today's scale of population and consumption we require high dependence on nonrenewables as well as overexploitation of renewables. Our dependence on the natural world takes two forms—that of a source of low-entropy inputs and that of a sink for high-entropy waste outputs. Capital stocks are open systems whose maintenance requires a continual exchange with the environment, a continual throughput of matter-energy. This throughput may be negligible for low levels of stock, but for high levels it involves sacrifices (especially if the stocks are made of nonrenewables) and becomes a cost—the final uncancelled real cost. This cost consists of the benefits sacrificed as a result of the entropic degradation of the natural world that is speeded up by economic activity. The physical potential for present and future want satisfaction is diminished. Alternatives are being sacrificed. More capital requires for its maintenance more throughput, which means more depletion and pollution, which means more rapid entropic degradation of the natural world. Moreover, the high-entropy wastes often interfere with the functioning of natural capital and inhibit the life-supporting services rendered by air, water, and soils. Pollution also inhibits the ability of manmade capital to render services. These costs are usually unintentional, and hence inframarginal in their incidence. Even if the costs are recognized beforehand, there is often no way to shift their burden to the margin. (Air pollution must be borne by the lungs and cannot be shifted to some less important place, say the little toe). Thus economic calculation becomes more difficult, but all the more necessary.

Figure 3 summarizes the point of view developed above. Service comes from two sources: the stock of artifacts and the natural ecosystem. The stock of artifacts requires throughput for its maintenance, which requires depletion and pollution of the ecosystem. In other words the structure and order (low entropy) of the economy is maintained by imposing a cost of disorder on the ecosystem. From the entropy law we know that the entropy increase in the ecosystem is greater than the entropy decrease in the economy. As the stock and its maintenance throughput grow, the increasing disorder exported to the ecosystem will at some point interfere with its ability to provide natural services. As we add artifacts we gain services from them, but beyond some point we pay a price in terms of diminished natural services from the ecosystem.

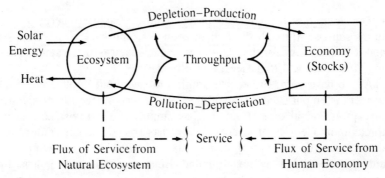

Figure 3

From this perspective it is clear that we can define an optimum stock as one for which total service (the sum of services from the economy and the ecosystem) is a maximum. This will occur when the addition to service arising from a marginal addition to the stock is equal to the decrement to service arising from impaired ecosystem services that result from the incremental throughput required by the increment in stock. In other words, marginal cost (service sacrificed) equals marginal benefit (service gained) is the rule defining the optimum level of stocks to be maintained in a steady state. The big problem in making this scheme operational is that marginal costs are determined by the web of ecological interdependence and cannot be incurred in an ordered sequence of gradually rising costs. Vital services may be sacrificed before trivial services. Marginal costs may soar to infinity and crash to zero. Therefore, "satisficing" is a better strategy than optimizing; that is, it is better to be safe than sorry. Minimizing future regret is wiser than maximizing present benefit.

The three basic magnitudes of stock, service, throughput can now be given more formal definitions.

Stock is the total inventory of producers' goods, consumers' goods, and human bodies. It corresponds to Fisher's definition of capital (1906) and may be thought of as the set of all physical things capable of satisfying human wants and subject to ownership.

Service is the satisfaction experienced when wants are satisfied, or "psychic income" in Fisher's sense (1906). Service is yielded by the stock. The quantity and quality of the stock determine the intensity of service. There is no unit for measuring service, so it may be stretching words a bit to call it a "magnitude." Nevertheless, we all experience service or satisfaction and recognize differing intensities of the experience. Service is yielded over a period of time and thus appears to be a flow magnitude. But unlike flows, service cannot be accumulated. It is probably more accurate to think of service as a psychic flux (Georgescu-Roegen, 1971).

Throughput is the entropic physical flow of matter-energy from nature's sources, through the human economy, and back to nature's sinks, and it is necessary for the maintenance and renewal of the stocks (Boulding, 1966; Daly, 1968; Georgescu-Roegen, 1971).

As we have seen, Fisher had nothing to say about throughput, but this concept is emphasized by Boulding (1966), who shares Fisher's concepts of capital and income. Boulding has emphasized the *cost* nature of the throughput. Georgescu-Roegen (1971) has traced the cost nature of the throughput (or the entropic flow, as he calls it) to its origin in the entropy law, which, as already noted, Einstein considered the least likely law in science to be overthrown. Entropy is the basic physical coordinate of scarcity. Were it not for entropy, we could burn the same gallon of gasoline over and over, and our capital stock would never wear out. Technology is unable to rise above the basic laws of physics, so there is no question of ever "inventing" a way to recycle energy, some economists (to be cited in Chapter 5) notwithstanding.

All of this leads to the following formulation. Service (net psychic income) is the final benefit of economic activity. Throughput (an entropic physical flow) is the final cost. The throughput flow does not yield services directly; it must first be accumulated and fashioned into a stock of useful artifacts (capital). All services are yielded by stocks not flows, a fact that is sometimes obscured because some stocks are short-lived and their services seem to stem from their destruction—but this is an illusion. Common sense recognizes that the service of transportation is yielded by the stock of autos. We cannot ride to town on the production flow of autos on the assembly line nor on the depreciation flow of autos decaying in the junk yard but only in an existing auto that is a member of the current stock. Less obviously to common sense, but just as logically, we can consider, in the case of short-lived assets such as gasoline, that what yields service is the stock of gasoline in the tank. This stock depreciates rapidly, it is true, but it is nevertheless the stock that satisfies our wants—not the flow of petroleum from well to gas station pump nor the flow of combustion products out the tailpipe. If we achieve the same service of passenger miles with a more slowly deteriorating stock (i.e., more miles per gallon), then the maintenance cost is less and we are better off, not worse off, even though production has diminished. Capital stocks are intermediate magnitudes, accumulated throughput temporarily frozen in ordered structures, which on the one hand yield services and on the other hand require continued throughput for physical maintenance and replacement. This can be expressed in the following identity (Daly, 1974):

$$\frac{\text{service}}{\text{throughput}} \equiv \frac{\text{service}}{\text{stock}} \times \frac{\text{stock}}{\text{throughput}}$$

$$(1) \qquad\qquad (2) \qquad\qquad (3)$$

Stocks are in the center of the analysis because they are the intermediate magnitude. It is stocks that directly yield services (ratio 2). It is the stocks that directly require throughput for maintenance and replacement (ratio 3). In the final analysis stocks cancel out just as they wear out in the real world, and we see that ultimately the benefit is service, not stocks, and that the cost of services is throughput, or rather the sacrificed ecosystem services provoked by the throughput.

Stock is neither a benefit nor a cost, but both benefits and costs are functions of the stock. The steady-state paradigm suggests three different modes of behavior regarding these three separate dimensions. For stocks, the indicated mode of behavior is *satisficing,* choosing some level of stocks that is sufficient for a good life and sustainable for a long future. Throughput is to be *minimized,* subject to the maintenance of the constant stocks. Service is to be *maximized,* subject to the constant stocks.

Ratio 1 represents the final service efficiency of the throughput—final benefit over final cost. Ratio 2 is the service efficiency of the stock, ratio 3 the stock-maintenance efficiency of the throughput. Economic *development* consists in increasing ratios 2 and 3, thus getting more service per unit of throughput. *Growth* consists of increasing service by increasing the size of stocks, but with no increase (and possibly a decrease) in the efficiency ratios 2 and 3. The steady-state economy, by holding stocks constant, would force an end to pure growth but would not curtail, and in fact would stimulate, development.

The increase of ratio 3 (maintenance efficiency) is limited by the second law of thermodynamics. Maintenance efficiency is essentially a measure of the durability of the stock, and the second law tells us that we cannot approach infinite durability. Limits to increasing ratio 2 (service efficiency) are less clear. Perhaps there is no limit to the amount of service (psychic satisfaction) derivable from a given stock. Even if true, this would not be inconsistent with the steady state, which is defined in physical terms only. Evidently ascetics believe that once the body is maintained at minimal levels, further stocks just get in the way of true welfare. Without going that far, we may question whether there are not some basic limits on service imposed by the limited capacity of the human nervous system to experience the service. For example, high-fidelity sound systems, beyond some degree, reproduce vibrations that we simply cannot hear. Moreover, time is limited, and we experience a congestion of the temporal dimension with stocks of commodities. If a man buys golf clubs, then he will have less time to enjoy his tennis racket, his boat, and so forth. At some point the marginal yield must become very low or even negative. To the extent that there are such limits on service, then development as well as growth will be limited. But the limit to service efficiency is not crucial to the steady-state view; only the limit to maintenance efficiency is crucial. Service is a psychic magnitude and the steady state is defined only in terms of physical magnitudes.

These considerations lead us quite naturally to ask how much capital stock is enough and how that sufficient stock could be maintained with the least possible throughput, that is, the least possible entropic degradation of the physical world. The goal would then become to maintain the sufficient capital stock with a low throughput. In other words, the goal becomes a steady-state economy.

The contrast between this common-sense formulation and conventional economic thinking has been vividly pointed out by Boulding:

> Throughput is by no means a desideratum, and is indeed to be regarded as something to be minimized rather than maximized. The essential measure of the success of the economy is not production and consumption at all, but the nature, extent, quality, and complexity of the total capital stock, including in this the state of the human bodies and minds included in the system. In the spaceman economy, what we are primarily concerned with is stock maintenance, and any technological change which results in the maintenance of a given total stock with a lessened throughput (that is, less production and consumption) is clearly a gain. The idea that production and consumption are both bad things rather than good things is very strange to economists, who have been obsessed with the income-flow concepts to the exclusion, almost, of capital-stock concepts [Boulding, 1966, p. 9].

We should be concerned with the "nature, extent, quality and complexity of the capital stock" because that determines how much service, how much want satisfaction, is yielded by the stock. It determines the ratio $\frac{service}{stock}$, or the service efficiency of the stock. We are concerned to minimize throughput because that increases the ratio $\frac{stock}{throughput}$, or the maintenance efficiency of the throughput. Thus for a given sufficient stock we should seek to maximize service by improving the quality and usefulness of the stock, while minimizing the maintenance and replacement costs of throughput. The first ratio measures service yielded by the stock *per unit of time*. The second ratio measures the *number of units of time* during which the stock yields services before it must be replaced. We will return to these concepts of efficiency in Chapter 4.

Looking at things in Fisher's way, as further developed by Boulding and Georgescu-Roegen, leads away from growthmania and toward the steady-state paradigm. It forces recognition of ultimate means and ultimate ends, and their more operational counterparts, final costs and final benefits. It shifts attention to stocks, the quality of the stocks, and the distribution of stock ownership. It leads to impolite questions about inequality, and to the realization that redistribution is the only cure for poverty, because growth simply cannot do the job. It forces the throughput into the focus of analysis, along with the "external" costs of depletion and pollution. It forces out the concept of GNP, in which many have a large professional investment. Most of all, it threatens the Faustian covenant with Big Science and High Technology and forces the more humble view that not all things are possible through technology—that the big problems of overpopulation and overconsumption have no technical fixes, but only difficult moral solutions. For all these reasons, the steady-state view is resisted by many, especially by orthodox economists. However, for the very same reasons the steady-state view is gaining support. As the consequences of growthmania become more apparent and more costly, the steady-state paradigm will be taken ever more seriously. The world cannot stand another decade of narrow economists who have never thought about ultimate means or the Ultimate End, who are unable to define either entropy or a sacrament, yet behave as if there were no such thing as entropy and as if nothing were sacred except growth.

Scarcity, Wants, and the SSE

It has been argued that a proper reinterpretation of the basic concepts of capital and income, following Fisher, leads naturally to the concept of a SSE. Similarly, it can be shown that a fresh look at the basic concepts of scarcity and wants will also lead us to the notion of a SSE. The logical path to the SSE via an analysis of scarcity and wants is very similar to the path already traveled in our discussion of ultimate means and the Ultimate End. Even at the risk of repetition, it is useful to develop the argument in terms of the more traditional concepts of scarcity and wants, since these are probably the two most fundamental ideas in economics. Each concept has an absolute and a relative aspect, and the failure to adequately distinguish these aspects and their changing importance, or rather the tendency to treat each concept in terms of one of the aspects alone, has produced much confusion. To understand the origins and consequences of this confusion we must first define our terms.

All scarcity is relative to wants or needs, but that is not the sense in which we use the term "relative scarcity." Rather, this term refers to the scarcity of a particular resource relative to another resource, or relative to a different (lower) quality of the same resource. The solution to relative scarcity is substitution. Relatively abundant resources are eventually substituted for relatively scarce resources by the combined adjustment of the price system and new technologies.

Absolute scarcity, by contrast, refers to the scarcity of resources in general, the scarcity of ultimate means. Absolute scarcity increases as growth in population and per-capita consumption push us ever closer to the carrying capacity of the biosphere. The concept presupposes that all economical substitutions among resources will be made. While such substitutions will certainly mitigate the burden of absolute scarcity, they will not eliminate it nor prevent its eventual increase.

Barnett and Morse (1963), in their classic statement of what is now the orthodox view of the economics of natural resource availability, make essentially the same distinction between Malthusian scarcity (an absolute limit to natural resources, beyond which availability is nil) and Ricardian scarcity (unlimited resources in total, but nonhomogeneous in quality). Their study leads them to conclude that Malthusian or absolute scarcity is not relevant: "Nature imposes particular scarcities, not an inescapable general scarcity" (p. 11). Thus only Ricardian or relative scarcity is of concern, and even that is being overcome: "Science, by making the resource base more homogeneous, erases the restrictions once thought to reside in the lack of homogeneity. In a neo-Ricardian world, it seems, the particular resources with which one starts increasingly become a matter of indifference" (p. 11). In sum, absolute scarcity is dismissed from further consideration, and even relative scarcity is deemed likely to be vanquished by the march of science. This is the dominant view of current orthodox economic theory: only relative scarcity matters.*

Turning now to relative and absolute wants or needs, we can do no better than to quote the definitions given by J. M. Keynes:

> Now it is true that the needs of human beings may seem to be insatiable. But they fall into two classes—those needs which are absolute in the sense that we feel them whatever the situation of our fellow human beings may be, and those which are relative in the sense that we feel them only if their satisfaction lifts us above, makes us feel superior to, our fellows. Needs of the second class, those which satisfy the desire for superiority, may indeed be insatiable: for the higher the general level, the higher still are they. But this is not so true of the absolute needs—a point may soon be reached, much sooner perhaps than we are all of us aware of, when these needs are satisfied in the sense that we prefer to devote our further energies to non-economic purposes [Keynes, 1931, p. 365].

This is a very clear and important distinction of concepts. The importance lies in the fact that only one class of wants or needs is insatiable, namely, relative wants. Modern economic theory treats wants in general as insatiable, and refuses to make such distinctions as the above in order not to introduce value judgments into economic theory, thereby jeopardizing its coveted status as a "positive" science. Even wants created by

---

*That the denial of absolute scarcity was still dogma in 1973 is evidenced by the papers in the section "Natural Resources as a Constraint on Economic Growth," *American Economic Review,* Papers and Proceedings, May 1973. See also the survey article, "The Environment in Economics" (Fisher and Peterson, 1976), which begins with the revealing sentence, "Man has probably always worried about the environment because he *was once* totally dependent on it" (emphasis supplied). If we can see the absurdity of that statement we are well on the way to the steady-state paradigm.

advertising are granted absolute status, Galbraith being the exceptional economist who proves the rule. By treating all wants on equal footing we are not, of course, avoiding value judgments. Instead, we are making a particularly inept value judgment, namely, that relative wants (the insatiable needs of vanity) should be accorded equal status in economic theory with satiable absolute wants, and that wants in general should be considered insatiable. Most economists would deny that this is a value judgment. We do behave as if relative wants had equal status with absolute wants, (or so it is claimed), and economic theory, it is argued, merely describes this behavior without judging. However, always saying "is" and never "ought" tends to apologize for the status quo. The theory by which we try to understand our economic behavior cannot help but be an element in determining that behavior. The medium becomes the message. But even if we admit infinite wants, it does not follow that attempting infinite production via continuous growth is capable of satisfying infinite wants. Many wants simply cannot be satisfied by increasing aggregate production (relative wants), and many wants are rendered less capable of satisfaction by further growth (wants for leisure, wilderness, silence, etc.). Growth cannot overcome existential scarcity—the basic limits on our time, energy, attention, and devotion. Recognition of limits does not require rejection of the infinite wants dogma. But it should be rejected anyway, or at least confined to the class of relative wants.

The upshot is that in orthodox economics all scarcity is considered merely relative, while the class of all wants is accorded the insatiability of relative wants but is invested with the moral earnestness of absolute wants. The implication of the doctrines of the relativity of scarcity and the insatiability of wants is growthmania. If there is no absolute scarcity to limit the *possibility* of growth (we can always substitute relatively abundant resources for relatively scarce ones), and no merely relative or trivial wants to limit the *desirability* of growth (wants in general are infinite and all wants are worthy of and capable of satisfaction by aggregate growth, even if based solely on invidious comparison), then "growth forever and the more the better" is the logical consequence. It is also the *reductio ad absurdum* that exposes the growth orthodoxy as a rigorous exercise in wishful thinking.

It is a brute fact, however, that there *is* such a thing as absolute scarcity, and there *is* such a thing as purely relative and trivial wants. And, if these aspects are dominant at the margin, the implication is the opposite of growthmania, namely, the steady-state economy. Nature does impose an absolute general scarcity in the form of the laws of thermodynamics and the finitude of the earth. Low entropy is the common denominator of all useful things and is scarce in an absolute sense. The stock of terrestrial low entropy is limited in total amount, while the flow of solar low entropy is limited in its rate of arrival. These facts, in the face of growing population and growing per-capita consumption, guarantee the existence and increasing importance of absolute scarcity. Substitution is always of one source of low entropy for another. There is no substitute for low entropy itself, and low entropy is scarce.

It may be objected that these physical limits do not constitute scarcity because low entropy is superabundant relative to our needs. But this objection loses plausibility when it is recognized that "our needs" include the job of running the entire biosphere—of powering the vast web of life-support services. As economic growth lowers the entropy (increases the order, reduces the randomness) of the human sector of the biosphere, it raises the entropy (reduces the order, increases the randomness) of the nonhuman sector. The increase of order in one sphere is compensated by a reduction of order in the other sphere, and the second law tells us that for the two sectors taken together there is a net reduction in order. But in increasing the entropy of the nonhuman part of the biosphere we interfere with its ability to function, since it also runs on low entropy. The fact that such interferences are now much more noticeable than in the past indicates that low entropy is increasingly scarce. Absolute scarcity is becoming more important.

One of the major differences between absolute and relative scarcity is that the price system handles the latter admirably but is, by itself, largely powerless against the former. Correctly adjusted relative prices allow us to bear the burden of absolute scarcity in the least uncomfortable manner. But even an efficiently borne burden can eventually become too heavy. When the relative price of the relatively scarce resource rises, as it eventually will, it induces the substitution of relatively abundant resources. Price cannot deal with absolute scarcity because it is impossible to raise the relative prices of *all* resources in general. Any attempt to do so merely raises the absolute price level, and instead of substitution (What substitute is there for resources in general, for low entropy?) we merely get inflation. Maybe that is one of the root causes of inflation in advanced economies. Perhaps we respond to increasing absolute scarcity as if it were relative scarcity, that is, by trying to raise the relative price of everything. To the extent that inflation results, greater money price increases are required to achieve a given relative price increase, present consumption is speeded up, and the increase in absolute scarcity becomes self-feeding. Given the large measure of monopoly power in our economy and the tendency of each power group to protect and extend its relative share of total income, then any price increase for whatever reason becomes amplified and generalized as other prices are marked up to protect profits and incomes from the eroding effects of the first price increase. Be that as it may, the inability of the price system to deal with absolute scarcity is probably another reason for orthodox economics'

having wished it out of existence. Malthus has been buried many times, and Malthusian scarcity with him. But as Garrett Hardin remarked, anyone who has to be reburied so often cannot be entirely dead.

The same exclusive focus on relative scarcity leads economists to the advocacy of "internalization of externalities" via pollution taxes as the sufficient cure for environmental ills. In the words of economist Wilfred Beckerman: "The problem of environmental pollution is a simple matter of correcting a minor resource misallocation by means of pollution charges . . ." (1972, p. 327). But internalization is insufficient in that it acts only on relative prices. Growth in population and per-capita consumption lead to increasing absolute scarcity, which is manifested in the increasing prevalence of external costs. To charge these external costs to the particular resources and activities within the total interrelated system that seem most directly responsible for them is a good fine-tuning policy for bearing the burden most efficiently and inducing substitution. But it does not stop the increase in absolute scarcity resulting from continuing population growth and growth in per-capita consumption. The price system could halt growth only if it were possible to raise the relative price of everything (i.e., relative to total income). But this is impossible, since one man's price is another man's income, so that, in the aggregate, supply generates its own demand, as Say's Law tells us. Aggregate income, if spent, is always sufficient to purchase whatever is produced, regardless of prices. And if aggregate demand should lag a bit, then Keynesian policy is there to make up the difference. Aggregate physical limits must be placed on the causative factors of population and per-capita consumption growth, with the price system achieving the fine-tuning adjustment within those limits. (This will be further discussed in Chapter 3.) Internalizing externalities into relative prices deals only with relative scarcity, not at all with absolute scarcity. Orthodox economics has treated all scarcity as relative, so naturally it considers internalization of externalities to be the whole answer. But of course it is not.

At some point, absolute scarcity makes growth impossible, and, quite independently, at some (probably earlier) point, further satisfaction of the self-cancelling relative wants of vanity makes growth either futile or undesirable. Either case is, by itself, a sufficient argument against the apotheosis of growth. Clearly, both the relative and the absolute aspects of both scarcity and wants exist and are important. But their relative importance has undergone an evolutionary change. At low levels of population and low per-capita consumption there was little need to worry about absolute scarcity. In addition, since only basic absolute wants could be satisfied, there was no possibility of relative wants becoming dominant (except for elite minorities). But this situation has been reversed by a long period of growth. At the current margin, relative wants are dominant, and absolute scarcity can no longer be ignored. To catch up with this dialectical change in the real world, we need a new economic theory that recognizes absolute scarcity and relative wants (and their increasing dominance at the margin), and consequently shifts its perspective from growthmania to the steady state.

The continued existence of unsatisfied absolute wants among the poor is more an argument for redistribution than for further growth. Further growth dedicated mainly to the satisfaction of relative wants faces a grave dilemma. If the aggregate growth is evenly distributed, then the satisfaction of the relative wants will be cancelled out, because everyone cannot improve his position relative to everyone else. But to avoid the cancelling effect, those who are already relatively well off must become relatively better off, that is, inequality must increase. Beyond some point, growth in the pursuit of relative want satisfactions must lead either to increasing futility, increasing inequality, or a mixture of both.

Underlying Value Assumptions of the SSE

Our discussion of the steady state has been based on some fundamental assumptions of a physical and moral nature. The biophysical assumptions (the first and second laws of thermodynamics and the complex evolutionary adaptation of the biosphere to a fixed flow of solar energy) have already been discussed. The moral or ethical assumptions have been alluded to, but they merit more explicit discussion.

Nearly all traditional religions teach man to conform his soul to reality by knowledge, self-discipline, and restraint on the multiplication of desires, as well as on the lengths to which he will go to satisfy some desire. The modern religious attitudes of technological scientism and growthmania seek, after the manner of magic, to subjugate reality and bend it to the uninstructed will and whim of some men, usually to the unmeasured detriment of other men. We often forget that what we call the increasing dominance of man over nature is really the increasing dominance of some men over other men, with knowledge of nature serving as the instrument of domination (Lewis, 1946). This may not be intentional or always a bad thing, but it should be recognized for what it is. There is a limit beyond which the extra costs of surrendering control over our lives to the experts becomes greater than the extra benefits. For scientism and growthmania there is no such thing as "enough," even on the material plane. Indeed, the whole idea seems to be to try to fill a spiritual void with material commodities and technological razzle-dazzle. The usual objection to limiting growth, made ostensibly in the name of the poor, only illustrates the extent of the void because it views growth as an alternative to sharing, which is considered unrealistic. For the traditional religious attitude, there is such a thing as material sufficiency, and beyond that admittedly vague and historically changing amount, the goal of life becomes wisdom, enjoyment, cultivation of the mind and soul, and community. It may even be that community requires a certain degree of scarcity, without which cooperation, sharing, and friendship would have no organic reason to be, and hence community would atrophy. Witness the isolated self-sufficiency of households and lack of community in affluent middle-class suburbs.

The role of money fetishism in supporting the ideology that there is no such thing as enough has been noted by Lewis Mumford:

> Now, the desire for money, Thomas Aquinas points out, knows no limits, whereas all natural wealth, represented in the concrete form of food, clothing, furniture, houses, gardens, fields, has definite limits of production and consumption, fixed by the nature of the commodity and the organic needs and capacities of the user. The idea that there should be no limits on any human function is absurd: all life exists within very narrow limits of temperature, air, water, food; and the notion that money alone, or power to command the services of other men, should be free of such definite limits is an abberation of the mind.
>
> The desire for limitless quantities of money has as little relevance to the welfare of the human organism as the stimulation of the "pleasure center" that scientific experimenters have recently found in the brain. This stimulus is subjectively so rewarding, apparently, that animals under observation willingly forgo every other need or activity, to the point of starvation, in order to enjoy it [Mumford, 1966, p. 276].

Has growthmania, aided by money fetishism, become a kind of pleasure center in our collective brain that is so much fun to stimulate that we willingly sacrifice objective organic well-being and viability to a self-induced, subjective good feeling? This may be carrying an analogy too far, but the story of King Midas as well as the opposition of the medieval scholastics to interest indicate that thinking people of all ages have been suspicious of any notion implying the limitless growth of wealth. As Frederick Soddy pointed out, compound interest is the law of increase of debt, not wealth:

> Debts are subject to the laws of mathematics rather than physics. Unlike wealth which is subject to the laws of thermodynamics, debts do not rot with old age and are not consumed in the process of living. On the contrary they grow at so much percent per annum, by the well-known mathematical laws of simple and compound interest. . . .
>
> As a result of this confusion between wealth and debt we are invited to contemplate a millennium where people live on the interest of their mutual indebtedness [Soddy, 1926, pp. 68, 89].

Another ethical first principle is a sense of stewardship for all of creation and an extension of brotherhood to future generations and to subhuman life. Clearly, the first demands on brotherhood are those of presently existing human beings who do not enjoy material sufficiency. The answer to a failure of brotherhood is not simply more growth but is to be found mainly in more sharing and more population control. Both sharing and population control are necessary. Without population control, sharing will simply make everyone equally poor while driving other species to extinction. Without sharing, population control will at best reduce the number of the poor but will not eliminate poverty. Both sharing and population control are basically moral problems, whose solutions require sound values far more than clever techniques.

The virtue of humility is also high on the list of moral first principles. Much of the drive to convert the ecosphere into one big technosphere comes from the technological hubris of quite ordinary men, who think that the scientific method has somehow transfigured them into little godlings who can collectively accomplish anything—if only society will give them more and more research funds! At a more basic level, the drive comes from the need for doing and controlling as a verification of knowledge. There is no reason that we must do everything we know how to do, but there is a sense in which we cannot be sure we know how to do something unless we have done it. If we are going to avoid doing certain things, we will have to sacrifice the forbidden knowledge that would have been gained.* Basically, the steady-state view conceives of man as a fallible creature whose hope lies in the benevolence of his Creator not in the excellence of his own creations. Scientistic growthmania sees man as a potentially infallible creator whose hope lies in his marvelous scientific creativity and not in any superstitions about an unobservable creator. Our age is enormously biased in favor of the latter view, yet the traditional wisdom of all great religions favors the former. As H. Richard Niebuhr remarked: "This-worldliness may seem more objective than otherworldliness to those who have never faced their own presuppositions. When they do face them they become aware that their ultimate dogma is at least as much a matter of faith as is the dogma of the otherworldly man" (1937, p. 13).

Another important virtue is holism, the attitude that recognizes that the whole is greater than the sum of its parts, that reductionist analysis never tells the whole story, and that the abstractions necessary to make mechanistic models always do violence to reality. Those who habitually think in terms of abstract, reductionist models are especially prone to the fallacy of misplaced concreteness, that is, of applying to one level of

---

*Any notion of forbidden knowledge provokes charges of obscurantism and worse. Inevitably, someone will quote the Biblical passage most frequently carved on laboratory and library lintels, "Know the truth, and the truth will make you free" as high sanction for pulling apart anything that arouses our curiosity. Contrary to the thought implied by the fragment, the full quotation reads, "Jesus said to the Jews who had believed in him, 'If you continue in my word, you are truly my disciples, and you will know the truth, and the truth will make you free'" (John 8:31). The statement is decidedly conditional, and the freedom referred to is freedom from sin, not ignorance. Pascal saw things more clearly: "We make an idol of truth itself; for truth apart from charity is not God, but his image and idol, which we must neither love nor worship" (quoted in Huxley, 1944, p. 82).

abstraction conclusions arrived at from thinking on a different (higher) level of abstraction. Given a fulcrum and a long enough lever, Archimedes could move the earth. Given ceteris paribus, internalization of externalities, and exponentially increasing technology, economists can make the economy grow forever. Archimedes' boast was no more vacuous than that of the growth economist.

In sum, the moral first principles are: some concept of enoughness, stewardship, humility, and holism. In social science today we hear little of moral values or ethics (even though economics began as a branch of moral philosophy). Appeals to moral solutions, to a correction of values, are considered as an admission of intellectual defeat, as a retreat from the rules of the game—as cheating. The quest is for mechanistic and sophisticated technological resolutions, not straightforward moral solutions. Power-yielding techniques have been assiduously sought, while the cultivation of right purposes has been neglected—some even consider the latter a meaningless question. We now have increasing power governed by diminishing purpose, but seem reluctant to shift our attention toward the clarification of purpose. The issue has been well put by Huxley:

> Has the ability to travel in twelve hours from New York to Los Angeles given more pleasure to the human race than the dropping of bombs and fire has given pain? There is no known method of computing the amount of felicity or goodness in the world at large. What is obvious, however, is that the advantages accruing from recent technological advances—or, in Greek phraseology, from recent acts of *hubris* directed against Nature—are generally accompanied by corresponding disadvantages, that gains in one direction entail losses in other directions, and that we never get something except for something. Whether the net result of these elaborate credit and debit operations is a genuine Progress in virtue, happiness, charity and intelligence is something we can never definitely determine. It is because the reality of Progress can never be determined that the nineteenth and twentieth centuries have had to treat it as an article of religious faith. To the exponents of the Perennial Philosophy, the question of whether Progress is inevitable or even real is not a matter of primary importance. For them, the important thing is that individual men and women should come to the unitive knowledge of the divine Ground, and what interests them in regard to the social environment is not its progressiveness or non-progressiveness (whatever those terms may mean), but the degree to which it helps or hinders individuals in their advance towards man's final end [Huxley, 1944, p. 79].

As is evident from the discussion in this chapter, the steady-state position is arrived at by simple deduction from first principles. If the world is a finite complex system that has evolved with reference to a fixed rate of flow of solar energy, then any economy that seeks indefinite expansion of its stocks and the associated material and energy-maintenance flows will sooner or later hit limits. This is trivial logically, a tautology, but it is not trivial psychologically and politically. Some people seem to believe that if a proposition is tautological, or arrived at by a short chain of reasoning, it is so uninteresting that it can be safely dismissed and forgotten! If man's behavior should be governed by values of enoughness, steward-ship, humility, and holism, then it follows that attitudes of "more forever," *"après moi le deluge,"* technical arrogance, and aggressive analytical reductionism—all important components of growthmania—must be rejected. Again the proposition is obvious, which is too bad, because if it required a difficult mathematical proof probably more people would accept it! The one thing about truisms that we should never forget is that they are, after all, true.

REFERENCES

Barnett, Harold, and Chandler Morse. *Scarcity and Growth.* Baltimore: Johns Hopkins University Press, 1963.

Beckerman, Wilfred. "Economists, Scientists, and Environmental Catastrophe," *Oxford Economic Papers,* November 1972, 327–344.

Boulding, Kenneth E. "The Economics of the Coming Spaceship Earth," in H. Jarrett, ed., *Environmental Quality in a Growing Economy.* Baltimore: Johns Hopkins University Press, 1966.

Cook, Earl. *Man, Energy, Society.* San Francisco: W. H. Freeman, 1976.

Daly, Herman E. "The Economics of the Steady State," *American Economic Review,* May 1974, 15–21.

Daly, Herman E. "On Economics as a Life Science," *Journal of Political Economy,* May/June 1968, 392–406.

Eddington, Arthur. *The Nature of the Physical World.* New York: Cambridge University Press, 1953.

Fisher, Anthony C., and Frederick M. Peterson. "The Environment in Econom-ics: A Survey," *Journal of Economic Literature,* March 1976, 1–33.

Fisher, Irving. *The Nature of Capital and Income.* London: Macmillan, 1906.

Georgescu-Roegen, Nicholas. "Economics and Mankind's Ecological Problem," in Joint Economic Committee of the Congress of the United States, *U.S. Economic Growth from 1976 to 1986: Prospects, Problems, and Patterns,* Vol. 7. Washington, D.C.: U.S. Government Printing Office, December 17, 1976.

Georgescu-Roegen, Nicholas. *The Entropy Law and the Economic Process.* Cambridge, Mass.: Harvard University Press, 1971.

Huxley, Aldous. *The Perennial Philosophy.* New York: Harper & Row, 1944.

Jevons, W. S. *The Theory of Political Economy.* London: Macmillan, 1924.

Keynes, J. M. "Economic Possibilities for Our Grandchildren," in *Essays in Persuasion.* New York: Norton, 1963.

Kuhn, Thomas. *The Structure of Scientific Revolutions.* Chicago: University of Chicago Press, 1962.

Lewis, C. *The Abolition of Man.* London: Macmillan, 1946.

Lotka, A. J. *Elements of Mathematical Biology.* New York: Dover, 1956. Previously published in 1925 under the title *Elements of Physical Biology.*

Mill, John Stuart. *On Liberty.* Chicago: Encyclopedia Brittanica Great Books, 1952. Originally published in 1859.

Mishan, E. J. "Growth and Anti-Growth: What Are the Issues?" *Challenge,* May/June 1973.

Mumford, Lewis. *The Myth of the Machine.* New York: Harcourt Brace Jovanovich, 1966.

Niebuhr, H. Richard. *The Kingdom of God in America.* New York: Harper & Row, 1937.

Pigou, A. C. *The Economics of Welfare,* 4th ed. London: Macmillan, 1932.

Ruskin, John. "Unto This Last," in Lloyd J. Hubenka, ed., *Four Essays on the First Principles of Political Economy.* Lincoln: University of Nebraska Press, 1967. Originally published in 1860.

Schlipp, P. A., ed. *Albert Einstein: Philosopher Scientist,* Vol. 7. New York: Harper & Row, 1959.

Schumpeter, Joseph. *History of Economic Analysis.* New York: Oxford University Press, 1954.

Soddy, Frederick. *Cartesian Economics: The Bearing of Physical Science Upon State Stewardship.* London: Hendersons, 1922.

Soddy, Frederick. *Wealth, Virtual Wealth and Debt.* London: George Allen and Unwin, Ltd., 1926.

Woodwell, George M. "Short-Circuiting the Cheap Power Fantasy," *Natural History,* October 1974.

3

INSTITUTIONS FOR
A STEADY-STATE ECONOMY

If you jump out of an airplane, you are better off with a
parachute than an altimeter.

Robert Allen (1973)

Drawing blueprints for future societies is a favorite pastime of intellectu-
als and dreamers, and it is often dismissed as a waste of time. Detailed
blueprints no doubt are a waste of time judged by the likelihood that
future people will precisely follow their specific impositions. But a general outline or image of a desirable future is an absolute logical necessity
for any kind of policy that is not a mere repetition of past practices.
Indeed, even such repetition tacitly assumes a desirable image of the
future that is identical to the present, and that image, if spelled out in
detail, has as small a chance of fulfillment as any other. The following
speculations represent a general outline rather than a detailed blueprint
and are meant to show that the desirable image of a steady-state economy
is feasible. There are perhaps better means for attaining it than the institutions I suggest, but a start must be made somewhere. We will first
consider the question: Could a steady-state economy function if people
accepted it? Then we will speculate on the separate question: How likely
are people to accept it? These questions should not be confused, because

they are quite independent, except that a prior demonstration that something could work if accepted may increase its likelihood of being accepted. There are plenty of workable schemes that for good reasons are not acceptable, and contrary to rational expectation, there are unworkable schemes that are politically acceptable, for example, Project Independence.

Three institutions for attaining and maintaining a steady-state economy are outlined. These institutions build on the existing bases of the price system and private property and are thus fundamentally conservative, but they are extended to areas previously not included: control of aggregate births and control of the aggregate throughput. Property rights and markets are extended to these vital areas in order to stabilize population and capital stock. Moreover, control is exercised in the form of aggregate physical quotas, since, as argued in the last chapter, price controls deal only with relative scarcity and cannot limit the increase of absolute scarcity. Markets allow these quota rights to be allocated efficiently. Extending the discipline of the market to such vital areas of life makes it urgent to establish the institutional preconditions of mutually beneficial exchange, namely, to limit the degree of inequality in the distribution of income and wealth and to limit the size and monopoly power of corporations.

The guiding design principle for the three institutions is to provide the necessary social control with a minimum sacrifice of personal freedom, to provide macrostability while allowing for microvariability, to combine the macrostatic with the microdynamic. To do otherwise, to aim for microstability and control is likely to be self-defeating and to result in macroinstability, as the capacities for spontaneous coordination, adjustment, and mutation (which always occur on the micro level) are stifled by central planning with its inevitable rigidities and information losses. The micro is the domain of indeterminacy, novelty, and freedom. The macro, or aggregate, is the domain of determinacy, predictability, and control. We should strive for macrocontrol and avoid micromeddling. A second design principle, closely related to the first, is to maintain considerable slack between the actual environmental load and the maximum carrying capacity. The closer the actual approaches the maximum the less is the margin for error, and the more rigorous, finely tuned, and microoriented our controls will have to be. We lack the knowledge and ability to assume detailed control of the spaceship, so therefore we must leave it on "automatic pilot," as it has been for eons. But the automatic pilot only works when the actual load is small relative to the conceivable maximum. A third important design principle for making the transition to a steady-state economy is to build in the ability to tighten constraints gradually and to begin from existing initial conditions rather than unrealistically assuming a clean slate.

In the definition of a steady-state economy in the previous chapter, the level at which stocks of physical wealth and people should be stabilized was not specified, beyond some "sufficient, sustainable level." Naturally, we would like to be able to define an optimum level of population and artifacts. If this could be done, it would immediately follow that, once having reached the optimum levels, the optimum growth rates of population and physical capital would be zero. It is very difficult, probably impossible, to define such an optimum level. Some people go on to argue that unless we can specify the optimum it makes no sense to advocate a SSE. That is not so. Stability and viability are more important than, and logically independent of, questions of optimality. If we knew the precise optimum without knowing how to be stable at that optimum, it would profit us nothing. It would merely enable us to recognize and wave goodbye to the optimum as we grew through it. If we knew how to be stable without knowing the precise optimum, it would profit us a great deal. Survival requires limiting physical growth, achieving stability. Optimality is nice, but feasibility is essential. Furthermore, the actual levels of population and artifact stocks are historically given, at least initially. We must learn to be stable at existing or nearby levels, simply because that is where we are. Later we can chase the optimum.

If it is required that the optimum levels chosen for the United States be generalizable to the whole world and to many future generations, then in all likelihood we will have to reduce our current population, stock of artifacts, and their associated maintenance throughput. The question of optimum is so difficult because it requires that we simultaneously decide the size of population, the standards for per-capita resource use, the relevant time period, and the kinds of technology. There are trade-offs among the four issues. Obviously, we could choose many people at low per-capita resource use or fewer people at higher per-capita use rates. We could choose many people and high per-capita use for just a few generations. We could reject certain technologies as socially unacceptable and accommodate our numbers and consumption to fit the capacity of acceptable technologies.

Before we argue about these trade-offs, the first issue remains to stop the momentum of growth and to learn to run a stable economy at historically given initial conditions. These given conditions may be far from optimal. Maintaining existing levels may require onerous technologies and a short life for the system. But we cannot go into reverse without first coming to a stop. Step one is to achieve a SSE at existing or nearby levels. Step two is to decide whether the optimum level is greater or less than present levels. This decision involves the trade-offs mentioned, which in turn depend on our value judgments regarding posterity, technology, and the worth of material consumption beyond some level of sufficiency. My own judgments on these issues lead me to think we have overshot the optimum. But even those who think we have not yet reached the optimum should be interested in learning to live in a SSE before reaching the optimum. Otherwise we would not know how to stay at the optimum once we arrived. To argue that we must first know the optimum and arrive at it before learning to be stable is a classic case of the best being the enemy of the good.

Economist Michael Goldberg (1976) has made a similar point in distinguishing two concepts of stability. Equilibrium-centered stability is point oriented and maximizes speed of return to the optimum point after disturbance. Boundary-oriented stability, on the other hand, maximizes the range of disturbances that can be encountered without pushing the system beyond a set of feasible boundaries. In boundary-oriented stability, generality of resilience takes precedence over speed of adjustment, and "satisficing" takes precedence over optimizing. Equilibrium-centered stability attempts to reduce all uncertainty to measurable risk and include it in the optimizing calculus. Boundary-oriented stability recognizes pure uncertainty (unpredictable novelty) and, in so far as possible, prepares to be surprised by leaving open a range of options that would be considered wasteful from the optimizing view. The equilibrium-centered view concentrates on finding the peak of the mountain as quickly as possible. The boundary-oriented view builds fences along the edges of all chasms and argues that all the fenced-in high area is worth preserving because someday it might get very cold and windy on the peak. Boundary-oriented stability tends to minimize future regrets rather than maximize present satisfaction. The policies to be advocated below aim at boundary-oriented stability.

The kinds of institutions required follow directly from the definition of a SSE: constant stocks of people and artifacts maintained at some chosen, sufficient level by a low rate of throughput. We need (1) an institution for stabilizing population (transferable birth licenses); (2) an institution for stabilizing the stock of physical artifacts and keeping throughput below ecological limits (depletion quotas auctioned by the government); and (3) a distributist institution limiting the degree of inequality in the distribution of constant stocks among the constant population (maximum and minimum limits to personal income and a maximum limit to personal wealth).

In discussing each institution separately, it will be convenient to begin with the last mentioned of the three.

The Distributist Institution

The critical institution is likely to be the minimum and maximum limits on income and the maximum limit on wealth. Without some such limits, private property and the whole market economy lose their moral basis, and there would be no strong case for extending the market to cover birth quotas and depletion quotas as a means of institutionalizing environmental limits. Exchange relations are mutually beneficial among relative equals. Exchange between the powerful and the powerless is often only nominally voluntary and can easily be a mask for exploitation, especially in the labor market, as Marx has shown.

There is considerable political support for a minimum income, financed by a negative income tax, as an alternative to bureaucratic welfare programs. There is no such support for maximum income or maximum wealth limits. In the growth paradigm there need be no upper limit. But in the steady-state paradigm there must be an upper limit to the total, and consequently an upper limit to per-capita income as well. A minimum wealth limit is not feasible, since we can always spend our wealth and could hardly expect to have it restored year after year. The minimum income would be sufficient. But maximum limits on both wealth and income are necessary, since wealth and income are largely interchangeable and since, beyond some point, the concentration of wealth becomes inconsistent with both a market economy and political democracy. John Stuart Mill put the issue very well:

> Private property, in every defense made of it, is supposed to mean the guarantee to individuals of the fruits of their own labor and abstinence. The guarantee to them of the fruits of the labor and abstinence of others, transmitted to them without any merit or exertion of their own, is not of the essence of the institution, but a mere incidental consequence, which, when it reaches a certain height, does not promote, but conflicts with, the ends which render private property legitimate [Mill, 1881].

According to Mill, private property is legitimated as a bastion against exploitation. But this is true only if everyone owns some minimum amount. Otherwise, private property, when some own a great deal of it and others have very little, becomes the very *instrument* of exploitation rather than a guarantee against it. It is implicit in this view that private property is legitimate only if there is some distributist institution (as, for example, the Jubilee year of the Old Testament) that keeps inequality of wealth within justifiable limits. Such an institution is now lacking. The proposed institution of maximum wealth and income plus minimum income limits would remedy this severe defect and make private property legitimate again. It would also go a long way toward legitimating the free market, since most of our blundering interference with the price system (e.g., farm program, minimum wage, rent controls) has as its goal an equalizing alteration in the distribution of income and wealth. Thus such a distributist policy is based on impeccably respectable premises: private property, the free market, opposition to welfare bureaucracies and centralized control. It also heeds the radicals' call of "power to the people," since it puts the source of power, namely property, in the hands of the many people, rather than in the hands of the few capitalist plutocrats and socialist bureaucrats.

The concept of private property here adopted is the classical view of John Locke, Thomas Jefferson, and the Founding Fathers. It is emphatically not the apologetic doctrine of big business that the term "private property" evokes today. Limits are built into the very notion of property, according to Locke:

> Whatsoever, then, a man removes out of the state that nature hath provided and left it in, he hath mixed his labor with it, and joined to it something that is his own, and thereby makes it his property. But how far has God given property to us to enjoy? As much as anyone can make use of to any advantage of life before it spoils, so much may he by his labor fix his property in. Whatever is beyond this is more than his share, and belongs to others [Quoted in McClaughry, 1974, p. 31].

Clearly, Locke had in mind some maximum limit on property, even in the absence of general scarcity. Locke assumed, reasonably in his time, that resources were superabundant. But he insisted that the right to property was limited. Growing resource scarcity reinforces this necessity of limits. Some of the correlates of this view of private property are listed by McClaughry:

> Property should be acquired through *personal effort;* it is a reward for diligent industry and fair dealing. An inheritance or windfall may look and feel like property, and even be used as property, but it lacks this essence of reward for personal effort.
>
> Property implies *personal control* and individual responsibility. Where the putative owners are far removed from the men who make the decisions about the use of their wealth, this aspect of personal and individual responsibility is absent, and this wealth becomes something less than true property.
>
> Property is relative to *human need.* That which is accumulated beyond an amount necessary to suffice for the human needs of its owner and his family is no longer property, but surplus wealth.
>
> Although to own a home and a car is to own property, and although possession of these consumer goods may have important effects upon the owner and his community, Locke and his successors thought of property as productive—yielding goods or services for exchange with others in the community —concentrated wealth means concentrated power—power to dominate other men, power to protect privilege, power to stifle the American Dream [McClaughry, 1974, p. 32].

Maximum limits on income and wealth were an implicit part of the philosophy of all the prominent statesmen of early America except Alexander Hamilton.

Maximum income and wealth would remove many of the incentives to monopolistic practices. Why conspire to corner markets, fix prices, and so forth, if you cannot keep the loot? As for labor, the minimum income would enable the outlawing of strikes, which are rapidly becoming intolerably exploitative of the general public. Unions would not be needed as a means of confronting the power of concentrated wealth, since wealth would no longer be concentrated. Indeed, the workers would have a share of it and thus would not be at the mercy of an employer. In addition, some limit on corporate size would be needed, as well as a requirement that all corporate profits be distributed as dividends to stockholders.

With no large concentrations in wealth and income, savings would be smaller and would truly represent abstinence from consumption rather than surplus remaining after satiation. There would be less expansionary pressure from large amounts of surplus funds seeking ever new ways to grow exponentially and leading to either physical growth, inflation, or both.

The minimum income could be financed out of general revenues, which, in addition to a progressive income tax within the income limits, would also include revenues from the depletion quota auction (to be discussed below), and 100-percent marginal tax rates on wealth and income above the limits. Upon reaching the maximum, most people would devote their further energies to noneconomic pursuits, so that confiscatory revenues would be small. But the opportunities thus forgone by the wealthy would be available to the not-so-wealthy, who would still be paying taxes on their increased earnings. The effect on incentive would be negative at the top but positive at lower levels, leading to a broader participation in running the economy. If the maximum and minimum were to move so close together that real differences in effort could not be rewarded and incentives were insufficient to call forth the talent and effort needed to sustain the system, then we should have to widen the limits again or simply be content with the lower level of wealth that could be maintained within the narrower distributive limits. Since we would no longer be anxious to grow, the whole question of incentives would be less pressing. There might also be an increase in public service by those who have hit the maxium. As Jonathan Swift argued:

> In all well-instituted commonwealths, care has been taken to limit men's possessions; which is done for many reasons, and, among the rest, for one which, perhaps, is not often considered; that when bounds are set to men's desires, after they have acquired as much as the laws will permit them, their private interest is at an end, and they have nothing to do but to take care of the public [Swift, 1958, p. 1003].

Transferable Birth Licenses

This idea was first put forward in 1964 by Kenneth Boulding (1964, pp. 135–136). Hardly anyone has taken it seriously, as Boulding knew would be the case. Nevertheless, it remains the best plan yet offered, if the goal is to attain aggregate stability with a minimum sacrifice of individual freedom and variability. It combines macrostability with microvariability. Since 1964 we have experienced a great increase in public awareness of the population explosion and an energy crisis, and we are now experiencing the failures of the great "technological fixes" (Green Revolution, Nuclear Power, and Space). This has led at least one respected demographer to take Boulding's plan seriously, and more will probably follow (Heer, 1975).

So many people react so negatively to the birth license plan that I should emphasize that the other two institutions (distributive limits and depletion quotas) do not depend on it. The other two proposals could be accepted and the reader can substitute his own favorite population control plan if he is allergic to this one.

The plan is simply to issue equally to every person (or perhaps only to every woman, since the female is the limitative factor in reproduction, and since maternity is more demonstrable than paternity) an amount of reproduction licenses that corresponds to replacement fertility. Thus each woman would receive 2.1 licenses. The licenses would be divisible in units of one-tenth, which Boulding playfully called the "deci-child." Possession of ten deci-child units confers the legal right to one birth. The licenses are freely transferable by sale or gift, so those who want more than two children, and can afford to buy the extra licenses, or can acquire them by gift, are free to do so. The original distribution of the licenses is on the basis of strict equality, but exchange is permitted, leading to a reallocation in conformity with differing preferences and abilities to pay. Thus distributive equity is achieved in the original distribution, and allocative efficiency is achieved in the market redistribution.

A slight amendment to the plan might be to grant 1.0 certificates to each individual (or 2.0 to each woman) and have these refer not to births but to "survivals." If a female dies before having a child, then her certificate becomes a part of her estate and is willed to someone else, for example, her parents, who either use it to have another child or sell it to someone else. The advantage of this modification is that it offsets existing class differentials in infant and child mortality. Without the modification, a poor family desiring two children could end up with two infant deaths and no certificates. The best plan, of course, is to eliminate class differences in mortality, but in the meantime this modification may make the plan initially easier to accept. Indeed, even in the absence of class mortality differentials the modification has the advantage of building in a "guarantee."

Let us dispose of two common objections to the plan. First, it is argued that it is unjust because the rich have an advantage. Of course the rich *always* have an advantage, but is their advantage increased or decreased by this plan? Clearly it is decreased. The effect of the plan on income distribution is equalizing because (1) the new marketable asset is distributed equally; and (2) as the rich have more children, their family per-capita incomes are lowered; as the poor have fewer children their family per-capita incomes increase. From the point of view of the children, there is something to be said for increasing the probability that they will be born richer rather than poorer. Whatever injustice there is in the plan stems from the prior existence of rich and poor not from Boulding's idea, which actually reduces the degree of injustice. Furthermore, income and wealth distribution are to be controlled by a separate institution, dis-cussed above, so that in the overall system this objection is more fully and directly met.

A more reasonable objection concerns the problem of enforcement. What to do with law-breaking parents and their illegal children? What do we do with illegal children today? One possibility is to put the children up for adoption and encourage adoption by paying the adopting parents the market value, plus subsidy if need be, for their license, thus retiring a license from circulation to compensate for the child born without a license. Like any other law breakers, the offending parents would be subject to punishment. The punishment need not be drastic or unusual. Of course, if everyone breaks a law no law can be enforced. The plan presupposes the acceptance by a large majority of the public of the morality and necessity of the law. It also presupposes widespread knowl-edge of contraceptive practices and perhaps legalized abortion as well. But these presuppositions would apply to any institution of population control except the most coercive.

Choice may be influenced in two ways: by acting on or "rigging" the *objective* conditions of choice (prices and incomes in a broad sense), or by manipulating the *subjective* conditions of choice (preferences). Bould-ing's plan imposes straight-forward objective constraints and does not presumptuously attempt to manipulate peoples' preferences. Preference changes due to individual example and moral conversion are in no way ruled out. If preferences should change so that, on the average, the population desired replacement fertility, the price of a certificate would approach zero and the objective constraint would automatically vanish. The current decline in the birth rate has perhaps already led to such a state. Maybe this would be a good time to institute the plan, so that it would already be in place and functioning, should preferences change toward more children in the future. The moral basis of the plan is that everyone is treated equally, yet there is no insistence upon conformity of preferences, the latter being the great drawback of "voluntary" plans that rely on official moral suasion, Madison Avenue techniques, and even Skinnerian behavior control. Which is the greater affront to the indi-vidual—to be forbidden what he wants for objective reasons that he and everyone else ought to be able to understand, or to get what he "wants" but to be badgered and manipulated into "wanting" only what is collectively possible? Some people, God bless them, will never be brainwashed, and their individual nonconformity wrecks the moral basis (equal treatment) of "voluntary" programs.

Kingsley Davis points out that population control is not a technological problem.

> The solution is easy as long as one pays no attention to what must be given up. For instance a nation seeking ZPG could shut off immigration and permit each couple a maximum of two children, with possible state license for a third. Accidental pregnancies beyond the limit would be interrupted by abortion. If a third child were born without a license, or a fourth, the mother would be sterilized and the child given to a sterile couple. But anyone enticed into making such a suggestion risks being ostracized as a political or moral leper, a danger to society. He is accused of wanting to take people's freedom away from them and institute a Draconian dictatorship over private lives. Obviously then reproductive freedom still takes priority over population control. This makes a solution of the population impossible because, by definition, population control and reproductive freedom are incompatible [Davis, 1973, p. 28].

The key to population control is simply to be willing to pay the cost. The cost of the plan here advocated seems to me less than the cost of Davis' hypothetical suggestion because it allows greater diversity—families need not be so homogeneous in size, and individual preferences are respected to a greater degree. Moreover, should it become necessary or desirable to have negative population growth (as I believe it will) the marketable license plan has a great advantage over those plans that put the limit on a flat child-per-family basis. This latter limit could be changed only by an integral number, and to go from two children to one child per family in order to reduce population is quite a drastic change. In the Boulding scheme of marketable licenses issued in deci-child units or one-tenth of a certificate, it would be possible gradually to reduce population growth by lowering the issue to 1.9 certificates per woman, to 1.8, and so on, the remaining 0.1 or 0.2 certificates being acquired by purchase or gift.

Part of our difficulty in accepting the transferable license plan is that it is so direct. It frankly recognizes that reproduction must henceforth be considered a scarce right and logically faces the issue of how best to distribute that right and whether and how to permit voluntary reallocation. But there is an amazing preference for indirect measures—find new roles for women, change the tax laws, restrict public housing to small families, encourage celibacy and late marriage, be more tolerant of homosexuality, convince people to spend their money on consumer durables rather than having children, make it popular to have children only between the ages of twenty and thirty, and so forth.

Whence this enormous preference for indirectness? It results partly from our unwillingness to really face the issue. Limiting reproduction is still a taboo subject that must be approached in contorted and roundabout ways rather than directly. Furthermore, roundaboutness and indirectness are the bread and butter of empirical social scientists, who get grants and make their reputations by measuring the responsiveness of the birth rate to all sorts of remote "policy variables." The direct approach makes estimation of all these social parameters governing tenuous chains of cause and effect quite unnecessary. If the right to reproduce were directly limited by the marketable license plan, then the indirect measures would become means of adjusting to the direct constraint. For example, with reduced childbearing, women would naturally find other activities. The advantage of the direct approach is that individuals would be free to make their own personal specific adjustments to the general objective constraint, rather than having a whole set of specific constraints imposed on them in the expectation that it would force them indirectly to decide to do what objectively must be done. The direct approach is more efficient and no more coercive. But the direct approach requires clarity of purpose and frank objectives, which are politically inconvenient when commitment to the objective is halfhearted to begin with.

There is an understandable reluctance to couple money and reproduction—somehow it seems to profane life. Yet life is physically coupled to increasingly scarce resources, and resources are coupled to money. If population growth and economic growth continue, then even free resources, such as breathable air, will become either coupled to money and subject to price or allocated by a harsher and less efficient means. Once we accept the fact that the price system is the most efficient mechanism for rationing the right to scarce life-sustaining and life-enhancing resources, then perhaps rather than "money profaning life" we will find that "life sanctifies money." We will then take the distribution of money and its wise use as serious matters. It is not the exchange relationship that debases life (indeed, the entire biosphere runs on a network of material and energy exchanges), it is the underlying inequity in wealth and income beyond any functional or ethical justification that loads the terms of free exchange against the poor. The same inequality also debases the "gift relationship," since it assigns the poor to the status of a perpetual dependent and the rich to the status of a weary and grumbling patron. Thus gift as well as exchange relationships require limits to the degree of inequality if they are not to subvert their legitimate ends. The sharing of resources in general is the job of the distributist institution. Allocation of particular resources and scarce rights is done by the market within the distribution limits imposed.

In view of the fact that so many liberals, not to mention the United Nations, have declared it to be a human right to have whatever number of children the parents desire, it is worthwhile to end this discussion with a statement from one of the greatest champions of liberty who ever lived, John Stuart Mill:

> The fact itself, of causing the existence of a human being, is one of the most responsible actions in the range of human life. To undertake this responsibility—to bestow a life which may be either a curse or a blessing—unless the being on whom it is to be bestowed will have at least the ordinary chances of a desirable existence, is a crime against that being. And in a country either over-peopled, or threatened with being so, to produce children, beyond a very small number, with the effect of reducing the reward of labor by their competition, is a serious offence against all who live by the remuneration of their labor. The laws which, in many countries on the Continent, forbid marriage unless the parties can show that they have the means of supporting a family, do not exceed the legitimate powers of the State: and whether such laws be expedient or not (a question mainly dependent on local circumstances and feelings), they are not objectionable as violations of liberty. Such laws are interferences of the State to prevent a mischievous act—an act injurious to others, which ought to be a subject of reprobation and social stigma, even where it is not deemed expedient to superadd legal punishment. Yet the current ideas of liberty, which bend so easily to real infringements of the freedom of the individual in things which concern only himself, would repel the attempt to put any restraint upon his inclinations when the consequence of their indulgence is a life or lives of wretchedness and depravity to the offspring, with manifold evils to those sufficiently within reach to be in any way affected by their actions [Mill, 1952, p. 319].

Depletion Quotas

The strategic point at which to impose control on the throughput flow seems to me to be the rate of depletion of resources, particularly non-renewable resources. If we limit aggregate depletion, then, by the law of conservation of matter and energy, we will also indirectly limit aggregate pollution. If we limit throughput flow, then we also indirectly limit the size of the stocks maintained by that flow. Entropy is at its minimum at the input (depletion) end of the throughput pipeline and at its maximum at the output (pollution) end. Therefore, it is physically easier to monitor and control depletion than pollution—there are fewer mines, wells, and ports than there are smokestacks, garbage dumps, and drainpipes, not to mention such diffuse emission sources as runoff of insecticides and fertilizers from fields into rivers and lakes and auto exhausts. Land area devoted to mining is only 0.3 percent of total land area (National Commission on Materials Policy, 1973).

Given that there is more leverage in intervening at the input end, should we intervene by way of taxes or quotas? Quotas, if they are auctioned by the government rather than allocated on nonmarket criteria, have an important net advantage over taxes in that they definitely limit aggregate throughput, which is the quantity to be controlled. Taxes exert only an indirect and very uncertain limit. It is quite true that given a demand curve, a price plus a tax determines a quantity. But demand curves shift, and they are subject to great errors in estimation even if stable. Demand curves for resources could shift up as a result of population increase, change in tastes, increase in income, and so forth. Suppose the government seeks to limit throughput by taxing it. It then spends the tax. If government expenditures on each category of commodity were equal to the revenues received from taxing that same category, then the limit on throughput would be largely cancelled out, with the exact degree of cancelling depending on the elasticity of demand. If the government taxes resource-intensive items and spends on time-intensive items, there will be a one-shot reduction in aggregate physical throughput but not a limit to its future growth. A credit expansion by the banking sector, an increase in velocity of circulation of money, or deficit spending by the government for other purposes could easily offset even the one-shot reduction induced by taxes. Taxes can reduce the amount of depletion and pollution (throughput) per unit of GNP down to some irreducible minimum, but taxes provide no limit to the increase in the number of units of GNP (unless the government runs a growing surplus) and therefore no limit to aggregate throughput. The fact that a tax levied on a single resource could, by inducing substitution, usually reduce the throughput of that resource very substantially should not mislead us into thinking that a general tax on all or most resources will reduce aggregate throughput (fallacy of composition). Recall that there is no substitute for low-entropy matter-energy. Finally, it is *quantity* that affects the ecosystem, not price, and therefore it is ecologically safer to let errors and unexpected shifts in demand result in price fluctuations rather than in quantity fluctuations. Hence quotas.

The same point can be made in another way. Suppose the government taxes automobiles heavily and that people take to riding bicycles instead of cars. They will save money as well as resources (Hannon, 1975). But what will the money saved now be spent on? If it is spent on airline tickets, resource consumption would increase above what it was when the money was spent on cars. If the money is spent on theater tickets, then perhaps resource consumption would decline. However, this is not certain, because the theater performance may entail the air transport of actors, stage sets, and so on, and thus indirectly be as resource consumptive as automobile expenditures. If people paid the high tax on cars and continued buying the same number of cars, then they would have to cut other items of consumption. The items cut may or may not be more resource intensive than the items for which the government spends the revenue. If the revenue is spent on B-1 bombers, there would surely be a net increase in resource consumption. The only way to be sure that resource consumption will, in fact, be limited is directly to impose aggregate quantitative limits on resource extraction and let prices allocate or ration the fixed aggregate among firms,

Pollution taxes would provide a much weaker inducement to resource-saving technological progress than would depletion quotas, since, in the former scheme, resource prices do not necessarily have to rise and may even fall. The inducement of pollution taxes is to "pollution avoidance," and thus to recycling. But increased competition from recycling industries, instead of reducing depletion, might spur the extractive industries to even greater competitive efforts. Intensified search and the development of technologies with still larger jaws could speed up the rate of depletion and thereby lower short-run resource prices. Thus new extraction might once again become competitive with recycling, leading to less recycling and more depletion and pollution—exactly what we wish to avoid. This perverse effect could not happen under a depletion quota system.

The usual recommendation of pollution taxes would seem, if the above is correct, to intervene at the wrong end with the wrong policy tool. Intervention by pollution taxes also tends to be microcontrol, rather than macro. There are, however, limits to the ability of depletion quotas to influence the qualitative nature and spatial location of pollution, and at this fine-tuning level pollution taxes would be a useful supplement, as would a bureau of technology assessment. Depletion quotas would induce resource-saving technological change, and the set of resource-saving technologies would probably overlap to a great degree with the set of socially benign technologies. But the coincidence is not complete, and there is still a need, though a diminished one, for technology assessment.

How would a depletion quota system function? The market for each resource would become two tiered. To begin with, the government, as a monopolist, would auction the limited quota rights to many buyers. Resource buyers, having purchased their quota rights, would then have to confront many resource sellers in a competitive resource market. The competitive price in the resource market would tend to equal marginal cost. More efficient producers would earn differential rents, but the pure scarcity rent resulting from the quotas would have been captured in the depletion quota auction market by the government monopoly. The total price of the resource (quota price plus price to owner) would be raised as a result of the quotas. All products using these resources would become more expensive. Higher resource prices would compel more efficient and frugal use of resources by both producers and consumers. But the windfall rent from higher resource prices would be captured by the government and become public income—a partial realization of Henry George's ideal of a single tax on rent (George, 1951).

The major advantage is that higher resource prices would bring increased efficiency, while the quotas would directly limit depletion, thereby increasing conservation and indirectly limiting pollution. Pollution would be limited in two ways. First, since pollution is simply the other end of the throughput from depletion, limiting the input to the pipeline would naturally limit the output. Second, higher prices would induce more recycling, thereby further limiting materials pollution and depletion up to the limit set by the increased energy throughput required by recycling. The revenue from the depletion quota auction could help finance the minimum-income component of the distributist institution, offsetting the regressive effect of the higher resource prices on income distribution. Attempts to help the poor by underpricing resources are totally misguided, because the greatest benefit of subsidized prices for energy, for example, goes to those who consume the most energy—the rich not the poor. This is hardly progressive.

Higher prices on basic resources are absolutely necessary. Any plan that refuses to face up to this necessity is worthless. Back in 1925, economist John Ise made the point in these words:

> Preposterous as it may seem at first blush, it is probably true that, even if all the timber in the United States, or all the oil or gas or anthracite, were owned by an absolute monopoly, entirely free of public control, prices to consumers would be fixed lower than the long-run interests of the public would justify. Pragmatically this means that all efforts on the part of the government to keep down the prices of lumber, oil, gas, or anthracite are contrary to the public interest; that the government should be trying to keep prices up rather than down [Ise, 1925, p. 284].

Ise went on to suggest a general principle of resource pricing: that nonrenewable resources be priced at the cost of the nearest renewable substitute. Therefore, virgin timber should cost at least as much per board foot as replanted timber; petroleum should be priced at its Btu equivalent of sugar or wood alcohol, assuming they are the closest renewable alternatives. In the absence of any renewable substitutes, the price would merely reflect the purely ethical judgment of how fast the resources should be used up—that is, the importance of the wants of future people relative to the wants of present people. Renewable resources are assumed to be exploited on a sustained-yield basis and to be priced accordingly.

The Ise principles could also be used in setting the aggregate quota amounts to auction. For renewables, the quota should be set at an amount equivalent to some reasonable calculation of maximum sustainable yield. For nonrenewables with renewable substitutes, the quota should be set so that the resulting price of the nonrenewable resource is at least as high as the price of its nearest renewable substitute. For nonrenewables with no close renewable substitute, the quota would reflect a purely ethical judgment concerning the relative importance of present versus future wants. Should these resources be used up by us or by our descendants? The price system cannot decide this, because future generations cannot bid in present resource markets. The decision is ethical. We have found it too easy to assume that future generations will be better off due to inevitable "progress" and therefore not to worry about the unrepresented claims of the future on exhaustible resources.

In addition to the Ise principles, which deal only with depletion costs that fall on the future, the quotas must be low enough to prevent excessive pollution and ecological costs that fall on the present as well as on the future. Pragmatically, quotas would probably at first be set near existing extraction rates. The first task would be to stabilize, to get off the growth path. Later, we could try to reduce quotas to a more sustainable level, if present flows proved too high. Abundant resources causing little environmental disruption would be governed by generous quotas, and therefore relatively low prices, and a consequently strong incentive to technologies that make relatively intensive use of the abundant resource.

Depletion quotas would capture the increasing scarcity rents but would not require the expropriation of resource owners. Quotas are clearly against the interests of resource owners, but not unjustly so, since rent is by definition unearned income from a price in excess of the minimum supply price. The elimination of this unearned increment would no doubt reduce the incentive to exploration and new discovery. Geological exploration has many aspects of a natural monopoly and probably should, in any case, be carried on by a public corporation. As the largest resource owner by far, the government should not have to lease public lands to private companies who have more geological information than the government about the land. If private exploration is thought desirable, it could be encouraged by a government bounty paid for mineral discoveries. The current resource owners would suffer a one-time capital loss when depletion limits are imposed and, in fairness, should be compensated.

For many readers a graphical exposition of the depletion quota scheme will be helpful, as shown in Figure 4. DD' is the market demand curve for the resource in question. SS' is the supply curve of the industry. A depletion quota, in the aggregate amount Q, is imposed, shown by the vertical line QQ'. The total price paid per unit of the resource (price paid to resource owner plus price paid to government for the corresponding

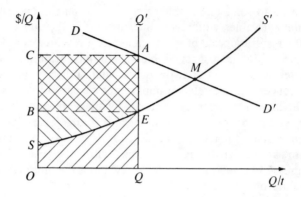

Figure 4

quota right) is *OC*. Of the total price *OC*, the amount *OB* is the price paid to the resource owner for one unit of the resource, and *BC* is the price paid to the government for a quota right to purchase one unit of the resource. Of the total amount paid, *OQAC*, the amount *OSEQ* is cost, reflecting the necessary supply price. The remainder, *SEAC*, is surplus, or rent.

Rent is defined as payment in excess of necessary supply price. Of the total rent area, the amount *BES* is differential rent, or surplus that arises from the difference in the supply price of the marginal amount produced, which is *QE*, and all previous amounts produced. Price is determined at the margin, and is equal to *QE*, the marginal cost of production. Since the cost of production of all inframarginal units is less than *QE*, and since all units sell at the same price, equal to *QE*, a profit, or differential rent, is earned on all inframarginal units produced. The profit on the first unit is *BC* and declines slightly for each additional unit until it is zero for the last unit at *Q*. Thus *BES* is the sum of the diminishing series of inframarginal per-unit profits. It is called differential rent because its amount depends on the schedule of cost differences between the first and last units. The remainder of the surplus, the amount *CAEB*, is pure scarcity rent. It does not arise from cost differentials but simply from the excess of the market price above the marginal cost of production, by the amount *AE*. In effect, *AE* represents a kind of price per unit of resources in the ground that prior to the quota auction had implicitly been priced at zero. At the market equilibrium *M*, the entire surplus would be differential rent, and scarcity rent would be zero. Hence scarcity rent, as the name implies, emerges when the resource is made scarce relative to the quantity corresponding to market equilibrium, which, of course, is what happens when quotas are imposed.

The scarcity rent *CAEB* is captured by the government quota auction. The differential rent *BES* remains in the hands of the resource owners.

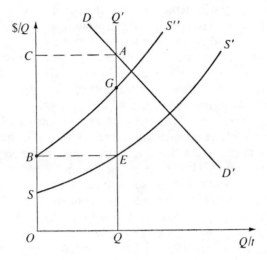

Figure 5

The reason for this particular division of the surplus is that the resource market is assumed to be competitive (many sellers and buyers), while the quota auction market is monopolistic (many buyers, one seller). The government has monopoly power; the resource owners and buyers have none. The price in the resource market is set by competition at an amount equal to marginal cost, QE. The government, by charging what the market will bear with no fear of being undercut by competitors, is able to extract the remainder of the full demand price, or the amount AE. If the resource market were also monopolized, then the division of scarcity rent between the government and private monopolies would be indeterminate. Even in that case, however, the government would have an advantage in that the quota right has to be purchased *first*. Thus even if competition is less than perfect in the resource market, we would still expect the government to capture all monopoly profits (scarcity rents), because it constitutes the first tier of the market and controls the entry of buyers into the second tier.

Over time the supply curve for nonrenewable resources would shift upward as more accessible resources become depleted and previously submarginal mines and wells have to be used. In Figure 5 the higher supply curve is represented by BS'', which may be thought of as the "unused" segment of the original supply curve, ES', shifted horizontally to the left until it touches the vertical axis. Assuming an unchanged demand curve and quota, it is clear from Figure 5 that rising cost of production (now shown by the larger area, $OBGQ$) will eventually eliminate the pure scarcity rent, leaving only differential rent. Quotas will slow down the upward shift of the supply curve relative to what it would have been with faster depletion, but of course they cannot arrest the inevitable process. Probably the quota would have to be reduced as the supply curve shifted up in order to pass along the higher cost signals to users and to maintain some scarcity rent for public revenue.

For renewable resources, where the quota is set at maximum sustainable yield, there would be no upward shift of the supply curve. However, the demand curve for renewables would shift up as nonrenewable resource usage became more restricted and expensive and efforts were made to substitute renewables for nonrenewables. The quota on renewables would then protect those resources from being exploited beyond capacity in order to satisfy the rising demand while at the same time rationing access to the limited amount and diverting the windfall profits into the public treasury. In sum, the depletion quota auction is an instrument for helping us to make the transition from a nonrenewable to a renewable resource base in a gradual, efficient, and equitable manner.

The depletion quota scheme allows a reconciliation between the two conflicting goals of efficiency and equity. Efficiency requires high resource prices. However, equity is not served by high prices, because they have a regressive effect on income distribution in the same way that a sales tax does, and also because the windfall rents arising from the higher prices accrue to resource owners, not to the poor. The latter effect can be reversed by capturing the scarcity rent through the depletion quota auction and using it to finance a minimum income, and/or to replace the most regressive taxes.

Two further efficiency increases could be expected. First, taxing rent causes no allocative distortions and is the most efficient way to raise government revenue. To the extent that a rent tax (or its equivalent in this case) replaces other taxes, then static allocative efficiency should be improved. Second, as conservatives and radicals alike have noted, the minimum income could substitute for a considerable number of bureaucratic welfare programs. Of course, the major increase in efficiency would result directly from higher resource prices, which would give incentives to develop resource-saving techniques of production and patterns of consumption. Equity is not served by low prices, which, in effect, give a larger subsidy to the rich than to the poor, since the rich consume more resources. Equity is served by higher incomes to the poor and by a maximum limit on the incomes of the rich.

A Coordinated Program

Let us now consider all three institutions as a unified program.

The allocation among firms of the limited aggregate of resources extracted during the given time period would be accomplished entirely by the market. The distribution of income within the maximum and minimum boundaries imposed would also be left to the market. The initial distribution of reproductive licenses is done outside the market on the basis of strict equity—one person, one license—but reallocation via market exchange is permitted in the interest of efficiency. The combination of the three institutions presents a nice reconciliation of efficiency and equity and provides the ecologically necessary macrocontrol of growth with the least sacrifice in terms of microlevel freedom and variability. The market is relied upon to allocate resources and distribute incomes within imposed ecological and ethical boundaries. The market is not allowed to set its own boundaries, but it is free within those boundaries. Setting boundaries is necessary. No one has ever claimed that market equilibria would automatically coincide with ecological equilibria or with a reasonably just distribution of wealth and income. Nor has anyone ever claimed that market equilibria would attain demographic balance. The very notions of "equilibrium" in economics and ecology are antithetical. In growth economics equilibrium refers not to physical magnitudes at all but to a balance of desires between savers and investers. As long as saving is greater than depreciation, then net investment must be positive. This implies a *growing* flow of physical inputs from and outputs to nature, that is, a biophysical *dis*equilibrium. Physical conditions of environmental equilibrium must be imposed on the market in aggregate quantitative physical terms. Subject to these quantitative constraints, the market and price system can, with the institutional changes just discussed, achieve an optimal allocation of resources and an optimal adjustment to its imposed physical system boundaries. The point is important because the belief is widespread among economists that internalization of externalities, or the incorporation of all environmental costs into market prices, is a sufficient environmental policy and that once this is accomplished the market will be able to set its own proper boundaries automatically. This is not so. Nor, as we have already seen, is it possible to incorporate all ecological costs in rigged money prices.

The internalization of externalities is a good strategy for fine-tuning the allocation of resources by making relative prices better measures of relative marginal social costs. But it does not enable the market to set its own absolute physical boundaries with the larger ecosystem. To give an analogy: proper allocation arranges the weight in a boat optimally, so as to maximize the load that can be carried. But there is still an absolute limit to how much weight a boat can carry, even optimally arranged. The price system can spread the weight evenly, but unless it is supplemented by an external absolute limit, it will just keep on spreading the increasing weight evenly until the evenly loaded boat sinks. No doubt the boat would sink evenly, ceteris paribus, but that is less comforting to the average citizen than to the neoclassical economist.

Two distinct questions must be asked about these proposed institutions for achieving a steady state. First, would they work if people accepted the goal of a steady state and perhaps voted the institutions into effect? Second, would people ever accept either the steady-state idea or these particular institutions? I have tried to show that the answer to the first question is probably "yes." Let the critic find any remaining flaws; better yet, let him suggest improvements. The answer to the second question is clearly "no" in the short run. But several considerations make acceptance more plausible in the not-too-long run.

The minimum-income side of the distributist institution already has some political support in the United States; the maximum limits will at first be thought un-American. Yet, surely, beyond some figure any additions to personal income would represent greed rather than need, or even merit. Most people would be willing to believe that in most cases an income in excess of, let us say, $100,000 per year has no real functional justification, especially when the highly paid jobs are usually already the most interesting and pleasant.

In spite of their somewhat radical implications, the proposals presented in this chapter are, as we have seen, based on impeccably respectable conservative institutions: private property and the free market.

By fixing the rate of depletion we force technology to focus more on the flow sources of solar energy and renewable resources. The solar flux cannot be increased in the present at the expense of the future. Thus let technology devote itself to learning how to live off our solar income rather than our terrestrial capital. Such advances will benefit all generations, not just the present. Indeed, the main goal of the depletion quota plan is to turn technological change away from increasing dependence on the terrestrial stock and toward the more abundant flow of solar energy and renewable resources. As the stock becomes relatively more expensive, it will be used less in direct consumption and more for investment in "work gates" that increase our ability to tap the solar flow. Instead of taking long-run technical evolution as a parameter to which the short-run variables of price and quantity continually adjust, the idea is to take short-run quantities (and hence prices) as a social parameter to be set, so as to induce a direction of technological evolution more in harmony with mankind's long-run interests.

This new direction of technological change is likely also to be in mankind's short-run interests, if we accept the view that man's evolution in a solar-based and stable economy has programmed him for that kind of life rather than for the stresses of a growing industrial economy. The future steady state could be a good deal more comfortable than past ones and much more human than the overgrown, overcentralized, overextended, and overbearing economy into which growth has pushed us.

The depletion quota plan should appeal to both technological optimists and pessimists. The pessimist should be pleased by the conservation effect of the quotas; the optimist should be pleased by the price inducement to resource-saving technology. The optimist tells us not to worry about running out of resources because technology embodied in reproducible capital is a nearly perfect substitute for resources. As we run out of anything, prices will rise and substitute methods will be found. If we believe this, then how could we object to quotas, which simply increase the scarcity and prices of resources a bit ahead of schedule and more gradually? This plan simply requires the optimist to live up to his faith in technology.

Like the maximum limits on income and wealth, the depletion quotas could also have a trust-busting effect if accompanied by a limit—for example, no single entity can own more than x percent of the quota rights for a given resource or more than y percent of the resource owned by the industry of which it is a member. We could set x and y so as to allow legitimate economies of scale, while curtailing monopoly power.

The actual mechanics of quota auction markets for three or four hundred basic resources would present no great problems. The whole process could be computerized, since the function of an auctioneer is purely mechanical. It could be vastly simpler, faster, more decentralized, and less subject to fraud and manipulation than today's stock market. In addition, qualitative and locational variation among resources within each category, though ignored at the auction level, will be taken into account in price differentials paid to resource owners.

The depletion quota and birth quota systems bear an obvious analogy. The difference is that the birth quotas are privately held and equally distributed initially, and then redistributed among individuals through the market; the depletion quotas are collectively held initially and then distributed to individuals by way of an auction market. The revenue derived from birth quotas is private income; the revenue from depletion quotas is public income.

The scheme could, and probably must, be designed to include imported resources. The same depletion quota right could be required for importation of resources, and thus the market would determine the proportions in which our standard of living is sustained by depletion of national and foreign resources. Imported final goods would now be cheaper relative to national goods, assuming foreigners do not limit their depletion. Our export goods would now be more expensive relative to the domestic goods of foreign countries. Our terms of trade would improve, but we would tend to a balance of payments deficit. However, with a freely fluctuating exchange rate, a rise in the price of foreign currencies relative to the dollar would restore equilibrium. The balance of payments can take care of itself. If foreigners are willing to sell us goods priced below their true full costs of production, we should not complain.

It might be objected that limiting our imports of resources will work a hardship on the many underdeveloped countries that export raw materials. This is not clear, because such a policy will also force them to transform their own resources domestically rather than through international trade. Foreign suppliers of raw materials will be treated no differently than domestic suppliers. Finished goods would not be subject to quotas. In any case, it is clear that in the long run we are not doing the underdeveloped countries any favor by using up their resource endowment. Sooner or later (sooner, in the case of OPEC), they will begin to drive a hard bargain for their nonrenewable resources, and we had better not be too dependent on them. Probably they will limit their raw material exports, thus making unnecessary any limits that we might place on our raw material imports. Eventually, population control and environmental protection policies might become preconditions for membership in a new free-trade bloc or common market. Free trade would be the rule among all countries that limited their own populations and rates of domestic depletion, while controls could be put on trade with other countries whenever desirable.

Although the President's Commission on Population Growth and the American Future (1972) did not advocate a marketable license plan for population control, it did recommend that the nation "welcome and plan for a stabilized population" (p. 110). Furthermore, it listed some criteria for a good stabilization plan. The Commission prefers "a course toward population stabilization which minimizes fluctuation in number of births; minimizes further growth of population; minimizes the change required in reproductive habits and provides adequate time for such changes to be adopted; and maximizes variety and choice in life styles, while minimizing pressures for conformity (p. 111). Judged on these criteria, the marketable license plan scores better than any alternative that I have seen or am able to imagine. If we accept these criteria, then we should either accept the marketable birth license plan or be prepared to suggest something better.

The National Commission on Materials Policy (1973) still put major emphasis on increasing supplies but recognized that a balance must be struck "between the need to produce goods and the need to protect the environment by modifying the materials system so that all resources, including environmental, are paid for by users" (p. 1–4). Depletion quotas were not taken seriously but pollution taxes were. Economists have made the case that pollution taxes are superior to the alternatives of direct regulations and subsidizing pollution abatement. But the alternative of depletion quotas has not yet been widely debated. The 1952 President's Materials Policy Commission (the Paley Commission), though acknowledging that "We share the belief of the American people in the principle of Growth" (their capital G), also went on to make the following enlightened observation: "Whether there may be any unbreakable upper limit to the continuing growth of our economy we do not pretend to know, but it must be a part of our task to examine such limits as present themselves" (quoted in Ordway, 1953, p. III). This would have been a good point of departure for the 1972 Commission.

On the question of energy policy, the Ford Foundation's Energy Policy Project (1974) took seriously the alternative of zero energy growth and included it as one of their three possible scenarios for the future, thus giving a certain respectability to what the Materials Policy Commission and others evidently still consider a "far-out" idea.

The National Academy of Sciences' Committee on Mineral Resources and the Environment (1975), of which I was a member, took more seriously the idea of limits to growth than did the Materials Policy Commission and urged that at least as much attention be devoted to reducing demands on resources as to increasing supplies. While this was a step forward, it was nevertheless clear that a substantial number of the panel were unwilling to consider seriously, much less advocate, a steady-state economy. The illusion that growth could continue by becoming ever less material-intensive and ever more service-oriented dominated the minds of the majority.*

The minimum-income aspect of the distributist institution already has political support. How much support there will be for maximum income and wealth depends partly on where the limits are set. There are very, very few voters with more than $100,000 income and $500,000 net worth and not many citizens who really believe that anything beyond those limits should not be classed as greed rather than need. The same could be said of limits set at one-half the above. Exactly where we draw the line is less important than the principle that such lines must be drawn. A widespread recognition of the general closure of growth should increase the appeal of maximum limits and perhaps revive our populist heritage. If we really want decentralized decision making and participatory democracy rather than a plutonium-powered corporate kleptocracy, some such limit is essential. Yet there is still ample room for the principle of differential reward for differential effort and contribution. A jealous homogeneity is not the goal.

The politically precarious nature of the current distribution of wealth and income has been noted by Arthur Okun:

> Neither rights to ownership of any class of physical assets nor rights to after tax income are given constitutional safeguards; in principle they could be curbed drastically by a vote of 51 percent of the elected representatives of the public. And a majority could easily wish to curb them drastically. The bottom

---

*This illusion will be considered in Chapter 5. See especially p. 118.

half of all American families has only about one-twentieth of all wealth and roughly a quarter of all income. How then does capitalism survive in a democracy? [Okun, 1975, p. 32]

The question should be: How does such inequality survive in a democracy, whether capitalist or socialist?

There are probably two reasons: the first and simplest is that money buys votes, and the second is that the bottom half is confused and divided regarding its own best interests and is mystified by the functioning of our economic system. Nevertheless, if the educational and political effort could be made, the basic arithmetic is favorable to limiting the domain of inequality. Okun calculates that less than 2 percent of GNP could raise every family of working age to half of mean family income (about $7,000 as of 1976), and he is "tempted to declare that every working age American family can and should be guaranteed half the average income" (p. 108). Okun does not consider a maximum income, but I am tempted to add that no American family should have more than five times the average income (about $70,000). Okun's otherwise excellent book is badly flawed by his refusal to take seriously any notion of limits to economic growth. Hence the absence of any consideration of a maximum income.

All three of the institutions we have discussed are capable of gradual application during the transition to a steady state. The birth quota does not have to be immediately set at negative or zero growth, or even at replacement, but could begin at any currently prevailing level and gradually approach replacement or lower fertility. Initially the certificate price would be zero, and it would rise gradually as the number of certificates issued to each person was cut from, for instance, 1.1, to 1.0, to 0.9, or to whatever level is desired. The depletion quotas could likewise be set at present levels or even at levels corresponding to a slower rate of increase than in the recent past. They could be applied first to those materials in shortest supply and to those whose wastes are hardest to absorb. Initial prices on quota rights would be low but then would rise gradually as growth pressed against the fixed quotas or as quotas were reduced in the interest of conservation. In either case, the increased scarcity rent would become revenue to the government. The distribution limits might begin near the present extremes and slowly close to a more desirable range. The three institutions are amenable to any degree of gradualism we may wish. However, the distribution limits must be tightened faster than the depletion limits if the burden on the poor is to be lightened. All three control points are price-system parameters and altering them does not interfere with the static allocative efficiency of the market, as will be shown in the following chapter.

But is it also the case that these institutions could be totally ineffective. Depletion quotas could be endlessly raised on the grounds of national defense, balance of payments, and so forth. Real estate and construction interests, not to mention the baby food and toy lobbies and the military, might convince Congress to keep the supply of birth licenses well above replacement level. People at the maximum income and wealth limit may succeed in continually raising that limit by spending a great deal of their money on TV ads extolling the Unlimited Acquisition of Everything as the very foundation of the American Way of Life. Everything would be the same and all justified in the sacred name of growth. Nothing will work unless we break our idolatrous commitment to material growth.

A definite U.S. policy of population control at home would give us a much stronger base for preaching to the underdeveloped countries about their population problem. So would the reduction in U.S. resource consumption resulting from depletion quotas. Without such a base to preach from, we will continue to waste our breath, as we did at the 1974 Population Conference in Bucharest. But more will be said on this in Chapter 6.

Thus we are brought back to the all-important moral premises discussed in Chapter 2. A physical steady state, if it is to be worth living in, absolutely requires moral growth. Future progress simply must be made in terms of the things that really count rather than the things that are merely countable. Institutional changes are necessary but insufficient. Moral growth is also necessary but insufficient. Both together are necessary and sufficient, but the institutional changes are relatively minor compared to the required change in values.

REFERENCES

Boulding, Kenneth E. *The Meaning of the Twentieth Century*. New York: Harper & Row, 1964.

Davis, Kingsley. "Zero Population Growth," *Daedalus*, Fall 1973, 15–30.

Energy Policy Project of the Ford Foundation. *A Time to Choose*. Cambridge, Mass.: Ballinger, 1974.

George, Henry. *Progress and Poverty*. New York: Robert Schalkenbach Foundation, 1951. Originally published in 1879.

Goldberg, Michael. "Less Is More," unpublished manuscript, 1976.

Hannon, Bruce. "Energy, Growth, and Altruism." Urbana: University of Illinois, Center for Advanced Computation, 1975 (mimeographed).

Heer, David M. "Marketable Licenses for Babies: Boulding's Proposal Revisited," *Social Biology*, Spring 1975, 1–16.

Ise, John. "The Theory of Value as Applied to Natural Resources," *American Economic Review*, June 1925, 284.

McClaughry, John. "The Future of Private Property and Its Distribution," *Ripon Quarterly*, Fall 1974.

Mill, John Stuart. *On Liberty*. Chicago: Encyclopedia Brittanica Great Books, 1952. Originally published in 1859.

Mill, John Stuart. "Of Property," in *Principles of Political Economy*, Book II. New York: Appleton-Century-Crofts, 1881.

National Academy of Sciences. *Mineral Resources and the Environment*. Washington, D.C.: U.S. Government Printing Office, 1975.

National Commission of Materials Policy. *Material Needs and the Environment Today and Tomorrow*. Washington, D.C.: U.S. Government Printing Office, 1973.

Okun, Arthur. *Equality and Efficiency: The Big Tradeoff*. Washington, D.C.: Brookings Institution, 1975.

Ordway, Samuel H., Jr. *Resources and the American Dream*. New York: The Ronald Press, 1953.

President's Commission on Population Growth and the American Future. *Final Report to President Nixon, Congress, and the American People*. Washington, D.C.: U.S. Government Printing Office, March 1972.

Swift, Jonathan. "Thoughts on Various Subjects," in G. B. Woods et al., eds., *The Literature of England*. Glenview, Ill.: Scott, Foresman, 1958.

4

EFFICIENCY IN THE STEADY-STATE ECONOMY

Preposterous as it may seem at first blush, it is probably true that, even if all the timber in the United States, or all the oil, or gas, or anthracite, were owned by an absolute monopoly, entirely free of public control, prices to consumers would be fixed lower than the long-run interests of the public would justify.

John Ise (1925)

In Chapter 2 the distinction was made between growth and development. Using the identity $\frac{\text{service}}{\text{throughput}} = \frac{\text{service}}{\text{stock}} \times \frac{\text{stock}}{\text{throughput}}$, "growth" was defined as an increase in total service resulting from an increase in stocks and throughputs, with the two efficiency ratios on the right-hand side of the identity held constant. "Development" was defined as an increase in either or both of the efficiency ratios, with stocks held constant. Since by definition growth is ruled out in the steady state, all progress must take the form of qualitative development or increases in maintenance efficiency $\left(\frac{\text{stock}}{\text{throughput}}\right)$, and in service efficiency $\left(\frac{\text{service}}{\text{stock}}\right)$. For this reason, it is worth our time to consider further these two concepts of efficiency and to break them down into subcategories.

Efficiency can be defined as the ratio of benefit to cost. Cost, in turn, is easily defined as "opportunity cost" or "the sacrificed benefit of the best alternative forgone." The problem, therefore, is to define benefit, and we have already defined benefit as *service*. Efficiency, then, is a ratio of service gained to service sacrificed. In Figure 3 (p. 35), the cost of economic growth was represented as "ecosystem services sacrificed" and benefit as "artifact services gained," with throughput providing the connecting link between the two. Thus

$$\text{efficiency} = \frac{\text{benefit}}{\text{cost}} = \frac{\text{artifact services gained}}{\text{ecosystem services sacrificed}}.$$

Sacrificed ecosystem services are certainly costs but, it may be objected, not the only cost. There are also disutility of labor and forgone consumption during accumulation. In the steady state there is no accumulation, so we can ignore costs of "abstinence" or "waiting" that are implied by accumulation. The disutility or disservice of labor is more troublesome, but we can follow the practice of Irving Fisher and subtract disservices of labor from artifact services, and treat the numerator as *net* artifact services gained. On the basis of this simplification we can define efficiency as it is defined above, and by means of an expanded identity analyze the single ratio into four component ratios:

$$\frac{\begin{array}{c}\text{artifact}\\\text{services}\\\text{gained}\end{array}}{\begin{array}{c}\text{ecosystem}\\\text{services}\\\text{sacrificed}\end{array}} \equiv \underbrace{\frac{\begin{array}{c}\text{artifact}\\\text{services}\\\text{gained}\end{array}}{\begin{array}{c}\text{artifact}\\\text{stock}\end{array}}}_{(1)} \times \underbrace{\frac{\begin{array}{c}\text{artifact}\\\text{stock}\end{array}}{\text{throughput}}}_{(2)} \times \underbrace{\frac{\text{throughput}}{\begin{array}{c}\text{ecosystem}\\\text{stock}\\\text{sacrificed}\end{array}}}_{(3)} \times \underbrace{\frac{\begin{array}{c}\text{ecosystem}\\\text{stock}\\\text{sacrificed}\end{array}}{\begin{array}{c}\text{ecosystem}\\\text{service}\\\text{sacrificed}\end{array}}}_{(4)}$$

Each of the four ratios on the right of the identity expresses a dimension of efficiency.

(1) *Artifact service efficiency.* The efficiency of a given amount of stock in satisfying wants (yielding services) depends on its *allocation* among different artifact embodiments and uses (commodity mix) and on the *distribution* of the stock among alternative people. Allocative efficiency is defined on the basis of a given distribution of wealth and income. The issue of distribution is usually treated as a question of justice not efficiency. Since this first category is the one economists have focused their attention on, we will treat it in more detail later. But first let us recognize the three neglected dimensions of efficiency.

(2) *Artifact maintenance efficiency* is essentially the turnover or renewal period of the artifact stock. The more durable, repairable, and recyclable

the stock, the longer things last; then the less maintenance and replacement they require and the greater is maintenance efficiency. Service efficiency reflects the intensity of service of the stock per unit of time, while maintenance efficiency reflects the number of units of time over which the artifact continues to yield services. Artifact maintenance efficiency is served by minimizing the throughput required to sustain a given stock.

(3) *Ecosystem maintenance efficiency* reflects the degree to which the ecosystem can maintain a supply of throughput on a sustainable basis, that is, without a depletion of the natural stocks. It depends on the replaceability or renewability of the environmental sources and sinks. Ecosystem maintenance efficiency is increased by using solar energy and renewable resources and by not overloading natural waste-absorption capacities. Also, maintenance efficiency is increased by using relatively abundant materials (even if nonrenewable) in preference to scarce materials. Ecosystem maintenance efficiency is diminished by using scarce materials, by using exotic man-made chemicals, by exploiting renewables beyond their sustainable yield, and by overloading biogeochemical cycles beyond their capacity. When renewable resources are exploited at a sustainable rate, a continual source of throughput is attained with practically no reduction of ecosystem stock.

(4) *Ecosystem service efficiency* depends on allocation and distribution, as in ratio 1, but this time on the allocation and distribution of *loss* rather than of gain. Is the loss of ecosystem stocks allocated among parts of the ecosystem in such a way as to minimize the total loss of ecosystem services? Are these lost ecosystem services evenly distributed among the people or do they fall entirely on one group? Are the people who bear the cost of lost services the same or different from the people who receive the benefits for the sake of which the costs were incurred? While the price system is of great importance in handling the allocation and distribution of services derived from artifact stocks, it is very limited in its ability to deal with the allocation and distribution of sacrificed ecosystem services. These costs are allocated and distributed mainly through a web of ecological interdependence that lies outside the market.

Technology can increase all four ratios, but it confronts limits. Ratios 2 and 3 are limited by the entropy law: nothing lasts forever; there is no such thing as a 100-percent renewable resource; depletion and pollution can never approach zero. Ratio 1 is limited by diminishing marginal utility; ratio 4 is limited by the law of increasing marginal costs, greatly complicated by the discontinuities arising from ecological thresholds and complex interdependencies. No doubt there are trade-offs among the various dimensions of efficiency. For example, the durability of a fiberglass boat is greater than that of a wooden boat (higher artifact maintenance efficiency), but fiberglass is made from nonrenewable resources (lower ecosystem maintenance efficiency).

All four dimensions of efficiency are served by the depletion quota auction. Limiting the volume of throughput at least slows down the rate at which ecosystem services are sacrificed (ratio 4). It allows us to incur these losses in a more cautious manner, although it does not by itself solve the problem of how best to allocate and distribute ecological costs. However, at least it allows us to face the question. The depletion quota system can be used to shift dependence from nonrenewables to renewables, thus increasing ratio 3. Higher resource prices resulting from the quota give an incentive to increase durability, repairability, and recyclability, thereby raising ratio 2. Higher prices also improve the allocative side of artifact efficiency (ratio 1) by forcing consumers to eliminate low-priority uses. The distributive side of service efficiency is adversely affected by higher prices, but that can be more than compensated for if the scarcity rents are captured by the government and reallocated to the poor, as was suggested in Chapter 3.

Economists have focused their attention on artifact service efficiency, and the result of their analysis is summarized below. Within this category the subdimension of allocative efficiency has received most attention, while distributive efficiency has been classed as a question of justice rather than efficiency. The central concept is that of Pareto optimality. A Pareto optimal allocation occurs when no consumer, given his income, could be made better off by a reallocation of any factor of production to any alternative use, or by any voluntary exchange of goods. In other words, the total stock is optimally allocated, since a position that cannot be improved upon is by definition an optimum.

There are, however, infinitely many Pareto optima—one for each of the infinitely many possible distributions of stock ownership. The distribution of the ownership of capital stock, and the distribution of the income flows generated by that capital stock, will clearly have an important effect on the intensity of total services yielded by the stock to all people. Common sense tells us that when the stock is so unequally distributed that the frivolous wants of the rich take precedence over the basic needs of the poor, then we could get more service from the same stock by redistributing some of it from the rich to the poor. However, this is not usually treated by economists under the heading of efficiency but rather of social justice. Since "service," the basic reason to be of economic activity, is unmeasurable, it is held that we really cannot be sure that the service derived from the rich lady feeding cream to her overweight cat is less than the service yielded by the same stock in the form of milk fed to the poor woman's undernourished child. This would require "interpersonal comparisons of utility," which are unscientific, because we have no measure of utility or service. Each individual, by introspection and experience, is entrusted to judge whether he himself is better off or worse off as a result of any change (though he cannot say by precisely how much), but no one is allowed to say that A is improved by more than B is harmed, at least not in the context of efficiency. Interpersonal welfare comparisons are considered a matter of justice and are to be dealt with by people other than economists.

Logically this is not an indefensible position. Ideologically and psychologically, however, it has resulted in sweeping distribution out of the economist's spotlight of efficiency and under someone else's rug of justice. Interpersonal comparisons of utility are not as entirely lacking in empirical base as is claimed. After all, we all suffer in the same way from the same diseases; are poisoned by the same poisons; made healthy by the same diets; cured by the same medicines; and delighted by the same beauties of art, music, and the natural world. At the margin, personal tastes differ, but inframarginally the similarities are overwhelming. Does a leg amputation hurt Smith more than a pin prick hurts Jones? Of course it does, and it is pure sophistry to feign ignorance of the answer. Minimizing pain is a more operational goal than maximizing pleasure precisely because of the basic, inframarginal character and commonality of pain. We are all hurt in much the same way by the same things, so that interpersonal comparisons are much easier for minimizing pain than for maximizing pleasure.

If we assume that people count equally and that the marginal utility of income diminishes for each person, then the presumption is that an equal distribution of wealth and income would maximize the interpersonal sum of utility or service. But as Joan Robinson has pointed out, economists have been strangely reluctant to question "an economic system in which so much of the good juice of utility is allowed to evaporate out of commodities by distributing them unequally" (Robinson, 1962, p. 54). There is, of course, the problem of incentives (would income remain constant if equally distributed?) and of differing degrees of irksomeness, danger, and effort required by different necessary tasks, so that equality in a more inclusive sense requires some degree of inequality in monetary income and wealth distribution. Furthermore, the goal of total equality can become a pathological quest for a jealous homogeneity at the lowest common denominator, as in Kurt Vonnegut's (1950, p. 7) fantasy of the Handicapper General who assigns equalizing handicaps to all—the strong and swift have sandbags tied around their necks to slow them down to average, and the intelligent have buzzers implanted in their heads that randomly go off and interrupt their thoughts, bringing their concentration span into line with average intelligence. To avoid the absurdities of too much equality as well as too much inequality, we should think in terms of limits to inequality; of a range within which inequality is necessary, efficient, and just, and beyond which it is unnecessary, inefficient, and unjust. The distributist institution discussed in Chapter 3 aims at such a balance.

In sum, distributive efficiency means not wasting the service-yielding power of the stock by allowing it to be too unequally distributed so that the trivial wants of some take precedence over the basic wants of others, while at the same time not making a self-defeating fetish out of equality by refusing to recognize and reward real differences in effort, skill, location, danger, and other conditions affecting work.

An interesting question is what range of difference in wealth and income is optimal? My own guess is that a factor of ten range should be enough. The maximum income in the civil service is around $36,000, and the minimum is probably at least $6,000; the range of kinds of jobs is probably as great as exists in the economy as a whole. Thus if a factor of six difference is sufficient for the civil service, I wonder why a factor of ten would not be sufficient for the whole economy. By way of comparison, in 1968 in the United States, the richest 10 percent had incomes twenty-seven times as high as those of the poorest 10 percent. The range between the richest and poorest 1 percent would, of course, be much greater (Budd, 1970, p. 253). Lester Thurow (1977) calculates that currently the richest 10 percent in the United States have incomes about fifteen times those of the poorest 10 percent, while the comparable ratios for Sweden and Japan are seven and ten, respectively. Just where the maximum and minimum limits should be in absolute terms can be worked out by trial and error once the principle of limits is established. The limits, of course, have to be consistent with the total amount of income, the total population, and the shape of the distribution curve between the limits.

The concept of allocative efficiency is the one that economists have emphasized and analyzed most fully. The result of that analysis is that, given certain assumptions, a price system (market system) leads to efficient allocation in the sense of Pareto optimality defined above. For this reason, considerable reliance was placed on the market in the institutions outlined in the previous chapter. Since the market is so thoroughly misunderstood by its opponents and so highly overrated by its friends, it is worthwhile here to review the assumptions and logic that lead to the conclusion that markets achieve allocative efficiency.

On the Allocative Efficiency of Competitive Markets

Let us analyze the price system by deriving and interpreting a basic market equation. The analysis is based on the three most common assumptions in economics: the behavioral and psychological assumption of diminishing marginal utility; the technological assumption of diminishing marginal physical product; and the institutional assumption of perfectly competitive markets (including the assumptions of individualistic maximizing behavior and absence of external costs and benefits). What is important here is not the existence or measurability of "utility," nor the precise meaning of marginal "product." It is sufficient to consider these two "laws" as heuristic expressions of the commonplace that individuals satisfy their most pressing wants first, and that producers first employ the best qualities and most efficient combinations of factors known to them. We could also substitute the laws of diminishing marginal rate of substitution and transformation, in which the heuristic analogy uses only the property of order of numbers without need of a unit. But the cardinal hypothesis is didactically simpler, so we will make use of it. The cardinalist-ordinalist controversy is mostly inflation, as are all attempts to measure utility. Even if utility could be measured, what difference would it make? My utility is still *qualitatively* different from your utility, and the ethical problems arising therefrom would not be resolved by a "utilometer."

The following symbols are employed:

MU_x^n = the marginal utility of good x to consumer n.

P_x = the market price of good x.

P_a = the market price of factor a.

MPP_x^a = the marginal physical product of factor a when used to make good x.

We assume *any* pair of goods x and y, *any* individual n, and *any* factor a. Hence the analysis will hold for all pairs of goods, all individuals, and all factors.

The basic market equation is the double equation:

$$\frac{MU_x^n}{MU_y^n} = \frac{P_x}{P_y} = \frac{MPP_y^a}{MPP_x^a}.$$

First we will demonstrate that the basic market equation follows logically from our assumptions. Next we will explain what the equation means and why it is important.

To derive the basic market equation we need appeal only to the common sense equimarginal principles of maximization. The left-hand equality is the condition for maximum consumer satisfaction (equal marginal utility per dollar in all alternative uses,* usually written

$$\frac{MU_x^n}{P_x} = \frac{MU_y^n}{P_y}.$$

---

*If $\dfrac{MU_x^n}{P_x} > \dfrac{MU_y^n}{P_y}$, then consumer n could take a dollar away from expenditure on y and spend it on x, and in so doing would gain more utility from more x than he lost from less y, thus increasing total utility. As the substitution of x for y continues, equality is approached, because the law of diminishing marginal utility tells us that as more x is purchased MU_x^n falls, and as less y is purchased MU_y^n rises. Further substitution of x for y ceases when equality is reached.

The right-hand equality can be derived by noting that in pure competition the following condition holds for *all* firms that use a to produce x; $P_a = P_x \cdot MPP_x^a$. The product $P_x \cdot MPP_x^a$ represents the marginal revenue derived from employing another unit of factor a to produce good x. P_a is the marginal cost of another unit of a. When marginal cost equals marginal revenue, the profit-maximizing amount of a is being employed. Likewise, for all firms using a to produce y, we have condition $P_a = P_y \cdot MPP_y^a$. In other words, profit maximization requires that all factors be employed in quantities such that the price of each factor equals the value of its marginal product.* Since P_a is the same for all firms, it follows that $P_x \cdot MPP_x^a = P_y \cdot MPP_y^a$, and that $\dfrac{P_x}{P_y} = \dfrac{MPP_y^a}{MPP_x^a}$, which is the right-hand equality in the basic equation.

In words the basic market equation says that prices of any two commodities are directly proportional to their marginal utilities and inversely proportional to the marginal products yielded by an increment of any factor. The inverse proportion between prices and marginal products could be stated as a direct proportion between prices and marginal costs. This is so because the MPP_y^a is the amount of y given up when we reallocate one unit of factor a from y-production to x-production. The true cost of x is the amount of y sacrificed in producing more x. Hence MPP_y^a is, in real terms, the marginal cost of x. Hence the equation states that prices of any two commodities are directly proportional to both their marginal utilities and their marginal costs.

On the left end of the basic equation we have the conditions of relative desirability (utility functions), that is, psychological forces and information. $\dfrac{MU_x^n}{MU_y^n}$ is the common marginal rate of psychological substitution at which all consumers arrive by maximizing utility subject to given prices and given individual incomes. On the right end of the equation we have conditions of relative possibility (production functions), that is, technological forces and information. $\dfrac{MPP_y^a}{MPP_x^a}$ is the common marginal rate of technical substitution at which the producing sector arrives by maximizing profits subject to given prices. Prices from the connecting link between relative desirability and relative possibility, between supply and demand in the market. $\dfrac{P_x}{P_y}$ is the marginal rate of market substitution. The equality

---

*Reasoning as before, if $P_a < MPP_x^a \cdot P_x$, then if the producer employs another unit of factor a his revenue $(P_x \cdot MPP_x^a)$ will increase by more than his costs (P_a). Hence it is profitable to employ the extra unit of a. But as more and more a is employed, we know from the law of diminishing marginal physical product (diminishing returns) that MPP_x^a will fall. When equality is attained, profits are no longer increased by using more a, so no more is used.

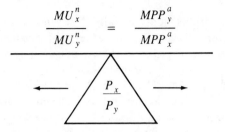

Figure 6

of these three rates of substitution means that the rates at which any consumer is *willing* to substitute commodities are equal to the rates at which he is *able* to substitute them, either by trade or through production.

Perhaps a more instructive way to state the same idea is to note that from the basic equation it follows (by cross multiplication of the first and last ratios) that $MU_x \cdot MPP_x^a = MU_y \cdot MPP_y^a$. In words, this states that the marginal utility of factor a in its x-use is equal to that of its y-use, as judged by consumer n.* Given the generality of our definitions, it follows that *no* consumer is able, given his income, to increase his utility by reallocating *any* factor to *any* alternative use. An allocation of resources that cannot be improved upon is, by definition, an optimal allocation. This sort of "optimum" is totally consistent with conditions of mass misery and social injustice, but it does represent the best attainable without redistributing wealth and income, and is usually called .a Pareto optimum. There are infinitely many Pareto optima just as there are infinitely many possible distributions of wealth and income.

To elucidate the role of prices in finding the optimum, let us first remember that what is essential in defining the optimum is the equality of the first and last terms in the basic equation. The middle term, relative prices, serves as a kind of adjustable fulcrum, keeping the two end terms in balance, as illustrated by the "see-saw" analogy shown in Figure 6. More precisely, the equality of the two end terms results from the axiom that things equal to the same thing are equal to each other, the "same thing" being relative prices. This "same-thing" or fulcrum function of prices has been called the "parametric function of prices" (Lange, 1938), because its operation depends on everyone treating price as beyond his control, as a parameter. Since no one can adjust prices to his plans, everyone must adjust his plans to prices. Prices are the same for all, and plans adjusted to the same prices become adjusted to each other, that is, balanced or made consistent. If the existing set of prices does not produce a balanced adjustment of plans, then the imbalances will show up as shortages or surpluses, which will cause prices of short items to

*Note that the units of the product are (utility/x) (x/a) = utility/a. The equation states that the utility yielded at the margin by factor a in its x-use is equal to that of its y-use.

rise and prices of surplus items to fall, thus tending to eliminate the imbalances. Therefore, the plans of producers and consumers are led by the parametric function of prices to a state of *balance,* which is also a *Pareto optimum.*

To understand the parametric function of prices more fully, we must consider two subsidiary functions of prices—the information and incentive functions. Instead of asking millions of consumers what their preferences are between all pairs of goods at the margin, producers get this information simply by consulting market prices! Instead of consumers asking thousands of production engineers what are the terms on which alternative goods are available at the margin, consumers get this information from market prices! The price system is thus able to sound out and communicate the scattered, piecemeal knowledge existing in the minds of all consumers and producers about their preference functions and production functions as well as about ephemeral circumstances of time and place. Thus prices summarize and communicate the fractionalized, inarticulate ends-means structure of society as a necessary precondition for allocating means in the service of ends. This knowledge of ends and means is never "given" in any operational sense. Like the gold in the ocean, it is there but of no value without some means of getting at it. The efficiency of the price system in using and communicating this dispersed knowledge is its most remarkable feature, and yet it is the most neglected by price theory (Hayek, 1945). In addition to collecting and communicating the necessary information for allocating resources, the price system also provides the incentive to act on that information, since only by so doing can consumers maximize satisfaction and producers maximize profit.

The above discussion has, following tradition, treated prices as very flexible relative to preferences and technology. That is, price changes are considered accommodating, while psychological and technological changes are treated as autonomous. It is obvious, however, that psychological and technological changes can also be accommodating, with prices assuming the autonomous role. In the real world of less than perfect competition, prices may become rigid for institutional reasons (oligopolistic price fixing, unions, etc.) or for legal or just-price reasons (price supports and ceilings, etc.), in which cases nonprice market adjustments assume greater relative importance. In terms of our basic equation, we have two general types of nonprice market adjustment; altering the marginal rate of psychological substitution (through advertising) to induce the consumer to buy more x at the fixed price (often cancelled out by similar advertising in favor of y); and altering the marginal rate of technical substitution (through research) so that, by lowering costs, more x can be profitably supplied at the fixed price. These two types of adjustment are obviously of great importance in the real economy. In terms of the see-saw analogy, we can leave the fulcrum fixed and adjust the two weights to attain balance. Vast resources are devoted to advertising and to research and development. Traditional theory, taking wants and techniques as given, thus leaves out two of the three possible mechanisms of market adjustment. Nevertheless, it is clear that the basic equation can be used to describe the market under conditions of producer or government sovereignty (rigid prices) as well as under consumer sovereignty (flexible prices), or any combination of the two. It is important to realize that as long as the basic equation holds, whether accompanied by price or nonprice adjustments or both, it defines a Pareto optimum. As long as everyone individually treats price as *given* (whether rigidly or flexibly so in the aggregate) the parametric function of prices still works to attain a Pareto optimum. In the producer sovereignty (rigid prices) case, we have simply altered tastes and technology and have redistributed income.

The conclusions, of course, are totally dependent on the assumptions. The laws of diminishing marginal utility and diminishing marginal physical product (diminishing returns both physically and psychically) are rather solid and can be easily defended by assuming their negation and showing that it leads to absurdities. Suppose a law of increasing (or constant) marginal utility. The consumer would spend his first dollar on the good yielding most satisfaction. The second unit of the good would yield as much or more satisfaction, likewise for the third, and so on. The consumer would spend his entire income on one commodity! Similarly, if the marginal physical product of labor or capital increased in agriculture, then the whole world's rice crop would be grown on the single most fertile acre. Such implications are grossly counterfactual and provide solid support for the two assumptions.

The problems arise with the assumption of perfect competition and the difficulties of institutionalizing this assumption. The condition of having many small buyers and sellers requires trust busting and limits to bigness, which is provided in the distributist institution of Chapter 3. This is nothing new. We have a long tradition favoring trust busting and competition. The early Chicago school of economists argued that there are only two ways to regulate the economy: competition and planning. Competition should be favored wherever possible, even at the expense of often exaggerated economies of scale. Where natural monopolies exist and economies of scale are enormous, the monopoly enterprise should be nationalized and run as a public corporation. To be avoided at all costs is the attempt to establish private monopolies and then to regulate them in the public interest, lest the industry end up regulating the regulators (Simons, 1948). This is an unworkable hybrid, neither fish nor fowl, yet it is what we now have.

The market system also assumes that all costs and benefits get reflected in money prices. When this is patently false, as it increasingly becomes thanks to economic growth, then the accounting of some of the relevant costs and benefits must take place outside the market, and corresponding limits must be placed on the market. How can this be done without obstructing the legitimate and efficient functions that the market does perform? In Chapter 3 it was argued that three institutions were required: depletion quota auctions, distributive limits, and a limit on aggregate births.

As argued earlier, growth in population, in artifact stocks, and in the necessary entropic throughput results in the increasing importance of absolute scarcity, which is manifested in the increasing prevalence of external costs. The biophysical system becomes more generally sensitive to particular interferences as the web of general interdependence is stretched ever tighter by growth in the population of people and artifacts. As a subsystem becomes a larger component of a total system, it has a larger area of interface with the total system and experiences more constraints and feedbacks. The maintenance of these increasingly large populations requires technologies that use enormous quantities and exotic qualities of material throughput and provoke unfavorable reactions from the biosphere, which we classify as "external" costs for no better reason than because we have made no provision for them in our economic theories. For example, there is nothing exotic or "external" about CO_2, yet it is being produced in such enormous quantities that it could affect the heat balance and climate of the earth (greenhouse effect). DDT and plutonium are exotic materials that we have been pushed into using by the demands for more food and more energy for more people. These two substances did not even exist until the 1940s. The biosphere evolved over billions of years without ever having had any evolutionary experience with DDT or plutonium. Consequently, the biosphere is totally unadapted to these substances, and their large-scale, or even small-scale, introduction cannot fail to be disruptive. Barry Commoner (1971) wants to blame technology for environmental ills and exempt population and per-capita consumption growth as minor factors. But nothing could be clearer than that growth itself is a major driving factor behind technological adventurism (Ehrlich and Holdren, 1972).

The market will certainly favor the introduction of exotic materials whenever it is profitable, and continued growth will surely make it profitable. Some economists advocate imposing taxes on ecologically disruptive activities so as to make them unprofitable. This, as we have seen, goes by the revealingly contradictory name of "internalizing externalities." It is, taken by itself, a recipe for frustration and failure. If we liken the market economy to a two-year-old child, and the biosphere to a living room full of irreplaceable antiques and complex TV and stereo equipment, then the internalization scheme would be analogous to telling the two-year old that he will get his hands slapped once for breaking a vase, twice for a lamp, and so forth, and then following him around and slapping his hand after he has damaged the furniture. A better procedure would be to build the largest feasible playpen in the living room and leave the child free to do what he wants with the limited resources within the playpen. This situation is analogous to the strategy of imposing quantitative limits on aggregate throughput, aggregate births, and distributional inequality. Conservative limits are set within which the market can safely function, and then the market is left alone. Distributional justice, ecological balance, and population restriction are matters that are too important to be left to determination by a market that is simply unable to take conscious account of such costs because the costs are usually not obvious, are delayed, and do not fall mainly on the decision maker. They involve time horizons and interdependence horizons beyond those of rational individuals acting independently.

Concluding Reflections on Efficiency

Some ecologists have defined an economist as a person who is seeking the optimal arrangement of deck chairs on the Titanic. The market will see to it that the deck chairs and umbrellas are optimally allocated, but it will not keep us from running into icebergs. The great advantage of the market is that it frees us from concern with the mass of day-to-day allocation problems and allows us to use our limited policy-making capacity to avoid the really big mistakes. It would be a foolish waste of effort and an intolerable imposition of microcontrol to refuse to use the market. But to trust the market to make decisions that are truly beyond its range can be suicidal. The market cannot, by itself, keep aggregate throughput below ecological limits, conserve resources for future generations, avoid gross inequities in wealth and income distribution, or prevent overpopulation.

The institutions of Chapter 3 were designed to face these issues and impose corresponding aggregate limits on the market but to leave all particular allocations to the market. Instead of internalizing external costs, the idea is to externalize them, that is, to take from the market sphere the possibility of incurring costs that it is unable to perceive or evaluate. Benefits and costs that do not register themselves as conscious short-run pleasure or pain at an individual level but that are organic, with interdependencies far exceeding market relationships, must be dealt with outside the market and must result in constraints on the market. Internalization of externalities attempts this, but in a way that seeks to reduce all forms of nonmarket interdependence to market interdependence reflected in prices. Externalization deals with natural nonmarket interdependencies on their own terms of quantity rather than price and communicates with the market via quantitative restrictions rather than rigged prices. The limited aggregate quantities will cause higher market prices, but the policy variable is external quantity limits rather than internal price manipulations. As noted in Chapter 3, the ecosystem is affected by quantity, not price, and it is therefore safer to let errors and unexpected changes be reflected in price movements rather than quantity movements. Only *aggregate* quantities are limited: the allocation of the aggregate amount of each resource among alternative users and uses is still determined by the market.

A rather strict distinction between allocative and distributive efficiency has been made. However, there are some important interconnections between the two. Factor prices are determined according to allocative efficiency, but factor prices, along with distribution of ownership of factor amounts, determine the distribution of income, and the distribution of income influences demand, which influences factor prices. Thus distributive efficiency is influenced by allocative efficiency. What is not so often recognized, yet in my view is more important, is that distributive efficiency can also affect allocative efficiency. In our society, labor and capital, the two funds or renewable-stock factors of production, represent major social classes as well as physical components of production. Each class possesses considerable monopoly power and strives to protect its distributive share of total income by keeping its price (wages and return to capital) as high as it can. In a capitalist market society, even with monopoly, the wage of labor and the rate of return on capital are related to the marginal productivities of labor and capital respectively. To a considerable degree, these two marginal productivities are in conflict. Cheap and abundant labor increases the marginal product of capital, while cheap and abundant capital increases the marginal product of labor. The two classes are in basic conflict.

But there is a third factor, the flow factor of natural resources. This factor is also associated with a social class—the landlord class. Landlords were the most powerful social class in feudal times, but in modern capitalism they are the least powerful class, and whatever power they might exert toward raising resource prices is undercut by the government, which is the largest resource owner and which follows a policy of cheap resources in order to benefit and ease the conflict between the two dominant classes, labor and capital. The way to raise both labor and capital productivity is to have cheap and abundant natural resources. Naturally, this will result in lower resource productivity, and landlord interests will be hurt. But landlord income is rent, which by definition is a payment in excess of supply price—unearned income. Resources have no cost of production, only a cost of extraction or collection. This cost of extraction is the necessary supply price. But resources also earn pure scarcity rent or royalties, which is unearned income, and this makes it difficult to defend high resource prices on ethical grounds when compared to the sweat and skill of the laborer and the initiative, risk, and managerial role of the capitalist. However, in today's world a good part of the income of labor and capital is also rent resulting from their monopoly power.

The distributive share struggle has resulted in a clear victory of the uneasy capital-labor alliance over landlords or resource owners. But the implications for efficiency of the resulting low price of resources needs to be considered. The nonrenewable component of this flow is very large in an industrial society and represents the limitative or ultimately scarce factor in the long run. Labor and capital can be reproduced as long as the resource flow holds out. Efficiency requires maximizing the productivity of the scarcest factor. We seem instead to be minimizing resource productivity in order to maximize the current incomes of labor and capital. There is clearly an enormous conflict here. As will be seen in Chapter 5, some economists seek to avoid the conflict by declaring capital a perfect substitute for resources, by denying that natural resources are scarce, or, in the extreme, by denying that such resources are necessary at all. Such evasions are totally inept.

The steady-state institutions of Chapter 3 attempt to meet the issue head-on by recognizing the need to maximize resource productivity and consequently to raise resource prices. This means higher scarcity rents on resources; however, instead of resulting in a private windfall to landlords, these scarcity rents are captured by the government through the depletion quota auction. The public revenue resulting from these scarcity rents on resources can be redistributed as desired, but the suggestion offered in Chapter 3 was to use them to finance the minimum-income feature of the distributist institution, thereby equalizing to some degree the distribution of income. This plan resolves the conflict between distributive efficiency and allocative efficiency that has evolved under present institutions.

The tendency to sacrifice resource efficiency in the service of capital and labor income does not totally resolve the capital-labor conflict, but it does soften it considerably. We might say that exploitation of nature by both laborers and capitalists has to some degree replaced the exploitation of labor by capital or at least restrained it. Quotas on resource use will surely sharpen the old Marxian class conflict between labor and capital and will certainly be unworkable without a complementary distributist institution. Similarly, a distributist institution (minimum income) requires a limitation on population. If we refuse to allow people to starve, yet are unwilling to limit fertility and population growth, then we merely generalize poverty. As Mill states, "Society can feed the necessitous, if it takes their multiplication under its control; . . . But it cannot with impunity take the feeding upon itself and leave the multiplying free" (1881, p. 447).

In sum, the institutions of Chapter 3 provide a context conducive to the improvement of each type of efficiency. Maintenance efficiency is promoted by higher resource prices, which encourage greater durability, more recycling, and more use of renewable resources and solar energy. Service efficiency is likewise stimulated, because the stock is constant and the only way to attain a higher intensity of want satisfaction is to improve service efficiency by increasing either allocative or distributive efficiency. Increased efficiency rather than increased throughput will be the focus of the profit motive. Allocative efficiency is achieved by the market, confined to its proper sphere. Distributive efficiency is attained outside the market via the distributist institution. Moreover, the impairment of the serviceability of natural systems is prevented by limiting the throughput, so as to keep market-determined physical processes from riding roughshod over life-sustaining biophysical processes. The birth quota system prevents all other gains from being overwhelmed by numbers of people.

The Study Group on Technical Aspects of Efficient Energy Utilization (American Institute of Physics, 1975) has developed the concept of second law efficiency, which is the ratio of the least available work that could have done the job to the actual available work used to perform the same job. The concept is task-oriented rather than device-oriented. The more usual concept of efficiency (first law efficiency) is device-oriented. Of the total amount of available work put into a device, what percentage comes out in the desired, useful form? There remains the further question of whether another (perhaps not yet invented) device could theoretically give the same useful output with a smaller input of available work. And what is the least input of available work that could accomplish the task without violating the second law? This concept is relevant to our discussion, because it provides an approximation to our efficiency ratio of $\frac{service}{throughput}$. If we take service as equivalent to the performance of a well-defined task, and throughput as equivalent to available energy used up, then the concept of second law efficiency would seem to give an operational approximation to this notion of efficiency. The physicists' study found that energy resources are presently being consumed at a second law efficiency of only 10–15 percent and concluded that such a performance is "not only wasteful; it is inelegant." Much room exists for improving efficiency, and in the SSE there would be abundant incentives for such improvement.

Some insightful observations on efficiency have been made by economic historian Richard Wilkinson (1973), who tells us that development is the adaptive response a society makes when it outgrows its resource base and productive system. For Wilkinson, development historically is "primarily the result of attempts to increase the output from the environment rather than produce a given output more efficiently" (1973, p. 4). The price of growing beyond our ecological niche is that the workload increases. As the workload increases, the development of labor-saving techniques becomes necessary. These adaptations do not necessarily increase efficiency above what it was before the adaptation became necessary. As often as not, they are accompanied by a decrease in the real efficiency of societies, that is, the new methods require more effort and supporting resources to satisfy the basic needs of the larger population or the same population in the face of whatever environmental deterioration made the change necessary. A plow culture is not more efficient than a bush-fallowing hoe culture. Cutting and turning the turf costs more work, requiring draft animals and the indirect work that goes into their maintenance. Industrialization requires mineral resources that are less accessible than vegetable or animal resources and requires increasing amounts of labor and transport. As long as there was abundant agricultural land for growing fodder, horses were more efficient than steam locomotives. The coal-burning locomotive was an adaptation to having outgrown the renewable resource base of agricultural land and timber—an iron horse that ate abundant, but nonrenewable and laboriously acquired, minerals. Wilkinson tellingly points out that the United States did not adopt British coal-burning technologies as soon as they were known, as we would expect if these techniques were more efficient, but waited instead until wood became scarce in the United States. Wood was more efficient than coal and horses more efficient than locomotives, until society outgrew its resource base. Thus historical economic development has not been pulled by the magnet of increasing efficiency but has been pushed by the necessity to increase total output as growth in population and per-capita consumption break the preexisting equilibrium with the resource base or ecological niche. For Wilkinson, efficiency seems to refer to the amount of labor required to meet basic necessities. Within ecological equilibrium there is a tendency for efficiency to increase, but in moving from one resource base to another, that is, between ecological equilibria, efficiency often seems to fall.

If economic development has been pushed by growing scarcity, and if it does not necessarily increase efficiency, then how can we maintain that it is *a priori* a good thing? This query is especially pertinent for class societies, which, as Wilkinson notes, throw the burden of increasing workload on to the lower class as one means of adaptation. Could we not make a good case for seeking to maintain ecological balance as an alternative to further growth and development, once some sufficient material standard has been attained? Does not the analysis point toward population control and consumption limits? Wilkinson notes that "Restraint on the growth of population and production seem to be an ecological necessity" (p. 193), and further remarks that "the continuous expansion of gross national product . . . should perhaps be regarded more as a reflection of the rising real cost of living rather than an indication of increasing welfare" (p. 185).

Thus if Wilkinson's interpretation of the historical process of development is correct, it would lend support to the position that conventional growth has not promoted efficiency and that efficiency is more likely to increase under steady-state conditions, though not indefinitely.

Our current notions of efficiency are grossly confused. We usually measure only the efficiency of the fund factors, labor and capital (excluding consumer goods). GNP divided by number of laborers or by value of the stock of producer's goods are the usual measures. GNP is a flow, reflecting mainly the flow of throughput, an index expressed in *value* units, but measuring change in a flow of *physical* quantities. Thus the greater the flow of throughput (the faster depletion, the more pollution, the sooner consumer goods wear out, the more time people devote to production), the higher is "efficiency." In other words, this notion of efficiency measures the efficiency with which we destroy what is valuable! The steady-state concept of efficiency seems much more sensible. Stocks should be "satisficed," throughput minimized, and service maximized, given the sufficient and ecologically sustainable level of stocks. The enormous irrationality of present economic institutions was underlined during the recession and oil shortage of 1974 by a perceptive comedian. "The best thing you can do for your country," he said, "is to junk your present car, buy the biggest new car you can afford, and then don't drive it." Or, as poet Wendell Berry has put it:

> And so when we examine the principle of efficiency as we now practice it, we see that it is not really efficient at all. As we use the word, efficiency means no such thing, or it means short-term or temporary efficiency; which is a contradiction in terms. It means hurrying to nowhere. It means the profligate waste of humanity and nature. It means the greatest profit to the greatest liar. What we have called efficiency has produced among us, and to our incalculable cost, such unprecedented monuments of destructiveness and waste as the strip-mining industry, the Pentagon, the federal bureaucracy, and the family car [Berry, 1973, p. 2].

In view of the lack of attention given to the Ultimate End and ultimate means, it is not surprising to find that efficiency in the use of ultimate means to satisfy the Ultimate End is a concept more honored in the breach than in fulfillment. We treat ultimate means as if they were not scarce. We ignore the issue of the Ultimate End yet illogically pay lip service to "priorities," which are necessarily confused if we deny the existence of an ordering principle. Efficiency is a ratio, and if we are confused about the denominator and refuse to think about the numerator, then it should not surprise us that efficiency is often inefficient. The link between growthmania and confused thinking about efficiency will be further considered in Chapter 5. Such anomalies as these will eventually discredit growthmania and lead to adoption of the steady-state paradigm with its more sensible concepts of efficiency. The following chapter provides a more extended catalog of the absurdities of growth economics.

REFERENCES

American Institute of Physics. "Efficient Use of Energy," *Physics Today,* 28, no. 8 (August 1975), A–H.

Berry, Wendell. Quoted in *Manas,* March 14, 1973.

Budd, E. C. "Postwar Changes in the Size Distribution of Income in the United States," *American Economic Review Papers and Proceedings,* May 1970, 247–260.

Commoner, Barry. *The Closing Circle,* New York: Knopf, 1971.

Ehrlich, Paul R., and John P. Holdren. "One-Dimensional Ecology," *Science and Public Affairs: The Bulletin of the Atomic Scientists,* 28, no. 5 (May 1972), 16–27.

Hayek, F. A. "The Use of Knowledge in Society," *American Economic Review,* 35, no. 4 (September 1945), 519–530.

Lange, Oskar, and Fred M. Taylor. *On the Economic Theory of Socialism.* New York: McGraw-Hill, 1964. Originally published in 1938.

Mill, John Stuart. *Principles of Political Economy.* New York: Appleton-Century-Crofts, 1881.

Robinson, Joan. *Economic Philosophy.* London: C. A. Watts, 1962

Simons, Henry C. *Economic Policy for a Free Society.* Chicago: University of Chicago Press, 1948.

Thurow, Lester C. "The Myth of the American Economy," *Newsweek,* February 14, 1977, p. 11.

Vonnegut, Kurt, Jr. "Harrisson Bergeron," in *Welcome to the Monkey House.* New York: Dell, 1950.

Wilkinson, Richard. *Poverty and Progress: An Ecological Perspective on Economic Development.* New York: Praeger, 1973.

II

THE
GROWTH
DEBATE

5

A CATECHISM
OF GROWTH FALLACIES

The part played by orthodox economists, whose common sense has been insufficient to check their faulty
logic, has been disastrous to the latest act.

J. M. Keynes (1936)

The first question asked of any critic of the status quo is: What would you put in its place? In place of the growth economy we would put a steady-state economy as elaborated in Part I. But such a theoretical alternative is not of great interest unless there is dissatisfaction with the business-as-usual growth economy. If you have eaten poison, it is not enough to simply resume eating healthful foods. You must get rid of the specific substances that are making you ill. Let us, then, apply the stomach pump to the doctrines of economic growth that we have been force-fed for the past four decades. Perhaps the best way to do that is to jump right into the growth debate and consider critically some fifteen to twenty general progrowth arguments that recur in various guises and either expose their errors or accommodate their valid criticisms.

First a preliminary point. The verb "to grow" has become so overladen with positive value connotations that we have forgotten its first literal dictionary denotation, namely, "to spring up and develop to *maturity.*" Thus the very notion of growth includes some concept of maturity or sufficiency, beyond which point physical accumulation gives way to physical maintenance; that is, growth gives way to a steady state. It is important to remember that "growth" is not synonymous with "betterment."

Can't Get Enough of That Wonderful Stuff

The American people have been told by no less an authority than the President's Council of Economic Advisors that, "If it is agreed that economic output is a good thing it follows by definition that there is not enough of it" (Economic Report of the President, 1971, p. 92). It is evidently impossible to have too much of a good thing. If rain is a good thing, a torrential downpour is, by definition, better! Has the learned council forgotten about diminishing marginal benefit and increasing marginal costs? A charitable interpretation would be that "economic" output means output for which marginal benefit is greater than marginal cost. But it is clear from the context that what is meant is simply real GNP. Perhaps this amazing nonsequitur was just a slip of the pen. At another point in the same document the council admits that "growth of GNP has its costs, and beyond some point they are not worth paying" (p. 88). However, instead of raising the obvious question—What determines the optimal point and how do we know when we have reached it?—the council relapses into non sequitur and quickly closes this dangerous line of thinking with the following pontification: "The existing propensities of the population and policies of the government constitute claims upon GNP itself that can only be satisfied by rapid economic growth" (p. 88). Apparently, these "existing propensities and policies" are beyond discussion. This is growthmania.

The theoretical answer to the avoided question is clear to any economist. Growth in GNP should cease when decreasing marginal benefits become equal to increasing marginal costs, as was discussed in Chapter 2. But there is no statistical series that attempts to measure the cost of GNP. This is growthmania, literally not counting the costs of growth. But the situation is even worse. We take the real costs of increasing GNP as measured by the defensive expenditures incurred to protect ourselves from the *unwanted* side effects of production and *add* these expenditures to GNP rather than subtract them. We count real costs as benefits. This is hypergrowthmania. Obviously, we should keep separate accounts of costs and benefits. But to do this would make it clear that beyond some point zero growth would be optimal, at least in the short run. Such an admission is inconvenient to the ideology of growth, which quite transcends the ordinary logic of elementary economics. More precisely, it is good growthmanship strategy to admit the theoretical existence of such a point way out in the future, but somehow it must always be thought of as far away. The ideological reasons for this are clear and have to do with the problem of distribution of output in an economy in which ownership of land and capital is highly concentrated and embodies labor-saving technology. Full employment at a living wage requires high aggregate demand, which requires high net investment to offset the large savings made possible by concentrated income. High net investment signifies rapid growth.

The Hair of the Dog that Bit You

One of the most popular arguments against limiting growth is that we need more growth in order to be rich enough to afford the costs of cleaning up pollution and discovering new resources. Economist Neil Jacoby says, "A rising GNP will enable the nation more easily to bear the costs of eliminating pollution" (1970, p. 42). Yale economist Henry Wallich makes a similar point:

> The environment will also be better taken care of if the economy grows. Nothing could cut more dangerously into the resources that must be devoted to the Great Cleanup than an attempt to limit resources available for consumption. By ignoring the prohibitionist impulse and allowing everybody to have more, we shall also have more resources to do the environmental job [Wallich, 1972, p. 62].

No one can deny that if we had more resources and were truly richer, all our economic problems would be more easily solved. The question is whether further growth in GNP will *in fact* make us richer. It may well make us poorer. How do we know that it will not, since we do not bother to measure the costs and even count many real costs as benefits? These critics simply assume that a rising per-capita GNP is making us better off, when that is the very question at issue!

If marginal benefits of physical growth decline while marginal costs rise (as elementary economic theory would indicate), there will be an intersection beyond which further growth is uneconomic. The richer the society (the more it has grown in the past), the more likely it is that marginal benefits are below marginal costs and that further growth is uneconomic. That marginal benefits fall follows from the simple fact that sensible people satisfy their most pressing wants first, whether in alternative uses of a single commodity or in alternative uses of income. That marginal costs rise follows from the fact that sensible people first exploit the most accessible land and minerals known to them, and that when sacrifices are imposed by the increase of any one activity, sensible people will sacrifice the least important alternative activities first. Thus marginal benefits of economic activity fall while marginal costs rise. Were this not the case, our previous "economic activity" would not have been economic —less pressing wants would have to have taken priority over more pressing wants, and the level of welfare could have been increased by reallocation with no increase in resources used.

The best attack on this simple argument is not to question the slopes of the benefit and cost curves but to argue that the curves themselves continually shift apart so that the intersection always stays ahead of us, and thus growth remains economic. But there are physical limits to efficiency (how far down cost curves can be shifted), and our rush toward exotic growth-permitting technologies, such as fission power and breeder reactors, is more likely to push the cost curve up than down, once all costs are counted. Moreover, our efforts to push the benefit curve up by creating new wants too rapidly and too artificially are more likely to pull down the benefit curve than to push it up. But even ignoring the possibility that the curves could shift in perverse directions, and assuming *very unrealistically* that the benefit curve will forever shift upward and the cost curve downward, there is *still* the question of timing. Why must the curves always shift *before* we reach the intersection? Might not technical progress occasionally be delayed? Might we not find it optimal to cease growth temporarily while waiting for the curves to shift? Or must we go beyond the optimum, just to keep up the momentum of growth for the sake of avoiding unemployment? Once we have gone beyond the optimum, and marginal costs exceed marginal benefits, growth will make us worse off. Will we then cease growing? On the contrary, our experience of diminished well-being will be blamed on the traditional heavy hand of product scarcity, and the only way the orthodox paradigm knows to deal with increased scarcity is to advocate increased growth—this will make us even less well off and will lead to the advocacy of still more growth! Sometimes I suspect that we are already on this "other side of the looking glass," where images are inverted and the faster we run the "behinder" we get.

Environmental degradation is an iatrogenic disease induced by the economic physicians who attempt to treat the basic sickness of unlimited wants by prescribing unlimited production. We do not cure a treatment-induced disease by increasing the treatment dosage! Yet members of the hair-of-the-dog-that-bit-you school, who reason that it is impossible to have too much of a good thing, can hardly cope with such subtleties. If an overdose of medicine is making us sick, we need an emetic, not more of the medicine. Physician, heal thyself!

Consistent Inconsistencies
and Avoiding the Main Issues

Growthmen are forever claiming that neither they nor any other economist worth his salt has ever confused GNP with welfare. Consider, however, the following four statements from the same article (Nordhaus and Tobin, 1970):

> (1) Gross National Product is not a measure of economic welfare. . . . maximization of GNP is not a proper objective of economic policy. . . . Economists all know that . . . [p. 6].
>
> (2) Although GNP and other national income aggregates are imperfect measures of welfare, the broad picture of secular progress which they convey remains after correction of their most obvious deficiencies [p. 25].
>
> *(3) But for all its shortcomings, national output is about the only broadly based index of economic welfare that has been constructed [p. 1, Appendix A].
>
> *(4) There is no evidence to support the claim that welfare had grown less rapidly than NNP. Rather NNP seems to underestimate the gain in welfare, chiefly because of the omission of leisure from consumption. Subject to the limitations of the estimates we conclude that the economic welfare of the average American has been growing at a rate which doubles every thirty years [p. 12].

It is asking too much of context and intervening qualification to reconcile statement 1 with statements 2, 3, and 4. Either GNP (or NNP) *is* an index of welfare, or it is *not*. The authors clearly believe that it *is* (in spite of the first statement). They offer many sensible adjustments to make GNP a better measure of welfare on the assumption that, although imperfect, it is nevertheless a measure of welfare. But all of this avoids the fundamental objection that GNP-flow is largely a *cost*. Wants are satisfied by the services of the *stock* of wealth. The annual production flow is the *cost* of maintaining the stock and, though necessary, should be minimized for any given stock level. If we want the stock to grow, we must pay the added cost of a greater production flow (more depletion, more labor, and ultimately more pollution). Depletion, labor, and pollution are real costs that vary directly with the GNP-throughput. If we must have some indices of welfare, why not take total stock per capita and the ratio of total stock to throughput flow? Welfare varies directly with the stock, inversely with the flow. Beyond some point, the benefits of additions to the stock will not be worth the costs in terms of additional maintenance throughput. A suggestion along these lines was made in Chapter 2, following the lead of Irving Fisher.

---

*These two statements were evidently omitted in the final 1972 published version. Reference is to the December 1970 National Bureau of Economic Research mimeographed conference paper. The omissions make the contradiction less obvious but do not remove it.

Kenneth Boulding has for many years been making the point that Gross National Product is largely Gross National Cost and has never been taken seriously. If this way of looking at things is wrong, why does not some economist deal it a decisive refutation instead of avoiding it? Certainly it is not a minor issue.

The source of this flow fetishism of orthodox economics is twofold. First, it is a natural concomitant of early stages of ecological succession (Odum, 1969). Young ecosystems (and cowboy economies) tend to maximize production efficiency, that is, the ratio of annual flow of biomass produced to the preexisting biomass stock that produced it. Mature ecosystems (and spaceman economies) tend to maximize the inverse ratio of existing biomass stock to annual biomass flow that maintains it. The latter ratio increases as maintenance efficiency increases. Economic theory is lagging behind ecological succession. The other reason for flow fetishism is ideological. Concentrating on flows takes attention away from the very unequally distributed stock of wealth that is the real source of economic power. The income flow is unequally distributed also, but at least everyone gets some part of it, and marginal productivity theory makes it appear rather fair. Redistribution of income is liberal. Redistribution of wealth is radical. Politically, it is safer to keep income at the center of analysis, because not everyone owns a piece of the productive stock, and there is no theory explaining wealth distribution. Putting stocks at the center of analysis might raise impolite questions.

Crocodile Tears from Latter-Day Marie Antoinettes

Economists and businessmen with no previous record of concern for the poor have now begun to attack steady-state advocates as upper-class social climbers, who, having gotten theirs, now want to kick the ladder down behind them and leave the poor forever on the ground floor. There may be such people, and certainly they should be condemned. But most advocates of the steady state accept and proclaim the absolute necessity of limits to inequality in the distribution of both wealth and income. Indeed, many people who have long favored less inequality in the distribution of wealth on ethical and political grounds have reached the same conclusion on ecological grounds. It is the orthodox growthmen who want to avoid the distribution issue. As Wallich so bluntly put it in defending growth, "Growth is a substitute for equality of income. So long as there is growth there is hope, and that makes large income differentials tolerable" (1972). We are addicted to growth because we are addicted to large inequalities in income and wealth. What about the poor? Let them eat growth! Better yet, let them feed on the hope of eating growth in the future!

We have been growing for some time, and we still have poverty. It should be obvious that what grows is the reinvested surplus, and the benefits of growth go to the owners of the surplus, who are not poor. Some of the growth dividends trickle down, but not many. The poor are given the sop of full employment—they are allowed to share fully in the economy's basic toil but not in its surplus—and unless we have enough growth to satisfy the dividend recipients, even the booby prize of full employment is taken away.

On the issue of growth and poverty, Joan Robinson noted:

> Not only subjective poverty is never overcome by growth, but absolute poverty is increased by it. Growth requires technical progress and technical progress alters the composition of the labor force, making more places for educated workers and fewer for uneducated, but opportunities to acquire qualifications are kept (with a few exceptions for exceptional talents) for those families who have them already [Robinson, 1972, p. 7].

Admitting the Thin Edge of a Big Wedge

"We know that population growth cannot continue forever" (Nordhaus and Tobin, 1970, p. 20). This is certainly a true statement. It is also the thin edge of a wedge whose thick end is capable of cracking the growth orthodoxy in half. This results from the fact that, in addition to the population of human bodies (endosomatic capital), we must also consider the population of extensions of the human body (exosomatic capital). Cars and bicycles extend man's legs, buildings and clothes extend his skin, telephones extend his ears and voice, libraries and computers extend his brain, and so on. Both endosomatic and exosomatic capital are necessary for the maintenance and enjoyment of life. Both are physical open systems that maintain themselves in a kind of steady state by continually importing low-entropy matter-energy from the environment and exporting high-entropy matter-energy back to the environment. In other words, both populations require a physical throughput for short-run maintenance and long-run replacements of deaths by births. The two populations depend upon the environment in essentially the same way. The same biophysical constraints that limit the population of organisms apply with equal force to the population of extensions of organisms. If the first limitation is admitted, how can the second be denied?

This simple logic has recently imposed itself on the population of books in college libraries (Gore, 1974). Academic library collections have for several decades been growing at a rate that doubles holdings every fifteen years. Microfilm technology has not substituted for bulkier acquisitions but has led to extra acquisitions. If we admit that every college cannot afford a Library of Congress, and that even that library cannot grow forever, we must accept some kind of a steady-state library. That is, some sufficient number of holdings must be maintained constant, and whenever a new book is added an old one must be discarded. Up to this point there is no escape from the simple logic of the problem.

Difficulties arise in setting the aggregate "birth" and "death" rates and especially in deciding which books are to be acquired and which are to be sacrificed. If to add a new book we must throw away an old one, then the new one must be judged better than the old one. This is surely a healthy discipline and will result in an improvement of the quality of the total stock of books. But the problem, as ever, is how to judge quality. A legitimate difference of opinion arises between the consumer sovereignty school (get rid of those books that are checked out least often) and the library responsibility school (rely on the judgment of librarians and scholars). This is a difficult issue and probably requires compromise. But what is certain is that the issue must be faced. No library can continue to buy books indefinitely and never discard any. What is true for books is true for cars, buildings, bicycles, and, of course, for human bodies. At some point, more births must be balanced by more deaths.

Misplaced Concreteness
and Technological Salvation

Technology is the rock upon which the growthmen built their church. Since rocks and foundations are concrete entities, it is natural that growthmen should begin to endow technology with a certain metaphorical concreteness, speaking of it as a *thing* that grows in *quantity*. From there, it is but a short step to ask whether this thing has grown exponentially, like many other things, and to consult the black art of econometrics and discover that indeed it has! Next, we can conceive of technology as a sort of antibody to the pollution and depletion germs. Ultimately, we conclude that depleting and polluting activities (production and consumption) can continue to grow exponentially, because we have a problem-solving antiparticle, technology, which can also grow exponentially!

Is this progression an unfair caricature? Consider the following statement from a review of *Limits to Growth* (Meadows et al., 1972) by two economists and a lawyer:

> While the team's world model hypothesizes exponential growth for industrial and agricultural needs, it places arbitrary, nonexponential, limits on the technical progress that might accommodate these needs.
>
> . . . It is true that exponential growth cannot go on forever if technology does not keep up—and if that is the case we might save ourselves much misery by stopping before we reach the limits. But there is no particular criterion beyond myopia on which to base that speculation. Malthus was wrong; food capacity has kept up with population. While no one knows for certain, technical progress shows no signs of slowing down. The best econometric estimates suggest that it is indeed growing exponentially [Passell et al., 1972, p. 12].

These few sentences are very valuable in that they unite in one short space so many of the misconceptions of orthodox growthmen. Note that technology has become an exponentially growing *quantity* of some *thing* that solves problems but does not create any. Note the clear implication that exponential growth could go on forever if technology (that problem-solving antiparticle) can keep up. Can it in fact keep up? Consult the entrails of a nameless econometrician and, behold! It has in the past, so it probably will in the future. Most econometricians are more cautious in view of the fact that technological change cannot be directly measured but is merely the unexplained residual in their regressions after they have included as many measurable factors and dummy variables as they can think of. Sometimes the residual technology component even includes the effect of increased raw material inputs! Note also the blind assertion that Malthus was wrong, when in fact his predictions have been painfully verified by the majority of mankind. But then majorities have never counted. Only the articulate, technically competent minority counts. But even for them Malthus was not really wrong, since this minority has heeded his advice and limited its reproduction.

The idea that technology accounts for half or more of the observed increase in output in recent times is a finding about which econometricians themselves disagree. For example, D. W. Jorgenson and Z. Grilliches found that "if real product and real factor input are accurately accounted for, the observed growth in total factor productivity is negligible" (1967). In other words, the increment in real output from 1945 to 1965 is almost totally explained (96.7 percent) by increments in real inputs, with very little residual (3.3 percent) left to impute to technical change. After taking account of critical reviews of their study, Jorgenson and Grilliches admitted the likelihood that a greater role was played by technological change but reaffirmed their basic conclusion "that total factor input, not productivity change, predominates in the explanation of the growth of output" (Jorgenson and Grilliches, 1972, p. 111). G. S. Maddala found that for the bituminous coal industry "growth in labor productivity can be explained almost totally by a rise in the horsepower per worker. Thus what formerly was considered as technical change now appears as a process of factor substitution" (1965, p. 352). Such findings cast doubt on the notion that technology, unaided by increased resource flows, can give us enormous increases in output. In fact, the law of conservation of matter and energy by itself should make us skeptical of the claim that real output can increase continuously with no increase in real inputs.

Norman Royall, a far more perceptive reviewer of *The Limits to Growth,* has noted a similar confusion and lucidly comments on it:

> Some critics of "Limits" berate the authors for not including exponentially growing technical knowledge as a sixth constituent of the World Model. Such

criticism elaborately misses the point. The other five constituents have real, physical referents that can be quantified: population can be counted, barrels of petroleum consumed can be enumerated and part per million of abrasive chemicals in the smog of Los Angeles can be measured.

Sheer "knowledge" means nothing for the world system until it enters one of the other five constituents, and the tacit assumption that all technical knowledge necessarily enters as a good is unwarranted. Is the technical knowledge that performance of gasoline engines can be improved by adding tetraethyl lead to their fuel a "good"? [Royall, 1972, p. 42].

In other words, the projections of physical growth trends already include the effects of past technical "progress" as these effects were registered in the five physical referents of the model. The tacit assumption is that the influence of technology on the physical world will, in the future, change in ways similar to the way it has changed in the past.

We need not accept *The Limits to Growth* in its entirety; it is clear, however, that whether or not technology has grown exponentially is largely irrelevant. The assumption of some critics that technological change is exclusively a part of the solution and no part of the problem is ridiculous on the face of it and totally demolished by the work of Barry Commoner (1971). We need not accept Commoner's extreme emphasis on the importance of the problem-causing nature of post–World War II technology (with the consequent downplaying of the roles of population and affluence) in order to recognize that recent technological change has been more a part of the problem than of the solution. The key questions are: What kind of technology is part of the solution? What type of institutional sieve will let pass the good kind of technology while blocking the bad kind? This issue was dealt with in the discussion in Chapter 3 of the depletion quota auction, which provides such a sieve in the form of higher resource prices.

Two-Factor Models with Free Resources and Funds That Are Nearly Perfect Substitutes for Flows

Economists routinely measure the productivity of the fund factors, labor and capital (and Ricardian land). But the productivity of the flow factors, natural raw materials and inanimate energy, are seldom even spoken of, much less calculated. This reflects an assumption that they are not really scarce, that they are the free and inexhaustible gifts of nature. The only limit to the flow of product is assumed to be the capacity of the fund factors to process the inputs and turn them into products. Nordhaus and Tobin are explicit on this point:

The prevailing standard model of growth assumes that there are no limits on the feasibility of expanding the supplies of nonhuman agents of production. It is basically a two-factor model in which production depends only on labor and reproducible capital. Land and resources, the third member of the classical triad, have generally been dropped [Nordhaus and Tobin, 1970, p. 14].

How is this neglect of resource flows justified? According to Nordhaus and Tobin, "the tacit justification has been that reproducible capital is a near perfect substitute for land and other exhaustible resources" (p. 15). If factors are near perfect substitutes, then there is, of course, no point in considering them separate factors. From the point of view of economic analysis they are identical. But it is very odd to have such an identity between factors whose very dimensionality is different. Capital is a fund, material and energy resources are flows. The fund processes the flow and is the instrument for transforming the flow from raw materials to commodities. The two are obviously complements in any given technology. But allowing for technological change does not alter the relationship. The usual reason for expanding (or redesigning) the capital fund is to process a larger, not a smaller, flow of resources, which we would expect if capital and resources were substitutes. New technology embodied in new capital may also permit processing different materials, but this is the substitution of one resource flow for another not the substitution of a capital fund for a resource flow.

Nordhaus and Tobin state that the "tacit assumption of environmentalists is that no substitutes are available for natural resources" (p. 15). They consider this an extreme position, but what substitute is there for natural resources? They offer "reproducible capital"; however, in addition to requiring natural resources for their very reproduction, capital funds are clearly complements to resource flows, not substitutes. The fact that one resource flow may substitute for another, if the capital fund is redesigned to allow it, is no basis for saying that the generic factor of capital is a substitute for the generic factor of natural resource! After we deplete one resource, we redesign our machines and set about depleting another. The assumption is that in the aggregate resources are infinite, that when one flow dries up there will always be another, and that technology will always find cheap ways to exploit the next resource. When the whales are gone, we will hunt dolphins, and so on until we are farming plankton. The ecologists tell us that it will not work, that there are other limits involved, and even if it would work, who wants it? But Nordhaus and Tobin see little connection between economic growth and ecological catastrophe: "As for the danger of global ecological catastrophe, there is probably very little that economics can say" (1970, p. 20). As long as economic growth models continue to assume away the absolute dimension of scarcity, this is quite true and is simply another way of saying that current growth economics has uncoupled itself from the world and has become irrelevant. Worse, it has become a blind guide. But it need not remain so.

But Resources Are Such a Small Percentage of GNP

Perhaps another "justification" for ignoring resources is the small value component of GNP they represent. In 1968 minerals production represented 1.7 percent of GNP and total fossil fuels, 2.0 percent (Goeller, 1972, p. 15).* Why is it that our price system imputes such a small share of total value produced to resources and such a large share (the remainder) to labor and capital? Does this vindicate the assumption that resources are ultimately not scarce? Or does it simply mean that they are underpriced? I believe the latter is the case** and that this underpricing results from the relative power of social classes that conditions the functioning of the market. Specifically, labor and capital are two powerful social classes, while resource owners, for good reasons, are not. Let us see how this rigs the market in favor of low resource prices.

In the short run, we have a given technology and given amounts of the fund factors, labor and capital. It takes time to change the capital stock and to change the size of the working-age population. Suppose we desire to increase the incomes of both capital and labor in the short run. Since the incomes of capital and labor are tied to their respective productivities, it becomes necessary to increase these productivities. Under short-run assumptions, the only way to increase the productivities of both fund factors is to increase the flow factors of raw materials and power. As the flow of resource throughput is increased with a given fund of labor and capital, the productivity of the resource flow must, by the law of diminishing returns, decrease. All three productivities cannot increase in the short run. It is clear that the flow factor's productivity is the one that is going to be sacrificed, since in the short run it is the only one whose quantity can be increased. Furthermore, even in the longer run, with all factors variable but no technological change, it is clear that resource productivity will also lose out. The tie between labor productivity and labor income, plus the monopoly power of labor unions, will keep labor productivity from being sacrificed. The tie between capital productivity and profit, along with the monopoly power of large corporations, will keep capital productivity from being sacrificed.

---

*The "optimistic" conclusion of Goeller's paper is that "assuming reasonable management the resource base of the *earth* is sufficient to maintain the *present state* of material affluence of the *United States,* and to share it to *some meaningful degree* with the rest of the world, for at least the next hundred years" (p. 1; my italics). In other words, if we move rapidly and efficiently to a steady state at present levels, and draw on all the world's resources, and limit our sharing with the rest of the world to some "meaningful degree," our system could continue for the next hundred years! Such optimism makes pessimism redundant.

**It would be interesting, following Ise's suggestion noted in Chapter 3, to calculate the value of nonrenewable resources priced at the price of their nearest renewable substitute—for example, petroleum priced at the Btu equivalent of, say, wood alcohol. No doubt the picture would be very different.

Capital and labor are the two social classes that produce and divide up the firm's product. They are in basic conflict but must live together. They minimize conflict by growth and by throwing the growth-induced burden of diminishing returns onto resource productivity. How do they get away with it? In earlier times it might not have worked; a strong landlord class would have had an interest in keeping resource prices from falling too low. But today we have no such class to exert countervailing upward pressure on resource prices. Although resource owners do exist and they do prefer higher to lower prices, other things being equal, it remains true that no social class is as effective in promoting resource productivity as the capitalists and laborers are in promoting the productivities of their respective factors.

Suppose we allow for technological change in the long run. Now it is possible for all three productivities to increase. But how likely is it? Given the desire to increase incomes of labor and capital, innovations that increase these two productivities will have first priority, while those that increase mainly resource productivity will not be stimulated. Given low prices for resources, it will not matter much to entrepreneurs what happens to resource productivity. And surely it is easier to invent a new technology that increases the productivity of two factors than to invent one that increases all three productivities.

Should we, by a kind of reverse land reform, reinstate a landlord class? Landlord rent is unearned income, and we find income based on ownership of that which no one produced to be ethically distasteful. No one loves a landlord. Adam Smith tells us that landlords love to reap where they have never sown, and not many lament the historical demise of the landowning aristocracy. But not all the long-run consequences of this demise are favorable. Rent may be an illegitimate source of income, but it is a totally legitimate and necessary price, without which efficient allocation of scarce resources would be impossible. Henry George said let rent be charged but then tax it away. Socialists, after trying to get along without rent, now say charge some rent but pay it to the government, who is now the landlord. In the United States neither of these things has happened. The largest resource owner, the government, has followed a give-away and low price policy, both on resources it owns and on those, such as natural gas, whose price it regulates (Energy Policy Project, 1974, Chapter 11). It has done this to favor certain capitalists, to promote growth, and to ease the labor-capital conflict and win votes in both camps.

Moreover, imports of resources from underdeveloped countries, which have not yet learned how to use them, have naturally been cheap because of the low short-run opportunity cost to the exporting country. This pattern is now changing, but in the past it has been a factor in keeping resource prices low. Some resources are owned by capitalists, who are likely to be much more interested in maximizing growth and minimizing conflict through low resource prices than in making profits on sales of resources. In fact, the capitalist's ownership of resources will generally be for the purpose of lowering the cost price of those resources to himself as capitalist, by means of vertical integration, in order to increase the returns to capital. Capital is the dynamic, controlling factor. It is not for nothing that our economic system is called "capitalism" rather than "resource-ism."

Evidence for this generalization is provided by the following statement from the National Commission on Materials Policy:

> The vertically integrated structure of the virgin materials industries discourages scrap use even when it is inexpensive. Their internalized operations and long term contracts tend to stabilize virgin material costs and lead to day-to-day decisions based more on constraints of prior investment and custom than on current price [National Commission, 1973, p. 4D–16].

The phrase "constraints of prior investment and custom" means keeping returns to capital high by keeping the accounting price of resources in vertically integrated "internal operations" so low that even cheap scrap is unattractive by comparison.

Let us consider briefly two similar analyses of resource productivity. Karl Marx had the following to say regarding the effect of capitalist production on soil productivity:

> Capitalist production . . . disturbs the circulation of matter between man and the soil, i.e., prevents the return to the soil of its elements consumed by man in the form of food and clothing; it therefore violates conditions necessary to the lasting fertility of the soil. . . . Moreover, all progress in capitalistic agriculture is a progress in the art, not only of robbing the laborer, but of robbing the soil; all progress in increasing the fertility of the soil for a given time is a progress toward ruining the lasting sources of that fertility. The more a country starts its development on the foundation of modern industry, like the United States, for example, the more rapid is the process of destruction! Capitalist production, therefore, develops technology, and the combining together of various processes into a social whole, only by sapping the original sources of all wealth—soil and the laborer [Marx, 1967, p. 505].

Marx sees capitalists exploiting the soil as well as the laborer. Our analysis sees capital and labor maintaining an uneasy alliance by shifting the exploitation to the soil and other natural resources. It follows that if some institution were to play the role of the landlord class and raise resource prices, the labor-capital conflict would again become severe; hence the radical implications of the ecological crisis and the need for some distributist institution, as we already noted in Chapter 3.

A more recent analysis of resource productivity, in the case of electric power, was made by Barry Commoner. He found the productivity of electric power to be falling in all individual industries considered and falling even more in the total economy, as power-intensive industries displaced other industries in relative importance. His empirical findings suggest to him an

> apparently unavoidable dilemma created by an effort to reduce overall power demanded by industrial production; either total production is curtailed, or power productivity is elevated; but if the latter course is taken, labor productivity must be reduced[*]. Thus, whichever course is taken, the effort to reduce power demand would appear to clash head on with one or both of the two factors that are widely regarded as essential to the stability of the United States economic system—increased production and increased labor productivity.
>
> These considerations raise the possibility—which it is to be hoped economists will investigate—that continued exponential increase in power consumption is not an accidental concomitant of industrial growth, but is rather a functional necessity for the continued operation of the United States economic system, as it is presently organized. If this should prove to be true, then the ultimate social choice signified by the power crisis becomes very stark. One course is to continue the present exponential growth in the supply of electric power, and risk our future on the ability to contain the huge mass of resultant chemical, radioactive, and thermal pollution. The other is to slow down the rate of power consumption, and accept as a necessary consequence that the economic system must be changed [Commoner, 1971b, p. 31].

The relative social power hypothesis presented as an explanation of low resource prices and productivities might be considered as a theoretical complement to Commoner's empirically based generalizations and conjectures. Social conflict is minimized in the short run by low productivity of the entire throughput, which is a consequence of high productivity (and income) for labor and capital. If we opt to avoid the risk of containing large masses of material, chemical, thermal, and radioactive pollution, not to mention aesthetic, moral, and social costs, we must limit growth in throughput. What is the most efficient and least painful way to limit throughput? In Chapter 3 it was suggested that the best way to limit throughput is with a depletion quota auction. Commoner (1976) leaps to the conclusion that socialism is the only answer, but such a conclusion does not follow at all.

---

*This is apparently an empirical generalization by Commoner, based on an observed inverse relationship between power productivity and labor productivity during the period 1946–1968 (see Commoner, 1971b, fig. 3).

Present Value and Positive Feedback

It is sometimes argued that the market automatically provides for conservation by offering high profits to farsighted speculators who buy up materials and resell them later at a higher price. There are at least two things wrong with this argument.

First, exponentially growing extraction leads to "unexpectedly" sudden exhaustion. Suppose the doubling time of the cumulative total amount extracted is on the order of 30 years, as it apparently is for many resources, and that there is enough of the resource to last for 300 years at present growth rates. At the end of 270 years the resource would only be half depleted. Yet in the final 30 years it would go from half to total depletion. Most resource owners probably find that surprising. For linear trends, the past is a good guide to the future. For exponential growth, the past is a deceptive guide to the future.

The second problem is that the future profit must be discounted to its present value. The investor has the alternative in an expanding economy of depleting now and investing the short-term profits in another line that will earn the expected going rate, which will be close to the growth rate of the economy. The discount rate he applies to future profit is the same as the rate at which he would expect his reinvested short-term profits to grow. This expected rate is determined largely by the current rate and by recent changes in the current rate. The result is that high and increasing current growth rates, based on high and increasing current depletion rates, lead to high and increasing discount rates applied to future values. The last condition in turn leads to a low incentive to conserve, which feeds back to high current depletion and growth rates, high discount rates, and so forth. Present value calculations thus have an element of positive feedback that is destabilizing from the point of view of conservation. Financial prudence usually advises depleting now and investing short-term earnings in depleting some other resource. The presumption again is infinite resources. There will always be more material and energy resources available to feed the march of compound interest, with its consequent discounting of future values and disincentive to conservation. This tacit assumption sometimes becomes explicit, as in the following statement from the president of a great oil company:

> The fact seems to be that the first [resource] storehouse in which man found himself was only one of a series. As he used up what was piled in that first room, he found he could fashion a key to open a door into a much larger room. And as he used up the contents of this larger room, he discovered there was another room beyond, larger still. The room in which we stand at the middle of the twentieth century is so vast that its walls are beyond sight. Yet it is probably still quite near the beginning of the whole series of storehouses.

> It is not inconceivable that the entire globe—earth, ocean and air—represents
> raw material for mankind to utilize with more and more ingenuity and skill
> [quoted in Ordway, 1953, p. 28].

Such is also the assumption of orthodox growth economics. Even if
this vision were correct, we should add that eventually we must *live* in the
same rooms we work in. Living in intimate contact with garbage and
noxious wastes is a by-product of growth. But optimists will argue that
there is another infinite series of ever larger garbage dumps! The whole
conceptual basis of the growth faith is equivalent to a generalization
of the chain-letter swindle. There will always be five new resources
for every depleted resource. The current beneficiaries of the swindle,
those at the beginning of the chain, try hard to keep up the illusion
among those doubters at the end who are beginning to wonder if there are
really sufficient resources in the world for the game to continue very
much longer.

Youth Culture and Frustrated Pyramid Climbers

A stationary population is a part of a steady-state economy. Assuming
present mortality rates, the attainment of a stationary population would
imply an increase in the average age of the population from the current
twenty-seven to about thirty-seven years. This raises fears of social senil-
ity, excessive conservatism, loss of adaptability and dynamism, and so
forth. This hardly seems a reasonable fear, even for devotees of the
"Pepsi generation." We need only compare Sweden, with one of the
oldest age structures, to Brazil, with one of the youngest. It would certainly be stretching things a bit to say that old Sweden is a reactionary,
noninnovative gerontocracy, while young Brazil is a progressive, innova-
tive country run by young people. We might just as well argue that Brazil
values youth less than Sweden because its infant mortality rates are
higher, and therefore Sweden is more youth-oriented than Brazil. Such
arguments are simplistic at best.

The stationary population "pyramid" would be shaped more like a
house (rectangular up to about age fifty, where the roof begins and
rapidly tapers to a peak). But the structure of authority in hierarchical
organizations remains a pyramid. Thus there would, in the future, be less
of a congruence between advancing age and advancing position. More
people would grow older at lower levels of authority, and many ambitions
would be frustrated. The observation is a highly interesting one and no
doubt has important sociological implications. But they are not all negative by any means. More individuals will learn to seek personal fulfillment outside hierarchical organizations. Within such organizations,

fewer people will be automatically promoted to their level of incompetence, thus thwarting the so-far relentless working of the "Peter Principle." Perhaps giant bureaucracies will even begin to dissolve and life will reorganize on a more human scale.

Pascal's Wager Revisited

The growthmania position rests on the hypothesis that technological change can become entirely problem solving and not at all problem creating and can continually perform successively more impressive encores as resources are depleted. There is sufficient evidence to make reasonable people quite doubtful about this hypothesis. Yet it cannot be definitely disproved. There is a certain amount of faith involved, and faith is risky. Let us then take a completely agnostic position and apply the logic of Pascal's wager and statistical decision theory. We can err in two ways: we can accept the omnipotent technology hypothesis and then discover that it is false, or we can reject it and later discover that it is true. Which error do we most wish to avoid? If we accept the false hypothesis, the result will be catastrophic. If we reject the true hypothesis, we will forgo marginal satisfactions and will have to learn to share, which, though difficult, might well be good for us. If we later discover that the hypothesis is true we could always resume growth. Thus even in the agnostic case, it would seem prudent to reject the omnipotent technology hypothesis, along with its corollary that reproducible capital is a near-perfect substitute for resources.

The Fallacy of Exponentially Increasing Natural Resource Productivity

In a previous section we considered the orthodox position that the productivity of reproducible capital increases exponentially, thanks to exponential technological progress. The problem noted was that exponential technological progress, as measured in two-factor production functions, is usually accompanied by exponential increases in resource throughput (depletion and pollution), which remain outside the analysis. It is of little comfort to contemplate increasing productivity of labor and capital if it is at the continuing expense of resource productivity and if resources are the ultimately scarce factor. Robert Solow has defended growth by directly appealing to increasing resource productivity. Solow concludes that "there is really no reason why we should not think of the productivity of natural resources as increasing more or less exponentially over time" (1973, p. 51). This remarkable conclusion, if true, would be a boon to those who advocate limiting the throughput of resources, because it would mean that such a limit is totally consistent with continued exponential growth in GNP and is therefore not such a radical proposal. The resource flow could be stabilized and GNP could continue to grow exponentially as resource productivity (i.e., GNP/resource flow) increased exponentially. Why, then, does limiting the resource flow provoke such strong opposition from growth economists?

The arguments Solow presents to support his conclusion are highly interesting. If the productivity of labor is measured by GNP/labor, he reasons, the productivity of iron is measured by GNP/iron output, that of aluminum by GNP/aluminum output, and so on. He calculates what has happened to the productivities of a number of particular resources between 1950 and 1970 and finds that some (iron, manganese, copper, lead, zinc, bituminous coal) have increased, while the productivities of others (nickel, petroleum) have remained the same and those of still others (aluminum, natural gas, electric power, columbium) have fallen. On the face of it, the evidence supports no generalization about resource productivity at all, even accepting Solow's definitions. But even more damaging is a hard look at the facile analogy between labor productivity and coal productivity, columbium productivity, and so forth, insofar as particular resource productivities are supposed to add up to, or convey some notion of, aggregate resource productivity, which is what Solow's conclusion clearly requires that it should do.

First of all, if the amount of labor used goes up, ceteris paribus, the productivity of labor goes down. If the quantity of all resources used goes up, then, ceteris paribus, the productivity of aggregate resources likewise goes down. But the productivity of a good many *particular* resources will still increase if the GNP happened to increase faster than the quantity of that resource used. Furthermore, the increase in GNP is in part made possible by the more rapid increase in quantity used of those particular resources whose productivities consequently fell over the given period. Solow recognizes this effect: "One of the reasons the productivity of copper rises is because that of aluminum falls, as aluminum replaces copper in many uses" (p. 51). This observation by itself could have restrained Solow from drawing his conclusion.

The meaning of these "resource productivities" is further obscured: "Sooner or later, the productivity of oil will rise out of sight, because the production and consumption of oil will eventually dwindle toward zero, but real GNP will not" (p. 51). Presumably, when production and consumption of oil approach zero, oil productivity will become infinite! The conclusion to be drawn is certainly not that increasing productivity compensates for diminishing supply of resources—otherwise we would be better off with nearly zero output of petroleum, which is absurd. Rather, the warranted conclusion is that Solow is playing around with meaningless numbers that support no conclusions at all.

Solow himself presents a good reason for doubting that there has been much resource-saving technological progress:

> First of all let me go back to the analogy between natural resources and labor. We are not surprised to learn that industry quite consciously tries to make inventions that save labor, i.e., permit the same product to be made with fewer man-hours of work. After all, on the average, labor costs amount to three-fourths of all costs in our economy. An invention that reduces labor requirements per unit of GNP by 1% reduces all costs by 0.75%. Natural resource costs are a much smaller proportion of total GNP, something nearer 5%. So industry and engineering have a much stronger motive to reduce labor requirements by 1% than to reduce resource requirements by 1%, assuming —which may or may not be true—that it is about as hard to do one as the other [Solow, 1973, p. 52].

We can agree with Solow that a well-functioning price system induces substitution and that this tends to dampen any overshoot and collapse behavior. But if that is his only point, then he is merely kicking at an open door and certainly does not need to "think of the productivity of natural resources as increasing more or less exponentially over time."

In his Richard T. Ely Lecture to the American Economic Association, Solow went as far as to proclaim not only the conditional possibility, but the empirical likelihood that "the world can, in effect, get along without natural resources" (1974, p. 11). Solow elaborates that this is so if we have a "backstop technology," such as breeder reactors, which will mean that "at some finite cost, production can be freed of dependence on exhaustible resources altogether" (1974, p. 11). Apparently, the world cannot get along without all natural resources, as he first suggested, but only without exhaustible ones. Just how to build and maintain a backstop technology of breeder reactors (the only example offered) without such exhaustible resources such as copper, zirconium, tungsten, and iron, not to mention initial stocks of enriched uranium or permanent depositories for radioactive wastes, is not explained by Solow. No doubt it is true that at "some finite cost" we could live on renewable resources, as mankind essentially did before the industrial revolution. But the finite cost is going to include a reduction in population and in per-capita consumption levels or, at the very least, a cessation of further growth. This is accepted by the steady-state view but not by Solow and other victims of the infinite substitutability fallacy, who are forced to lower the *deus ex machina* of backstop technologies onto the stage in order to save the awkward plot of growthmania. Even a perfect backstop technology, one that would deliver energy "too cheap to bear the cost of metering," to recall the early promises of fission advocates, cannot save the ever growing economy. In fact, "free" energy would simply enable the growth-maniacs to destroy the biosphere more quickly. Within the context of a SSE, free energy would be a blessing, but in the present growth context it would be a curse.

The explicit belief in the unlimited productivity of natural resources and the unlimited substitutability of other factors for natural resources has led economist Nicholas Georgescu-Roegen to the following verdict on Solow and the many other economists for whom he is the distinguished spokesman:

> One must have a very erroneous view of the economic process as a whole not to see that there are no material factors other than natural resources. To maintain further that "the world can, in effect, get along without natural resources" is to ignore the difference between the actual world and the Garden of Eden [Georgescu-Roegen, 1975, p. 361].

The Ever Expanding Service Sector and "Angelized GNP"

Advocates of growth frequently appeal to the increasing importance of services, which, it is assumed, can continue to grow indefinitely, since such activities are presumably nonpolluting and nondepleting. Thus while agriculture and industry will be limited by their necessary pollution and depletion flows, services are allegedly not so limited and will continue to grow. Therefore, an ever larger fraction of total GNP will originate in the service sector, and consequently the pollution and depletion flows per average dollar of GNP will fall continuously. Presumably, we will approach a nonphysical "angelized GNP."

There are two fatal flaws in this picture. While it is true that some activities are more throughput-intensive than others, it is not clear that these activities are always services, nor is it clear that the differences are very great once indirect effects are incorporated. Eric Hirst found that "services associated with food used almost as much energy as did farming and processing" (1974, p. 135). It is likely that when we add all the indirect as well as the direct aspects of service activities (inputs to service sector, inputs to inputs of service sector, etc.), we will find that services do not pollute or deplete significantly less than many industrial activities. That most services require a substantial physical base is evident from casual observation of a university, a hospital, an insurance company, a barber shop, or even a symphony orchestra. Certainly the incomes earned by people in the service sector will not all be spent on services but will in fact be spent on the average consumer basket of both goods and services.

The second flaw in this view is that there are limits to how high the proportion of services to goods can rise in the product mix without provoking a shift in the terms of trade in favor of goods and against services to such an extent that goods production would again expand and service production contract. Historically, employment in the service sector has grown relative to total employment, because productivity and total output of industry and agriculture have increased vastly. Once total output of physical goods is restricted, service sector growth will be increasingly restrained by a progressive deterioration in its terms of trade vis-à-vis physical goods.

It is true that "In 1969 a dollar's worth of GNP was produced with one-half the materials used to produce a dollar's worth of 1900 GNP, in constant dollars" (National Commission on Materials Policy, 1973, p. 3-3). Nevertheless, over the same period total materials consumption increased by 400 percent. We must resist being carried away by the halving of the material content of a GNP dollar. Remember the man who bought a new stove that cut his fuel bill in half and then reasoned that he could cut his fuel bill to zero by buying another such stove! More significant than the halving of the materials per dollar of GNP is the quintupling of the absolute material throughput and the similar increase in energy throughput over the same time period.

The idea of economic growth overcoming physical limits by angelizing GNP is equivalent to overcoming physical limits to population growth by reducing the throughput intensity or metabolism of human beings. First pygmies, then Tom Thumbs, then big molecules, then pure spirits. Indeed, it would be necessary for us to become angels in order to subsist on angelized GNP.

Kelso and the Second Economy

One of the most charitable, yet soft-headed manifestations of growth-mania is Louis O. Kelso's and Patricia Hetter's *Two Factor Theory: How to Turn Eighty Million Workers Into Capitalists on Borrowed Money* (1967). Kelso's rejection of full employment as a sufficient goal and his recognition that a system in which the vast majority are property-less workers and only a small minority are capitalists should be called proletarianism rather than capitalism go straight to the important issues. However, having arrived at the heart of the matter, he founders on twin rocks of redistribution and growth; in attempting to avoid the Scylla of redistribution he crashes headlong into the Charybdis of growthmania.

Kelso's idea is to give all workers a second income based on capital ownership. Instead of saving to accumulate capital, workers borrow to purchase stock and then earn dividends which allow them to pay off the loan and become sole owners of the stock with a net income from capital. Gradually, workers become capitalists. The notion is disarmingly simple and no doubt could work for some individual firms, but when generalized to the whole economy it runs into insurmountable problems. First, the workers borrow at the going interest rate and earn the going rate of return on stock that must be higher than the interest rate for the scheme to work. For the rate of return on stocks in general to be high, the economy must be growing rapidly in real terms. Kelso specifically assumed a growth rate several times the then current rates of 4 percent. His supporters envision rates on the order of 12 percent, which would mean a doubling of real GNP in less than six years. Kelso assumes without argument that such rates are physically possible for extended periods. That by itself dooms the scheme.

There is still another problem. Why should capitalists accept the workers as unneeded financial middlemen? Why would not capitalists buy the new stock themselves instead of lending to workers (to finance workers' stock purchases) at a lower rate than they could earn by buying the stock themselves? In a competitive market the rate of return on capital would tend to equality with the interest rate and thus eliminate or hold to a minimum that differential upon which the whole plan depends. Kelso's plan depends on the government's arranging tax incentives for capitalists to make it more profitable for them to lend to workers than to buy the stock themselves. This is not only a kind of hidden redistribution but may be a redistribution from workers to capitalists, instead of vice versa. If the government makes it more profitable for capitalists to lend to workers than to buy the stock that the workers are buying, then the capitalists are getting a better rate of return, counting tax advantages, than the workers are. These tax breaks are, in effect, subsidies to the capitalist that must be financed through the tax system—a subsidy or a lower effective tax for capitalists means a higher effective tax on the remainder of the population (or else reduced government services for all). The net effect is that the capitalists will become bigger capitalists faster than the workers will become little capitalists. Hardly a populist program, even assuming the 12 percent real rate of growth that would make the scheme environmentally disastrous regardless of whether its redistributive effects were progressive or regressive. The apparently regressive effects simply add insult to injury.

That Kelso has gained such a following is testimony to the power of wishful thinking—more for all with sacrifice by none. In Chapter 3 we discussed a set of institutions that could provide a kind of second income derived not from capital but from scarcity rents captured by the government through the auctioning of depletion quotas. The receipts could be redistributed as a social dividend, or rather a social royalty, which, it was suggested, should go mainly to the poor in the form of a minimum income. Rent is the best source of income to redistribute, from the point of view of efficiency as well as of equity. But it offers no magic formula for turning eighty million workers into capitalists on borrowed money!

The More-Is-Better Concept of Efficiency

Advocates of the steady-state economy are often accused of paying insufficient attention to the idea of efficiency. But could it be that orthodox economists are themselves rather muddled on the concept? That certainly seems to be the case in an otherwise valuable book by Arthur M. Okun (1975), who states that "efficiency means getting the most out of a given input." That is fair enough for a short definition, but Okun continues:

> This concept of efficiency implies that more is better, insofar as the "more" consists of items that people want to buy. . . . I, like other economists, accept people's choices as reasonably rational expressions of what makes them better off. To be sure, by a different set of criteria, it is appropriate to ask skeptically whether people are made better off (and thus whether society really becomes more efficient) through the production of more whiskey, more cigarettes, and more big cars. . . . Are there criteria by which welfare can be appraised that are superior to the observation of choices people make? Without defense and without apology, let me simply state that I will not explore those issues despite their importance. That merely reflects my choices, and I hope they will be accepted as reasonably rational [Okun, 1975, pp. 2, 3].

The first of several problems with this view is that the maxim "more is better" does not follow from the definition of efficiency. We could give an equivalent definition "efficiency means getting the same output with less input," and then argue that efficiency implied that "less is better," insofar as the "less" consists of items that people would like to avoid buying if only they could. The nonsequitur is enormously revealing and is not removed by specifying that "more" consists of items people want to buy. This simply confuses the definition of efficiency with the doctrine of consumer sovereignty. Once efficiency has been defined, we may argue that consumer sovereignty will increase it or decrease it, depending upon whether we accept any higher criteria for judging welfare than "the observation of the choices people make." Choices do not reveal much about welfare unless we know the alternatives available. And economic growth often narrows the range of alternatives. Is it any wonder that people choose automobiles if public transport is not available? If we really accept no higher criteria for judging welfare than the choices people make, then any behavior is as good as any other and it is meaningless to talk about right and wrong choices, or even about mistaken choices. Anything is right by virtue of the fact that it was chosen! Okun is at least consistent, because he justifies his refusal to face the issue by saying, "That merely reflects my choices, and I hope they are accepted as reasonably rational." I see no reason why they should be accepted as "reasonably rational" (whatever that means) or as anything other than self-imposed blinders that economists habitually wear in order to avoid facing up to some hard issues.

But Okun has not finished adjusting his blinders: "I have greater conviction in ignoring a second type of criticism of the 'more is better' concept of efficiency" (p. 3). This criticism turns out to be the "doomsday school," which worries that excessive economic growth will plunder and pollute the earth. This view is banished with a laudatory reference to Nordhaus and to Solow, whose views were critically considered above and found wanting.

To take a further example of loose thinking, agricultural efficiency has traditionally been measured by yield per acre or per man-hour of labor. These yields have been enormously increased by the growing use of fertilizers, insecticides, and inanimate energy, all of which are mainly nonrenewable mineral inputs. The efficiency of energy use, or yield per Btu, has been falling in U.S. agriculture. Nonrenewable minerals are the scarce factor in the long run. Elementary economic logic tells us that we should maximize the efficiency of the scarcest factor. Labor is renewable and the fertility of the soil is largely renewable if properly managed; minerals and fossil fuels are not renewable. The long-run economic interest of mankind requires the maximization of mineral productivity. Yet we have sacrificed mineral productivity in order to increase the returns to labor and capital (including land). This has resulted in higher incomes for labor and agricultural capitalists at the direct expense of long-run maintenance efficiency. The concepts of efficiency developed in Chapter 4 do not lead to the anomalies and confusions of the "more is better" school.

Misleading Views on Misallocation and Growth

Many growth economists (Beckerman, 1974, p. 20) have argued that in order to prove that the growth rate is excessive it is necessary to show that the resource misallocation at any point of time takes the form of excessive investment. This reflects a commonly held position among economists that the market will automatically limit growth at some optimal rate. But we must first ask just what "misallocation," or more specifically "excess investment," means in the context of the statement. It means that more is being invested and less consumed out of current production than would be the case under freely competitive markets and consumer sovereignty. Misallocation is defined with respect to the competitive market equilibrium of the plans of savers with the plans of investors, not with respect to physical relations of the economy with the ecosystem. Excessive "disinvestment" of geological capital (depletion), excessive pollution and destruction of ecosystems, and excessively onerous technologies are all consistent with the condition that savers in the aggregate are planning to save just what investors in the aggregate are planning to invest. The market seeks its *behavioral* equilibrium without regard for any ecological limits that are necessary to preserve *biophysical equilibrium*. There is no reason to expect that a short-run behavioral equilibrium will coincide with a long-run (or even a short-run) biophysical equilibrium. In fact, it is clear that under present institutions the two will not coincide. The behavioral equilibrium between planned saving and planned investment nearly always occurs at positive levels of net saving and investment. Positive net investment means growth, which means an increasing throughput and increasing biophysical disequilibrium.

Orthodox growth economists are likely to reply that if only we could internalize all true ecological costs into money prices, then market equilibrium would coincide with ecological equilibrium. This is a bit like Archimedes saying that if only he had a fulcrum and a long enough lever he could move the world. Even granting the impossible task of internalization, all that means is that all *relative* scarcities are properly evaluated. Growth could continue and *absolute* scarcity could become ever greater, even though relative prices were at all times perfect measures of relative scarcity. As was shown in Chapter 2, correct relative prices can help us bear the burden of absolute scarcity in the least uncomfortable way but cannot stop the weight of the burden itself from increasing.

Excessive growth is sometimes thought of by economists as a misallocation over time—the present is sacrificing too much current consumption to capital accumulation for the future. Conservationists looking at the same rapid growth attribute it to too little concern for the future, evidenced by rapid depletion of resources. Who is right? It depends on which is the limitative factor, capital stocks or resource flows. If resources are superabundant and capital scarce, the economist is right. As we have repeatedly seen, many economists effectively assume infinite resources. If resources are scarce, then the conservationist is right. The future inherits not only a positive bequest of more capital but also a negative bequest of depleted mines and polluted sinks. And refineries and supertankers are not very productive capital if there is not much petroleum left.

The intergenerational costs of growth are not at all clear, but as time goes on it would seem that the negative bequest of accelerated entropy increase would weigh increasingly heavily since low entropy is the ultimate means upon which all technologies depend. The market is not able to allocate goods temporally over more than one generation. Indeed, when different generations (different people) are involved, the issue is one of distribution not allocation. Future people cannot bid in present markets. Current markets cannot reflect the needs of future people, except as they are represented by concerned people in the present, whose concern rarely exceeds one or two generations. As Georgescu-Roegen (1975) points out, markets are temporally parochial, and consequently market prices cannot reflect the long-run value of resources any more than the market prices at an art auction held in Wink, Texas would determine the true value of the Mona Lisa. If prices are to measure values, all interested parties must be allowed to bid. For the future this is impossible. There is no objective market criterion for determining proper intergenerational allocation nor, consequently, for speaking of misallocation. In any case the proper word is "misdistribution."

Moreover, even within the present many natural values cannot be priced in markets at all. Consider the instructive case in which a juke box in a student cafeteria disturbed some students who preferred silence. They petitioned for the removal of the offending machine. The music lovers replied that the juke box was a democratic machine, like a free market, and if the disgruntled did not like what they heard they could vote with their money to hear something else. The objection, of course, was that the silence-lovers' money could not buy silence. The clever solution was to include a three-minute silent disc among the choices. This solution is notable for its uniqueness; in most cases, silence, clean air and water, and so forth cannot be purchased in discrete units by individuals, and their values cannot be defended against their opposites in competitive markets. They must be protected by physical boundaries that restrict the domain of the market without crippling the functioning of the market within its limited domain. This is the mode of operation of the three institutions proposed in Chapter 3.

The direct reply to the initial assertion then is: No, it is not necessary to show that excessive investment exists in order to argue that the growth rate is excessive. There are other criteria more basic than those of a competitive behavioral equilibrium for defining excessive growth. These are biophysical criteria that cannot be internalized in market prices. Market equilibrium under present institutions usually implies biophysical disequilibrium. Nor can the market handle intergenerational distribution. All interdependencies over time and space cannot be fit to the procrustean bed of an unrestricted price system.

What Second Law?

It was argued in Chapter 2 that growth economists were confused about ultimate means, or low-entropy matter-energy. It might be useful here to document a few examples of economists' disregard for the second law of thermodynamics.

In an article defending growth, Harvard economist Richard Zeckhauser tells us that "Recycling is not the solution for oil, because the alternate technology of nuclear power generation is cheaper" (1973, p. 117, n. 11). The clear meaning of the sentence is that recycling oil as an energy source is possible but just happens to be uneconomical, because nuclear energy is cheaper. The real reason that energy from oil, or any other source, is not recycled is of course the entropy law, not the relative price of nuclear power. This nonsensical statement is not just a minor slip-up that we can correct and forget; it indicates a fundamental lack of appreciation of the physical facts of life. No wonder Zeckhauser is unconvinced by limits to growth arguments; if he is unaware of the entropy law he could not possibly feel the weight of the arguments against which he is reacting in his article.

An article entitled "The Environment in Economics: A Survey" begins with the words: "Man has probably always worried about his environment because he was once totally dependent on it" (Fisher and Peterson, 1976, p. 1). The implication is that man is no longer totally dependent on his environment, or at least that he has become less dependent. Presumably, technology has made man increasingly independent of his environment. But, in fact, technology has merely substituted nonrenewable resources for renewables, which is more an increase than a decrease in dependence. How could man possibly become more independent of his environment without shutting off exchanges with the environment or reducing depletion and pollution, rather than increasing them? For man to exist as a closed system, engaging in no exchanges with the environment, would require suspension of the second law. Man is an open system. What was man three months ago is now environment; what was environment yesterday is man today. Man and environment are so totally interdependent it is hard to say where one begins and the other ends. This total interdependence has not diminished and will not in the future, regardless of technology.

The statement, already cited, by Barnett and Morse that "Nature imposes particular scarcities, not an inescapable general scarcity," is about as clear a denial of the second law as could be imagined. To drive the point home they add:

> Science by making the resource base more homogeneous, erases the restrictions once thought to reside in the lack of homogeneity. In a neo-Ricardian world, it seems, the particular resources with which one starts increasingly become a matter of indifference. . . . Advances in fundamental science have made it possible to take advantage of the uniformity of energy/matter—a uniformity that makes it feasible without preassignable limit to escape the quantitative constraints imposed by the character of the earth's crust [Barnett and Morse, 1973, p. 11].

It is, however, not the uniformity of matter-energy that makes for usefulness, but precisely the opposite. It is nonuniformity, differences in concentration and temperature, that makes for usefulness. If all materials and energy were uniformly distributed in thermodynamic equilibrium, the resulting "homogeneous resource base" would be no resource at all.

There would be a complete absence of potential for any process, including life. As noted in Chapter 2, the economist's notion of infinite substitutibility bears some resemblance to the old alchemists' dream of converting base metals into precious metals. All you have to do is rearrange atoms! But the potential for rearranging atoms is itself scarce, so the mere fact that everything is made up of the same homogeneous building blocks does not abolish scarcity. Only Maxwell's Sorting-Demon could turn a pile of atoms into a resource, and the entropy law tells us that Maxwell's Demon does not exist.

Zero Growth and the Great Depression

One of the more disingenuous arguments against the SSE was put forward by the editors of *Fortune,* who stated that "the country has just gone through a real life tryout of zero growth" (1976, p. 116). This was the period 1973–1975, a period remembered "not as an episode of zero growth but as the worst recession since the 1930s."

Fortune identifies a SSE with a failed growth economy. A condition of nongrowth can come about in two ways: as the failure of a growth economy, or as the success of a steady-state economy. The two cases are as different as night and day. No one denies that the failure of a growth economy to grow brings unemployment and suffering. It is precisely to avoid the suffering of a failed growth economy (we know growth cannot continue) that we advocate a SSE. The fact that an airplane falls to the ground if it tries to remain stationary in the air simply reflects the fact that airplanes are designed for forward motion. It certainly does not imply that a helicopter cannot remain stationary. A growth economy and a SSE are as different as an airplane and a helicopter. Growthmania reigns supreme when even the failures of a growth economy become arguments in its defense!

Conclusions from the Growth Debate

To a large degree, the growth debate involves a paradigm shift or a gestalt switch—a change in the preanalytic vision we bring to the problem. Conversion cannot be logically forced by airtight analytical demonstrations by either side, although dialectical arguments can sharpen the basic issues. But as the growing weight of anomaly complicates thinking within the growth paradigm to an intolerable degree, the steady-state view will become more and more appealing in its basic simplicity. In any case, orthodox economics will not easily recover from the weaknesses that some of its leading practitioners have revealed in their efforts at self-defense. It is, to say the least, doubtful that "the world can, in effect get along without natural resources." But it is certain that the world could do very well indeed without "the orthodox economists whose common sense has been insufficient to check their faulty logic."

REFERENCES

Barnett, Harold, and Chandler Morse. *Scarcity and Growth*. Resources for the Future. Baltimore: Johns Hopkins University Press, 1963.

Beckerman, Wilfred. *In Defence of Economic Growth*. London: Jonathan Cape, 1974.

Commoner, Barry. *The Closing Circle*. New York: Knopf, 1971a.

Commoner, Barry. "Power Consumption and Human Welfare." Paper presented to the AAAS Convention, Philadelphia, December 1971b.

Commoner, Barry. *The Poverty of Power*. New York: Knopf, 1976.

Economic Report of the President, 1971. Washington, D.C.: U.S. Government Printing Office, 1971.

Energy Policy Project of the Ford Foundation, 1974. *A Time to Choose*, Cambridge Mass: Ballinger, 1974.

Fisher, Anthony C., and Frederick M. Peterson. "The Environment in Economics: A Survey," *Journal of Economic Literature*, March 1976, 1–33.

Georgescu-Roegen, Nicholas. "Energy and Economic Myths," *Southern Economic Journal*, January 1975, 347–381.

Goeller, Harold E. "An Optimistic Outlook for Mineral Resources." Paper presented at Scarcity and Growth Conference, National Commission on Materials Policy, University of Minnesota, June 1972, mimeographed.

Gore, Daniel. "Zero Growth for the College Library," *College Management*, August/September 1974, 12–14.

Hirst, Eric. "Food-Related Energy Requirements," *Science*, April 12, 1974, 134–138.

Jacoby, Neil. "The Environmental Crisis," *Center Magazine*, November/December 1970.

Jorgenson, D. W., and Z. Grilliches. "The Explanation of Productivity Change," *Review of Economic Studies*, July 1967, 249–283.

Jorgenson, D. W., and Z. Grilliches. "Exchange with Edward Dennison," in *Survey of Current Business*, Part II. Washington, D.C.: U.S. Government Printing Office, May 1972.

Kelso, Louis O., and Patricia Hetter. *Two Factor Theory: How to Turn Eighty Million Workers Into Capitalists on Borrowed Money*. New York: Random House, 1967.

Keynes, J. M. *General Theory of Employment, Interest, and Money*. New York: Harcourt Brace Jovanovich, 1936.

Maddala, G. S. "Productivity and Technical Change in the Bituminous Coal Industry," *Journal of Political Economy*, August 1965, 352–365.

Marx, Karl. *Capital*. Vol. I. New York: International Publishers, 1967; originally published in 1867.

Meadows, D. H., et al. *The Limits to Growth*. New York: Universe Books, 1972.

National Commission on Materials Policy, 1973. *Material Needs and the Environment: Today and Tomorrow*. Washington, D.C.: U.S. Government Printing Office, 1973.

Nordhaus, William, and James Tobin. "Is Growth Obsolete?" National Bureau of Economic Research, December, 1970, mimeographed. Published with minor changes in 1972 under the same title, in *Economic Growth,* Fiftieth Anniversary Colloquium V, National Bureau of Economic Research. New York: Columbia University Press, 1972.

Odum, Eugene P. "The Strategy of Ecosystem Development," *Science,* April 1969, 262–270.

Okun, Arthur M. *Equality and Efficiency: The Big Tradeoff,* Washington, D.C.: Brookings Institution, 1975.

Ordway, Samuel H. *Resources and the American Dream*. New York: Ronald Press, 1953.

Passell, Peter, Marc Roberts, and Leonard Ross. Review of *Limits to Growth, New York Times Book Review,* April 2, 1972.

Robinson, Joan. "The Second Crisis of Economic Theory," *American Economic Review,* May 1972, 1–10.

Royall, Norman N. Jr. Review of *Limits to Growth, Kansas City Times,* April 28, 1972, p. 42.

Solow, Robert. "Is the End of the World at Hand?" in Andrew Weintraub et al., eds., *The Economic Growth Controversy,* I.A.S.P., 1973.

Solow, Robert. "The Economics of Resources or the Resources of Economics," *American Economic Review,* May 1974, 1–14.

Wallich, Henry C. "Zero Growth," *Newsweek,* January 24, 1972, p. 62.

"Well, How Do You Like Zero Growth?" *Fortune,* November 1976, 116.

Zeckhauser, Richard. "The Risks of Growth," *Daedalus,* Fall 1973, 103–118.

6

ENERGY AND
THE GROWTH DEBATE

> The decisive conflict of today is not between capitalists
> and communists, not between rich and poor, but be-
> tween the mass producers of plutonium and us who
> merely wish to survive.
>
> Hannes Alfvén (1974)

Probably the most impressive index of our blind commitment to growth is
the price we are willing to pay to keep growing. Reaction to the energy
crisis has been essentially to seek more energy at any cost. Fission power
and the breeder reactor have been given top priority as the best energy
source for the future *(The Plutonium Economy,* 1975*).* But the case for
continued energy growth is very weak. Let us consider the five common
arguments usually raised against any proposal to limit energy growth:

   (1) "Energy growth is necessary to maintain employment." This is
wrong for several reasons. First, the energy sector is the most capital-
intensive sector of the economy and offers the least new employment per
dollar invested of any major sector. The massive capital investments
required to maintain historical growth trends would put enormous pressure on the interest rate and choke off many other investments, most of
which would have provided more direct employment than that provided

by energy production. The net effect on employment is thus likely to be negative. As for the multiplier effects of the large investment, these are in no way peculiar to energy investments and would result from any expenditure of money. Therefore, it is special pleading to appeal to multiplier effects. The argument that inanimate energy is often a necessary complement to labor is misleading unless it is pointed out that energy also substitutes for human labor. The intensive use of energy is likely to increase the *productivity* of those laborers employed but to decrease the *number* of laborers employed. The productivity of all laborers (employed and unemployed) could conceivably decrease as the use of inanimate energy increased.

(2) "Unless energy production grows, the poor will be forever frozen at low levels of energy consumption and will never have the benefits of 'energy slaves,' or household appliances." This argument is not convincing, because the rich consume far more energy than the poor, and there is no evidence that the additional energy will go to the poor. The way to help the poor is to put more money in their hands through a minimum-income program, perhaps in the form of a negative income tax. As the poor spend the money on energy or whatever, it will trickle up into the profits of producers and will induce expansion in the output of things that the poor want to buy. The "trickle-up" approach is a much more sensible way to help the poor than the "trickle-down" theory and would permit energy growth for the poor. Yet the energy growth advocates seem to prefer the trickle-down approach.

(3) "We need more energy because our population growth requires it." This argument has force up to a point: specifically, that the energy growth rate should be as high as the population growth rate—currently less than 1 percent per year. Even so, I consider this more an argument for slowing population growth than for increasing energy growth.

(4) "We need energy growth for defense and military deterrence." We already have considerable overkill, so I wonder why we need more. Furthermore, there are cogent reasons for believing that continued growth in energy demand makes us less secure, because it is increasing our dependence on foreign countries for imports and is leading to the proliferation of nuclear reactors and stocks of plutonium that increase our vulnerability to both foreign enemies in case of war and to domestic terrorists, as well as to accidents.

(5) "We need energy growth to clean up the pollution and recycle the wastes that have resulted from past economic growth and will result from future growth. We need to grow so that we will be rich enough to afford the cost of cleaning up." The first problem is that the association between energy growth and economic growth, even as conventionally measured, is very loose. We can have economic growth, at least up to a point, without further energy growth. The second problem is the assumption that further

economic growth, as conventionally measured, is in fact making us richer in some meaningful sense. It may be making us poorer—the marginal costs of further growth may be greater than the marginal benefits. GNP is taken as a measure of benefits, when in fact it is a mixture of costs and benefits. To assume that increasing GNP really makes us better off, and thus more able to pay the increased costs of cleaning up, is just a way of begging the question. Cleaning up and repairing or substituting for natural services that have been disrupted are *themselves* costs, not the cancelling out or elimination of a cost.

The above arguments, fallacious on their own terms, all take it for granted that the supply of energy must be increased. The alternative of restraining demand is not considered.

One test of sanity is to put a man in a sealed room with the water tap open. As the room begins to fill up with water, a sane man will turn off the tap. The insane will go to work with mops and buckets and call for the production of more mops and buckets. Not only do we seem to have chosen the mop and bucket approach, we have picked the nuclear mop and bucket.

In addition to giving an extra push to the nuclear juggernaut, the energy crisis has scared people into accepting lower emission standards on air pollution, more strip-mining, more big pipelines and superports. Ecologist George Woodwell has noted an ironic result:

Reckless efforts to "solve" an energy problem that is unsolvable in the current context of growth threaten to speed destruction of renewable resources. Acid rains are a good example. Relaxation of air pollution standards for sulphur will result in continuation of the trend of rising acidity in rain in the Northeast. There is little doubt that a decade or more of precipitation with a pH of between 3.0 and 4.2 will reduce the net production of forests and agriculture. A 10 percent loss of net production in the New England states would be the equivalent of the power output of 15 1000-megawatt reactors. Would the people of New England agree to supply such a subsidy to the rest of the country if they had a choice?

There is no simple technical or social solution to the shortage of energy. Growth in energy consumption in the pattern of past years is over for the present. In addition, biotic flows of energy are now being lost, often irreversibly; the biota is being mined. Environmental problems are not simply those of adjusting techniques of energy production to reduce intrusions on the environment; they also include the preservation of the flows of energy—including food, materials, and services—through the biota to man. The shortage of fossil fuels presents a challenge to technologists to find more efficient ways of exploiting biotic energy flows on a renewable basis. . . . Facilities comparable to those of a major national laboratory should be devoted to the problems generated by the worldwide spread of biotic impoverishment that is caused in large degree by current rates of exploitation of nonrenewable energy sources. [Woodwell, 1972].

What is the benefit we are reaping from this costly mining of the biota? At the margin it could not be much and might well be negative. Consider that Sweden's per-capita energy consumption is one-half and Switzerland's is only one-third that of the United States. Even if we believe that Americans are better off than Swedes and Swiss (a debatable view), it would be absurd to argue that Americans are two or three times better off. Likewise, per-capita consumption of electrical energy in the United States in the early 1970s was twice that of the early 1960s. Has that recent doubling made much difference to welfare? Has it increased or decreased welfare? At the margin, it does not seem that our extra energy consumption is very productive of well-being.

Fission power is both an expensive white elephant and a dangerous Trojan horse. Even its proponents consider it a Faustian bargain (Weinberg, 1972). They see the historical trend of rapid energy growth projected into the future and treat it as if it were a constant of nature, like the speed of light, a fixed reference to which everything else must be fitted. Trend is elevated to destiny. How can we meet our destiny (i.e., stay on the projected curve)? Only fission power can save us from falling behind destiny's timetable—at least that is how it once appeared. Now it is recognized that fission will be rather slow in coming on line, and numerous responsible people are calling for a moratorium.

Let us consider the case for a nuclear moratorium, and begin our discussion with statements by two Nobel laureates:

> The decisive conflict of today is not between capitalists and communists, not between rich and poor, but between the mass producers of plutonium and us who merely wish to survive [Hannes Alfvén, Nobel laureate in physics, Pugwash Conference, 1974].

> I fear that when the history of this century is written, that the greatest debacle of our nation will be seen not to be our tragic involvement in Southeast Asia but our creation of vast armadas of plutonium, whose safe containment will represent a major precondition for human survival, not for a few decades or hundreds of years, but for thousands of years more than human civilization has so far existed [James D. Watson, Nobel laureate in medicine, 1974].

Are these two statements exercises in rhetorical hyperbole? A brief listing of a few facts about plutonium is sufficient to convince ourselves that they are, in truth, sober judgments that simply tell it like it is. Consider the following:

(1) Plutonium-239 is the most toxic element ever handled in quantity by man. How toxic? Dispersed as fine particles one micron in diameter, one pound of plutonium represents the potential for 9 billion lung cancers.

(2) Plutonium is the principal ingredient in an atomic bomb. It takes on the order of twenty pounds to make a respectable bomb. Lots of

people know how to make a bomb and could do so if they had the plutonium. Much more than twenty pounds is presently unaccounted for in the physical inventories.

(3) The half-life of plutonium is 24,000 years. Thus any large-scale contamination of the biosphere with plutonium must be considered permanent and irreversible.

(4) In the fully developed plutonium economy projected by the former AEC, the annual handling of plutonium would be on the order of 200,000 pounds. Thus even 99.999-percent containment would mean two pounds loose, which is more than enough for an enormous disaster. In other words, 100-percent efficient containment is *imperative.* What has man ever managed to do with 100-percent efficiency even for a year, let alone for millenia?

(5) The commercial value of plutonium, and especially its black market value, will be very high, much more per ounce than, say, gold or heroin. Has there ever been any substance of great value that man has not managed to steal?

In short, plutonium is very bad stuff and deserves its namesake, Pluto, the god of the underworld. If we go nuclear we will have a lot of plutonium around for incompetents and psychopaths to play with. No wonder Watson and Alfvén are alarmed!

It is true that Nobel laureates can also be cited in favor of nuclear power—Edward Teller and Willard Libby to name two—and, in any case, issues cannot be decided merely by counting Nobelites on each side. The undeniable fact, however, is that a lot of very capable people disagree very strongly on the desirability and safety of nuclear power. In the face of such profound disagreement, it is irresponsible, to say the least, for public utilities to trumpet, at rate payers' expense no less, Reddy Kilowatt's mindless commercial slogan "nuclear power is safe," and to proceed to build nuclear plants as fast as they can in advance of public debate and democratic expression of opinion. The more responsible procedure would be to call a moratorium on further nuclear plant construction for several years, to provide time for reflection, debate, and discussion.

The call for a moratorium is based mainly on seven specific arguments against fission power. All seven are important and relevant, but not all are equally conclusive in showing the need for a moratorium. The first four fall short of being conclusive, even when taken together. The last three, however, are each conclusive and taken together are overwhelmingly decisive.

Thermal or heat pollution. Although all types of power plants unavoidably produce waste heat, nuclear plants produce more waste heat per kilowatt-hour than do conventional plants. But this disadvantage can probably be corrected by engineers, if they spend the money. It is an example of a problem that is subject to a technical fix.

Eventually, thermal pollution will provide a limit to global energy use and will require that we maximize dependence on solar energy as well as achieve zero energy growth. According to Dr. Alvin Weinberg (1974), this must surely happen within 200 years, and quite probably within thirty to fifty years, if man is to avoid unacceptable meterological disruption. But I mention this only to put it aside, since it applies to any terrestrial energy source, not just nuclear.

Low-level routine releases of radioactivity from power plants and fuel reprocessing plants. This is a serious cause for concern and is specific to nuclear power. But thanks to the efforts of two former AEC scientists, Gofman and Tamplin (1970), the standards have been tightened 100-fold. The AEC and the nuclear establishment fought Gofman and Tamplin every step of the way, but they lost. Low-level radiation is not good for us, and even the new limits may be too permissive. Nevertheless, this problem may have a technical fix if sufficient money is spent. In fact, small-particle pollution from coal may be just as bad or worse. So I leave this issue to one side also.

Radiation exposure to uranium miners. There is a very high incidence of lung cancer among uranium miners, and that is certainly a grave social cost. But again, I set it aside, because it may be subject to a technical fix, if the money is spent to automate the mines. Coal miners die of pneumoconiosis, or black lung, which may be just as bad.

Shortage of uranium. The cumulative lifetime requirements of uranium needed to operate the 800 nuclear reactors commonly projected by the year 2000 amounts to about 4 million tons. The United States' potential uranium supply, counting hypothetical uranium resources up to the $30 per-pound category, is about 2.6 million tons. There have been no significant discoveries of uranium in the United States since 1965, despite intensified search (Kazman, 1975; Day, 1975). Does it make sense to build reactors that may not be able to operate for their full lifetimes because of uranium shortage? The only economic advantage nuclear power has is lower fuel costs, and continued skyrocketing of uranium prices erases even that advantage. Of course, we *may* discover more uranium, we *may* have a breakthrough in uranium mining or breeder reactor technology, but it hardly seems prudent to count on these mere possibilities. Should not nuclear proponents be required *first* to find the uranium before committing billions in capital for the construction of reactors that could easily be made anything from uneconomical to totally worthless because of a lack of fuel?

These four arguments can be debated pro and con and, though important, are not decisive in making the case for moratorium now. Let's turn now to the three decisive arguments.

Possible environmental contamination by large amounts of radioactive wastes. As yet, there is no solution to the permanent storage of high-level radioactive wastes that must be isolated from the environment for thousands of years with essentially perfect containment. Some say bury wastes in ice caps, others say rocket them into the sun (a truly insane idea), and some say put them in salt domes in Louisiana and Texas.

I doubt that this problem has a technical solution, but many think it does. If it does, then let us find the solution first before we produce any more long-lived radioactive waste. We should declare a moratorium until this problem is solved, if it can be solved.

The chance that the enormous inventory of radioactive materials in the reactor core might be accidentally released to the environment. This is the problem of a reactor core meltdown that could result in an enormous disaster. The Brookhaven report put the maximum damage at 3,000–4,000 deaths and $7 billion property damage. An updated 1965 version of that study, which was kept secret by the AEC until 1973, when it was pried loose by a lawsuit, set the maximum at 45,000 deaths and $17 billion property damage, and contamination of an area the size of Pennsylvania.

Obviously, a single accident that could inflict even $7 billion in damages is inherently uninsurable. Not even a coalition of the country's largest insurance companies would underwrite more than $110 million on nuclear plants. Another $450 million is provided by the government at tax payers' expense. Anything beyond $560 million is uninsured risk borne by the public at large. Normally, when a commercial venture is too novel and too large scale in its possible effects to be able to get adequate liability insurance, it simply does not take place. But this first line of defense against industrial irresponsibility was simply bypassed by the Price-Anderson Act that arbitrarily limited liability to the small amounts mentioned. If nuclear power is so safe, why isn't adequate insurance available? One of the often neglected costs of rapid growth is that our artifacts evolve in scale and quality too fast for us to accumulate actuarial experience sufficient to calculate the probability and cost of their malfunction. Thus sound insurance is rendered impossible when the nature and scale of our activities change too rapidly.

One reason nuclear plants cannot get more insurance coverage is that the emergency core cooling system designed to prevent a meltdown has never been successfully tested. Another reason may be that the alleged low probabilities of an accident given in the Rasmussen report (1974) are seen by actuaries for what they are—subjective estimates, not the objective relative frequency of actual occurrences needed for sound insurance. Since purposeful acts are omitted from the Rasmussen analysis, the results are of little value. In fact, physicist Donald Geesaman (1974) has argued that, in the absence of purposeful acts, the probability of a nuclear meltdown is zero, since without purposeful acts there could be no reactors in the first place. Geesaman further comments:

> Reactor accidents will happen when men want them to happen. The Second Law of Thermodynamics is an elegant way of stating that it is easier to destroy order than it is to construct it. Sabotaging or destroying a reactor is necessarily a minor technological task compared to building one. There is a technology of disordering order. In a relative sense it is a low technology and it cannot be ignored [Geesaman, 1974, p. 3].

Even a mere candle held by an electrician to test for wind currents was sufficient to accidentally start a fire at the TVA's Brown's Ferry nuclear station that resulted in the shutdown of two reactors and might have led to a meltdown.

3

The possibility that terrorists or psychopaths may sabotage a reactor or steal plutonium. This is the argument mentioned at the beginning. Managing plutonium with 100-percent efficiency is humanly impossible. But the attempt to make humans perform with superhuman efficiency and discipline will warp our institutions in drastic ways. Already, in order to deal with the security problems of plutonium recycle, the former AEC has suggested the need for a federal police force and for relaxation of certain protections of privacy in order that personnel security checks can be more stringent. To prevent traffic in heroin, police have asked for no-knock search laws. To prevent traffic in plutonium, such laws probably would be necessary. In the presence of nuclear blackmail, the imposition of martial law would be a foregone conclusion. In order to minimize risks and transport, there must be a concentration of as many nuclear facilities as possible in one place—hence nuclear parks consisting of fifteen to twenty reactors with support facilities. Such concentrations of power could not be left in private hands. The security problems imposed by plutonium would require the militarization of our economy, and the first step would be nationalization of key points of the nuclear fuel cycle, including public utilities.

It has not been generally appreciated that the dynamics of currently planned rapid growth in nuclear plants could make the whole nuclear program a net *consumer* of energy perhaps until the end of the century. This is so because, during construction periods of seven to ten years, nuclear plants are naturally net consumers of energy. Rapid growth means that there will be many plants under construction relative to operating plants, and if the number is too high (if growth is too rapid), the net energy produced by finished nuclear plants will be more than offset by the energy construction requirements of new plants (Price, 1974). This point would, of course, apply to the too rapid construction of any kind of power plant, not just nuclear.

Inevitably, we are told that we have no alternative. It is either nuclear power or back to caves. This is nonsense, but even if it were true some of us would prefer caveman life to life in a radioactive police state. It bears repetition that Sweden and West Germany have roughly one-half the per-capita energy consumption of the United States, yet people there live very well. "Whatever exists is possible" is an axiom we need to remember. The Ford Foundation Energy Policy Project (1974) has shown very clearly that continued energy growth at past rates presents far greater problems than does moderate or zero energy growth. The feasibility of even lower rates of energy growth, accompanied by a doubling or more of energy efficiency, has been ably argued by Amory Lovins (1976).

Ask a nuclear engineer why we can't eventually get along using mainly solar energy and adapt our technology and life styles to its benign requirements of decentralization and low-intensity use, and he will tell you that that presents insurmountable problems. Even though it is done by all other species, including those with no central nervous system and hence no brain at all, living on solar-energy income is just too big a challenge for our technologists. But ask him how he intends to solve any of the truly impossible problems just discussed, and he will tell you that science can do anything!

As indicated earlier, energy demand projections have played an important role in convincing many people of the necessity of fission power. The conventional "double every ten years" projections of electric power demand were based on a historical period in which the average real price of energy was falling. Between 1945 and 1969 the real price of electricity fell by 50 percent (Chapman et al., 1972). In 1970 the real price of electricity began to rise, and consequently projections based on a continuously falling price are sure to be upset. But there are also some more subtle preconceptions and attitudes in forecasting that merit discussion.

No one tries to predict what he will do tomorrow. Instead he *decides* what he will do tomorrow, and, subject to contingencies beyond his control, he carries out his decision. The domain of prediction does not include events under the control of the prediction maker. If it did, he could always ensure that his predictions were correct. We *plan* those events subject to our control, and we *predict* events that are not subject to our control. We may predict astronomical events, or the behavior of other people, or the contingencies that may limit our future options independently of our own wills; those events that we control are *planned*, not predicted.

Prediction sounds objective and scientific, while "planning" sounds subjective, arbitrary, and even socialistic. Hence the propensity to say prediction when we really mean planning. The dangers of such confusion are greatest in areas of collective behavior, where some events are beyond the control of individuals (subject to prediction) but are controllable by the society as a whole (subject to planning). Energy use is one such difficult area. Society can decide its energy use, just as an individual does and attempt to *shape* the future, or it can treat it as a problem in predicting other peoples' aggregate behavior and seek to *outguess* the future.

Suppose that a forecast shows that the future will very likely be X. Next it is shown that for X to happen, the necessary conditions Y and Z must also happen. Then it is concluded that to ease the transition toward our "destiny," X, we must strive for Y and Z. But as often as not, either Y or Z or both turn out to be not only necessary but also sufficient conditions for X, so that in preparing for the predicted future we in fact bring it to pass. The prediction is self-fulfilling because it was, from the beginning, more in the domain of planning than of prediction. Such self-fulfilling predictions represent implicit social planning and should not steal the mantle of objectivity by appropriating the favorable connotations of the word "prediction" and avoiding the unfavorable ones of the more proper word "planning." If the Edison Electric Institute makes a projection of energy demand for the year 2000, and the number is such that supply can meet it only with a crash program of building breeder reactors, and we undertake such a program, then barring technical failures and nuclear war, the Edison Electric Institute's projection will be borne out. Whether breeder reactors (or coal burners) should be built is not at issue here. The point is that such a question should be decided openly and politically and not by the stealth or confusion of treating recent trend as eternal destiny and investing the concept of demand with an imperial authority beyond its true meaning.

An example of the quasi-planning involved in energy forecasting is seen in the sensitivity of the AEC's cost-benefit analyses of breeder reactors to variations in energy demand forecasts. According to Thomas B. Cochran:

> Other current long range electrical energy demand projections (besides that of the FPC's 1970 National Power Survey which forms the basis of the AEC's projections), using independent forecasting techniques based on historical (national) trends in GNP growth, income and (gas and electricity) price elasticities, and per capita consumption, suggest that the 1970 analysis projections overestimate future electrical energy demand. The true demand could easily be 25 percent, and possibly 50 percent below the "probable" projection in the 1970 analysis for the year 2000. If the true demand is 25 percent less, then the projected discounted net benefits of the LMFBR program (assuming the rest of the economic and technologic projections remain unchanged from the AEC's most probable estimates in the 1970 Analysis) are reduced by one-half; if the actual demand is one-half the probable projection, the net benefits vanish, due to lower energy demand alone [Cochran, 1974, p. 221].

The point is that the major technological decision of our generation (Weinberg, 1972), the one with the most far-ranging social and environmental impacts, hinges on an energy-demand forecast whose error term encompasses a range of values that could completely reverse the cost-benefit decision. Make one projection and we get breeder reactors, make another equally plausible projection and we forgo (or escape) them. The distinction between planning and forecasting becomes very fuzzy.

The breeder reactor cost-benefit decision is, in addition, very sensitive to the discount rate at which present and future values are compared. The discount rate is itself a kind of forecast—a forecast of the average rate of return on new investment during the planning period, which serves as a measure of the opportunity cost of capital. Cochran points out that:

> The AEC used a 7 percent discount rate to compute present value benefits of the LMFBR program. With a 10 percent discount rate favored by many economists and now required by a 1972 Administration directive, the net benefits reported by the 1970 Analysis are reduced by 77 percent [Cochran, 1974, p. 221].

Once again, the element of implicit planning is inherent in the projection. Project a capital opportunity cost of 7 percent and the breeder is "economic"; project 10 percent and it is "uneconomic." It is no use pretending that those who make the projections are ignorant of, or disinterested in, the implications of their projections for economic policy making.

The implicit planning and self-fulfilling prophecies involved in forecasting are recognized, indeed formalized, in the concept of "indicative planning" used by the French and by some other European governments. Indicative planning is distinguished from imperative planning in that projected production targets for different industries are not enforced by the state (as in the Soviet Union) but are merely projected as a set of self-consistent guidelines. If every industry strives to produce the amount projected by the planners and balanced out with their input-output matrices, then no one will be disappointed in his expectations because the planners have made sure that their projections are consistent. Thus if one industry expects that most others will follow the indicated projections, then it will be in that firm's interest to follow the projection also, for by doing so it will avoid unprofitable surpluses or shortages. The job of the government is to follow the projections in its own sphere and to convince everyone else to do the same by methods short of coercion.

While the United States does not practice indicative planning officially, it is becoming apparent that there is an implicit indicative planning being practiced by corporations and government agencies that make projections of energy demand as if it were an external event located entirely in the domain of prediction and not overlapping into the domain of planning. If the state refuses to engage in planning, that simply means that utilities and other corporations do the planning for us, not that we avoid planning.

The tendency to treat demand as exogenous is perhaps another trap of thinking only in mechanistic terms. The economy is seen as an autonomous machine that inexorably generates energy requirements or demands. To keep the machine running, we must predict its exogenously determined energy appetite and then see to it by all means that supplies are adequate. Instead of perpetuating this mechanistic vision, we should think of the economy as an organism in coevolution with its environment, subject to biophysical constraints, and obliged to adjust to those constraints, either by conscious effort or by blind nemesis.

As discussed in Chapter 2, the economy, like an organism, lives on a continual throughput of matter and energy taken from the environment in the form of low-entropy raw materials (depletion), and returned to the environment in the form of high-entropy waste (pollution). The biomass of an organism, or a population of organisms, grows to some mature or equilibrium size. The throughput then functions to maintain the size and structure of the organism and is no longer the source of physical growth. The skill, knowledge, wisdom, love, and general welfare embodied in an organism may continue to increase even after physical growth has stopped. In like manner, the populations of human organisms and artifacts cannot grow forever but must cease growing at some level representing maturity or equilibrium. Beyond this point, economic growth must take place under the constraint of a constant population of people and artifacts, that is, births equal to deaths and physical production equal to physical consumption (or depreciation). Skill, wisdom, technical competence, love, and so on may continue to increase, and may lead to economic growth, depending on how it is measured, but gross physical accumulation of bodies and artifacts will have to cease. The throughput flow (depletion → pollution) is the *cost* of maintaining the population of people and artifacts and is not to be maximized, but rather minimized, subject to the requirement that the equilibrium stock of people and artifacts be maintained. Our current theories and institutions seem to consider the throughput flow (approximated by real GNP) as something to be maximized, as a benefit in itself rather than as the cost of maintaining a stock that yields benefits. If the stock can be maintained with a smaller throughput, we are better off not worse off. This steady-state paradigm (already discussed in Chapter 2) represents a radical shift from the standard growth paradigm. Nevertheless, it seems more logical and realistic, even though less appealing to politicians, in whatever walk of life, who prefer to promise more and more forever and ever. Probably the energy sector will be the first to have to come to terms with this steady-state or zero growth point of view.

As methods of demand forecasting have become increasingly arcane, the general public has once again been reduced to the status of layman under a priesthood of curve-fitters and multiple-regression testers. We probably hold multiple-regression techniques in higher veneration than the ancient Greeks held divination by consultation of chicken entrails, but the record of modern numerologists is probably no better, except in the case of self-fulfilling prophecies.

Demand projections usually attempt to measure the quantity of a given energy resource a given country or state will want, need, or require in some future year if the price of energy retains more or less its present relationship to other costs and if the ability to use and to supply the resource is not otherwise constrained. This notion of demand might better be called "requirements," so as not to confuse it with the economists' concept of demand. For the economist, demand is a relationship between the price of a commodity and the quantity purchased at that price over some time period. Demand is a function, not a quantity. Furthermore, requirements should not be confused with "quantity purchased or demanded," a concept that assumes a given price and all other influences constant. Nor should requirements be confused with "aggregate demand," which is simply the sum of all expenditures made during some time period. None of these demand concepts requires any specification of purpose, beyond the mere intent of making a purchase.

By contrast, the notion of requirements (or needs) is totally undefined until the purpose is specified, that is, requirements *for what?* Let us define "energy requirements" as the energy resource flows necessary to maintain or achieve a *population* of a certain size, living at a certain standard of *per-capita energy consumption,* during a certain *period of time,* using certain *kinds of technology.* It makes no sense at all to speak of energy requirements without having specified, at least in general terms, these four elements of purpose. Alternatively, if we speak of energy requirements, we must be making assumptions, explicitly or tacitly, about each of these four elements. What are the most common assumptions made and what are the most prudent assumptions to make about each element?

Probably the most common assumption is to extrapolate recent growth rates of population and per-capita consumption, assuming some arbitrary, round-numbered time period and assuming constant technology or a constant direction of technological change (i.e., that technology will change in the future in ways similar to the way it has changed in the past). The result is that total requirements grow as the product of population and per-capita consumption growth, usually exponentially, and energy requirements for maintaining such growth become overwhelming within the time period chosen. The conclusion is that such requirements, in all likelihood, cannot be met. *This means that the four assumptions of purpose are inconsistent and one or more must be modified.*

One way out is to shorten the time period, usually with arguments about the futility of looking very far ahead, and perhaps by arguing that at a 7-percent rate of discount what happens more than fifteen years from now will and should carry little weight in current decisions. Discounting can easily become a pseudoscientific way of making the ethical judgment that the future is not worth anything. This refers to only one reason for discounting, namely, pure time preference. Discounting for uncertainty (the future is usually less certain than the present) remains a matter of common prudence (a bird in the hand is worth two in the bush, because of uncertainty, but a sure bird today is not necessarily worth two sure birds in the future). Another way out is to assume new, *qualitatively different* kinds of technological progress that will reduce per-capita and per-dollar energy requirements as fast as growth increases population and per-capita GNP. Yet another way out is to assume reduced, eventually zero, rates of growth of population and per-capita consumption. Finally, there are the peacemakers and middle-of-the-roaders who argue that we ought to do a little of each: don't try to look too far ahead, have more faith in technology, and take comfort in the decreasing rate of population growth and the likely slowdown in economic growth. But, sensible though it seems, this eclectic approach is not terribly satisfactory.

Although we should avoid "living in the future" and being overly concerned about it, nevertheless, some reasonable interest in seeing to it that there will be a future for the human race is a very legitimate concern of the present. If present actions endanger that future, even if not within the "relevant time frame," it is not satisfactory to simply refuse to follow a logical chain of cause and effect beyond a decade or a generation. Nor is the counsel to have faith in technology very reassuring. The notion that technology has grown exponentially and that this somehow compensates for exponential growth in pollution and depletion is, as we have seen in the previous chapter, totally misleading. In the first place, technological change cannot be measured directly and is merely inferred from the permissive role that it has played in making possible an ever larger throughput (depletion and pollution). The technological change in the post–World War II period has been part of the problem not part of the solution. What we must appeal to is a *qualitative* change in the nature of technological progress, not a mere continuation of alleged quantitative trends of the recent past—and that requires a very strong faith indeed, especially since improvements in resource productivity probably will come at the expense of labor and capital productivity and will force the issue of income distribution into greater prominence.

Material and energy requirements to maintain the human body seem fixed, although really they are not. With known technologies of selective breeding, we could reduce the size of human beings considerably. Eventually we might achieve a race of mini-Tom Thumbs, making room for more people, and finally we might become totally immaterial, a race of angels, infinitely many of us. Probably there exists some minimum energy and material requirement for human consciousness, beyond which we become extinct rather than angels (or devils). Although no one advocates such a thing, this fantasy is instructive because some people who do not believe in angels nevertheless seem to believe in "angel commodities,"—that is, that technology can reduce the energy and material content of a dollar's worth of GNP indefinitely as growth continues, to the point where it becomes "angel GNP."

It would seem that the fundamentally most sensible adjustment to make among the four assumptions is to recognize that population and per-capita consumption must eventually be stabilized and that technological change should be relied on only for buying time—both time to make the adjustment to stable consumption levels and time in the sense of the life span of the stable system itself. The point that emerges is that the four elements of purpose, in relation to which energy requirements must be defined, are each subject to limits. Population cannot grow forever, per-capita consumption cannot grow forever, the relevant time period cannot be shortened forever, and technology cannot reduce material and energy intensity forever. Nevertheless, there are short- and middle-run trade-offs among the four elements.

What combination of values of the four variables is optimum? That is fundamentally an ethical question. Even if we could precisely and objectively specify the terms of the trade-offs, the choice of the optimum combination within the feasible set would still be an ethical choice. But unless we have made this choice we cannot answer the question "energy requirements *for what?*" and thus we cannot give any empirical content to the concept of energy requirements. Therefore, if we are going to construct a scenario of future energy requirements, it is absolutely necessary in the strictest logical sense to begin with a series of ethical propositions. Attempts to ride roughshod over this requirement, whether out of embarrassment at making ethical statements or eagerness to arrive at a number, are completely illogical and worse than useless.

One ethical proposition concerns the relevant time period—how long into the future do we care about? The tacit choice of our current growth mind-set is short run; if not "after me the deluge," then the attitude is at least "what has posterity done for me recently?" The alternative here recommended is the long-run view of stewardship for the indefinite future; that is, let us try to take good enough care of the ecosphere (keep our consumption demands well below the ecosphere's maximum capacity) so that it will last a long time. Exactly how long we do not need to know. The view is sometimes expressed that the best thing the present can do for the future is to grow and bequeath the future a larger capital stock. But the simultaneous bequest of depleted natural resources could reduce the productivity of that capital stock so that the net inheritance is diminished—not to mention the negative inheritance of polluted air and water and disrupted ecosystems.

A second ethical proposition is that there is or should be such a thing as *enough.* It will not be easy to agree on exactly how many people or what standard of consumption is enough. The good life has minimum energy and material requirements that may not be too hard to agree on. But beyond that minimum more consumption increases welfare only up to a further, less definable, maximum point.

A third ethical principle is that the claims on resources of those who are below the minimum should take precedence over the claims of those who are well above the minimum and certainly over the claims of those who are above the maximum and whose tastes have become so jaded that they must be artfully cajoled into further consumption. It has been suggested that as long as any are below the minimum, then the maximum should be no greater than the mean per-capita amount available. The similar maxim that no one has a right to luxury while his fellow man lacks necessities is a commonly cited principle of Christian ethics as well as of other ethical traditions.

A fourth ethical proposition is that the minimum requirements of people already born should take precedence over the population's reproductive desires in excess of replacement, or over a less than replacement birth rate if existing population size is too large.

If we accept these propositions, then our scenario for future energy requirements will have as its "for what" something like the following purpose: A stationary population should be maintained at a roughly stable average per-capita level of consumption that is bounded by a minimum and a maximum. The average level should not be so high as to require destruction of the ecosphere in other than the very long run. The spread between maximum and minimum should be sufficient to compensate for differences in work conditions and effort but should be considerably less than the present range, which is beyond any functional justification and tends to subvert the democratic process by excessively concentrating economic power. A technology should be developed that uses resources much more sparingly than presently and that strives to substitute renewables and solar energy for nonrenewables to the extent possible. Since technological progress cannot be foreseen, no particular degree of technological progress should be anticipated in defining future energy requirements; after technological progress has occurred, energy requirement figures can be readjusted. Institutions capable of bringing about this scenario were discussed in Chapter 3.

All forecasts are based on the belief that the future is to some extent discernible. Most forecasts require the stronger assumption that the future is discernible from evidence found in the recorded past. Many forecasts assume that the future is in some ways discernible from purely numerical evidence in the recorded past. Since forecasting has shifted from the prophet and seer to the statistician, the visionary element has been downplayed and the numerical element has received nearly exclusive emphasis. There is an approach that blends the visionary and the numerical in a fruitful way, the approach of considering alternative energy scenarios, as applied by the Ford Foundation Energy Policy Project (1974).

The basic assumption of the "numerological" forecasts is that the future is related to the past by means of a *stable* numerical relationship. Pure novelty, discontinuity, and emergence of the qualitatively different are ruled out. This is a metaphysical assumption and may lead to a kind of blindness that forecaster Daniel Yankelovich calls the McNamara Fallacy:

> The first step is to measure whatever can be easily measured. This is okay as far as it goes. The second step is to disregard that which cannot be measured or give it an arbitrary quantitative value. This is artificial and misleading. The third step is to presume that which cannot be measured easily is not really very important. This is blindness. The fourth step is to say what cannot be measured really does not exist. This is suicide [quoted in Hayes, 1974].

A further bias is inherent in the quantification of subjective probabilities. Thomas Schelling has written of "a tendency in our planning to confuse the unfamiliar with the improbable. The contingency we have not considered looks strange; what looks strange is thought improbable; what is improbable need not be considered seriously" (quoted in Hayes, 1974).

A basic conservative bias is imparted to some forecasting by the assumption of no discontinuity or emergent novelty. Most forecasting is paid for by big business, that is, by "the establishment," by persons and institutions that have something to conserve. These sponsors purchase the computer time and provide the often proprietary data without which the forecaster would be unable to practice his "science." Sponsor and forecaster are locked in a conservative symbiotic embrace: To the extent that the future is like the past only more so, the forecaster will make more accurate predictions, and the sponsor will be reinforced in the belief that whatever system had the wisdom to put him at the top must be a part of the eternal constitution of nature and certainly not a random fluke of capricious history. But this "mirror, mirror on the wall" bias is not limited to the establishment. Environmentalists and conservationists likewise have a tendency to forecast a self-justifying and self-congratulatory future. Hence the modern tendency to confuse trend with destiny and the prevalence of self-fulfilling predictions in which the future is implicitly planned under the guise of neutral scientific forecasting.

True science, by contrast, attempts to disprove its predictions, not to make them come true, and strives in so far as possible to avoid altering the system under study. Perhaps forecasting is limited by a generalized Heisenberg uncertainty principle: Any attempt to predict the future is likely to alter the future. Or as Karl Popper has argued, prediction may be subject to an impossibility theorem: Future events are partly determined by the content of future knowledge; the mind cannot predict today what it will know tomorrow (else it would already know it today); therefore future events cannot be predicted. The best that can be hoped for is to rule out some events that appear to contradict natural laws.

The above logical problems and conservative biases in forecasting are avoided in a more forthright and humble approach to the future—that of elaborating alternative possible energy scenarios, tracing out their implications, and then asking which total package is most desirable. This approach squarely faces up to the basic question of *requirements for what?* elaborated earlier.

An enormous literature on the subject of energy has grown up in recent years. This brief chapter has not attempted to review that literature but merely to relate the energy question to the growth debate. From previous chapters, it is clear that solar energy would be the major source in the SSE. Fission power was discussed because it is such a good example of how growth, whether actual or projected, forces us to adopt dangerous technologies that would never be acceptable and would never be needed with smaller populations living at less lavish standards of per-capita energy consumption.

REFERENCES

Chapman, D., et al. "Electricity Demand Growth and the Energy Crisis," *Science,* November 17, 1972, 703–708.

Cochran, Thomas B. *The Liquid Metal Fast Breeder Reactor.* Baltimore: Johns Hopkins University Press, 1974. Published for Resources for the Future, Inc.

Day, M. C. "Nuclear Energy: A Second Round of Questions," *Bulletin of the Atomic Scientists,* December 1975, 52–59.

Ford Foundation Energy Policy Project, 1974. *A Time to Choose.* Cambridge, Mass.: Ballinger, 1974.

Geesaman, Donald. "Comment on WASH1400," November 27, 1974 (mimeographed).

Gofman, John, and Arthur Tamplin. Testimony at Hearings of the Joint Committee on Atomic Energy, January 28, 1970.

Hayes, Denis. "Energy Forecasting." Background Paper for Committee on Mineral Resources and the Environment, National Academy of Sciences, 1974, mimeographed.

Kazman, Raphael G. "Do We Have a Nuclear Option?" *Mining Engineer,* August 1975, 35–37.

Lovins, Amory. "Energy Strategy: The Road Not Taken?" *Foreign Affairs,* October 1976, 65–96.

The Plutonium Economy. New York: Committee of Enquiry: The Plutonium Economy, National Council of the Churches of Christ in the USA, 1975.

Price, J. H. "Dynamic Energy Analysis and Nuclear Power." London: Friends of the Earth, December 18, 1974, mimeographed.

Rasmussen, Norman. *Reactor Safety Study* (WASH1400). Washington, D.C.: Atomic Energy Commission, August 1974.

Weinberg, Alvin. Editorial, *Science,* October 18, 1974, 205.

Weinberg, Alvin. "Social Institutions and Nuclear Energy," *Science,* July 7, 1972, 27–34.

Woodwell, George. Letter to the Editor, *Science,* February 1, 1972, 367.

7

DEVELOPING ECONOMIES
AND THE STEADY STATE

An increase in the rate of growth tends to aggravate
both external dependence and internal exploitation.
Thus higher rates of growth, far from reducing underdevelopment, tend to worsen it, in the sense of tending
to increase social inequalities.

Celso Furtado (1974)

It is absolutely a waste of time as well as morally backward to preach
steady-state doctrines to underdeveloped countries before the overdeveloped countries have taken any measure to reduce either their own population growth or the growth of their per-capita resource consumption.
Therefore, the steady-state paradigm must first of all be adopted and
applied in the overdeveloped countries. That does not mean, however,
that the underdeveloped countries can be left out of consideration. For
one thing, the underdeveloped countries are not ever going to develop (recall the "impossibility theorem" of Chapter 1) unless the overdeveloped countries moderate their demands on world resources and
absorption capacities. One of the major forces necessary to push the overdeveloped countries toward a SSE will be Third World outrage at their
overconsumption. In addition, underdeveloped countries will have to
revise their expectations downward regarding their own growth. Although
per-capita consumption levels are too low and must still grow, popula-

tion size need not grow and must, in fact, be significantly slowed down as a precondition for increasing the growth rate of per-capita consumption. Investment can be used either to increase the standards of a given population or to increase the population at given standards. Underdeveloped countries must, regardless of the actions of overdeveloped countries, reduce their population growth.

The starting point in development economics should be the "impossibility theorem" mentioned in Chapter 1: that a U.S.-style high mass consumption economy for a world of 4 billion people is impossible, and even if by some miracle it could be achieved, it would certainly be short lived. Even less realistic is the prospect of an ever growing standard of consumption for an ever growing population. The raw materials concentrated in the earth's crust and the capacity of ecosystems to absorb either large quantities or exotic qualities of waste materials and heat set a limit to the number of person-years that can be lived in the "developed state," as that term is understood today in the United States and in the Third World.

This impossibility theorem is arrived at by common sense reasoning and does not depend on opaque computer models with their "counterintuitive" results. Models such as those sponsored by the Club of Rome are useful and informative, but the steady-state position is not dependent on them. Just as in the Middle Ages all Holy Thought had to be expressed in Latin, so in the Age of Analysis all Correct Thought must, it would seem, be expressed in the binary language of computer codes. There is a real danger of the computer model of becoming a large black box containing a giant syllogism that carries us with the speed of light from dialectically fuzzy premises to analytically precise conclusions. While I have great admiration for the work sponsored by the Club of Rome (Meadows et al., 1972; Mesarovic and Pestel, 1974), I nevertheless think that we are wise to resist assurances of truth unless we can grasp the entirety of argument in intellectual intuition and see it illuminated as a whole by the natural light of reason. Complex computer models are aids to, but not substitutes for, this kind of more intimate understanding.

As a simple intuitive demonstration of the impossibility theorem, consider the following. If it requires roughly one third of the world's annual production of nonrenewable resources to support that 6 percent of the world's population residing in the United States in that developed condition to which the rest of the world is thought to aspire, then it follows that present resource flows would allow the extention of the U.S. standard to a maximum of 18 percent of the world's current population, with nothing left over for the other 82 percent. And without the services rendered by the other 82 percent, the rich 18 percent would have so much work to do that they could not possibly do it and, even if they could, they would have no time or energy left over to enjoy their riches. It is clear that a middle-class U.S. standard is possible for much less than 18 percent because it depends on having many poorer people available to do the dirty work; a significant share of resources must be devoted to sustaining them, even at their lower level, and hence would not be available to support the high consumption levels of the hypothetical 18 percent.

It will be objected by some that the solution is simply to increase world resource flows by some factor such that world resource use per capita will equal U.S. resource use per capita. That factor turns out to be about six.* In order to increase world resource flows sixfold, the rest of the world would have to attain the U.S. level of capitalization and technical extracting and processing capacity. This enormous increase in capital would require a long period of accumulation; moreover, even if it could be done overnight, it would require an immense increase in resource flows during that short accumulation period. To supply the rest of the world with the average per-capita "standing crop" of industrial metals already embodied in existing artifacts in the ten richest nations would require more than sixty years' production of these metals at 1970 rates (Brown, 1970).

But neglecting the enormous resource requirements of increasing the capital stock, for how long could the biosphere sustain the depletion and pollution generated by even the sixfold increase in the throughput of materials and energy required to maintain the miraculously accumulated capital? There is much evidence that present rates of usage are irreversibly damaging ecological life-support systems. Furthermore, a sixfold increase in *net, usable* throughput implies a much greater than sixfold increase in gross throughput and environmental impact, due to the law of diminishing returns. To mine poorer grade and less accessible minerals and to dispose safely of large quantities of wastes will require enormous increases in energy and capital devoted to mining, refining, transportation, and pollution control. To get our sixfold increase in net energy and materials throughput, the gross throughput must increase by much more than sixfold. There is a limit to the process of throwing ever larger quantities of capital into the exploitation of ever poorer, more remote, and more dangerous sources of energy and materials.

Nothing illustrates the amazing shallowness of orthodox development economics more convincingly than the realization that it has been for the last twenty years attempting an impossible goal. Yet the establishment worldwide of the Western, middle-class material lifestyle has been the explicit goal of most of our aid and development programs. As a means

---

*Let M be the factor, R be annual world resource production; 4 billion is the world population, and 210 million is the U.S. population; then:

$$\frac{M \cdot R}{4 \times 10^9} = \frac{0.33R}{2.1 \times 10^8} \rightarrow M = 6.35$$

to that end, as well as an end in itself, rich countries are urged to continue growing. According to former chairman of the Council of Economic Advisers, Dr. Paul W. McCracken, "The action most urgently needed in the world economy is for the strong economies to be willing to accept higher levels of living. Their reluctance to do so seems to be of Calvinistic proportions" (1975). In other words, the rich must consume more for the sake of the poor! How could such a respected economist make such an apparently absurd statement? Or, more instructively, what premises must be accepted for McCracken's statement to be reasonable? If resources were unlimited in supply, and the only limiting factor in economic growth were aggregate demand, and if the distribution of income did not matter as long as the absolute incomes of all were increasing, and if we look only at the short run—then the statement would be reasonable. Keynesian pump-priming is evidently the paradigm within which McCracken views world development.

But these assumptions are grossly unrealistic. Resource supplies are, in fact, increasingly limited; distribution is as important as absolute levels; we cannot ignore the long run, and the rich can remain at their more than sufficient material standard without necessarily being Calvinists. The rich should not be urged to devote their leisure to senseless consumption. Better that they should consume less, freeing resources for the poor, who can create their own markets by selling necessities to each other, instead of having to sell ever more extravagant luxuries to the jaded and harried rich.

From the impossibility theorem it follows that the important development questions for the remainder of the century will be:

(1) How will the limited number of person-years of "developed living" be apportioned among nations and among social classes within nations?

(2) How will the total be divided between the present generation and all future generations?

(3) Could not the total number of person-years lived from now until extinction be increased by having a smaller number of people simultaneously alive in each generation, thereby avoiding some of the permanent destruction of renewable resources and life support systems that results when their short-run carrying capacity is overstressed?

(4) Could not our standards of per-capita consumption be lowered in exchange for an increase in person-years lived?

(5) Should the burden of scarcity fall mainly on the present or the future? On the standard of per-capita consumption, or the numbers of people? On the rich or on the poor?

Lest we think that these questions are unanswerable, it should be noted that varying answers have been given in recent United Nations conferences in Stockholm (Environment), Bucharest (Population), and Rome (Food). The leaders of the overdeveloped countries seemed to say that the increasing world burden of scarcity should fall on numbers of people in Third World countries. Let the poor limit their populations. The leaders of the underdeveloped countries seemed to be saying that the burden should fall on the high per-capita consumption of the overdeveloped. Let the rich limit their consumption. Both seemed willing to pass as much of the burden as possible on to the future.

If we heroically assume goodwill on both parts, the solution is simple; without goodwill there is no solution at all. The overdeveloped should limit consumption growth (and population growth), and the underdeveloped should limit population growth, while increasing per-capita consumption only up to equality with the stabilized or reduced levels of the overdeveloped countries. Both groups should move to a steady state at a common level of capital stocks per person and stabilized or reduced populations. Welfare or service can still increase with improvements in efficiency as discussed in Chapter 4.

In principle, the solution is so simple. Why then does it strike us as so hopelessly utopian and unrealistic? Partly because of lack of goodwill internationally—it is hard to be optimistic about nations limiting goods when they cannot even agree to limit the production of "bads," to end the arms race. It could easily happen that increasing scarcity will lead nations to devote more rather than less resources to weapons, in order to appropriate by force the remaining resources from other countries. With proliferation of nuclear weapons to underdeveloped countries, however, this may become an expensive conquest.

In addition to lack of goodwill internationally, the existence of class conflicts within each group of nations makes our simple solution "unrealistic." The overdeveloped countries will not want to limit consumption, because growing consumption is what buys off social conflict and keeps attention diverted from the divisive issue of distribution of wealth and income. In the United States growth is a substitute for redistribution. The leaders of underdeveloped countries are often not anxious to limit the populations of their own lower-class majorities, because cheap and abundant labor is a benefit to the owners of land and capital, the ruling class, which of course limits its own progeny. Cheap labor means higher profits that can be reinvested for faster growth and thus more rapid attainment of international power and prestige for the elite (Daly, 1970). If we were just a little cynical we might suspect that the reluctance of some Third World elites to support population control, or even family planning, bore some analogy to the reluctance of foxes to advocate birth control for rabbits.

Thus internal class conflicts, as well as international enmity, will make agreement difficult and will predispose both parties to accept the wishful thinking of technological optimists who advocate that we have faith in the Great Breakthrough that will invalidate the impossibility theorem. All that is needed, they say, are larger research and development budgets, greater offerings to the Technological Priesthood who gave us the Green Revolution, Nuclear Power, and Space Travel. That these technological saviors have created more problems than they have solved is conveniently overlooked. The mythology of technological omnipotence is by itself very strong, but when backed by class interests in avoiding the radical policies required by the steady state, it becomes a full-fledged idolatry.

As long as we remain trapped by the ideology of competitive growth, there is no solution. We are reminded of the South Indian monkey trap, in which a hollowed-out coconut is fastened to a stake by a chain and filled with rice. There is a hole in the coconut just large enough for the monkey to put his extended hand through but not large enough to withdraw his fist full of rice. The monkey is trapped only by his inability to reorder his values, to recognize that freedom is worth more than the handful of rice. We seem to be in a similar position. The value of growth is rigidly held in first place, and we are trapped into a system of increasing environmental disruption and gross injustices by our inability to reorder values, to open our fist and let go of the growth paradigm. Although it is hard on rational grounds to be optimistic about our getting out of the growth trap, we must, nevertheless, adopt an existential attitude of hope, without which no efforts at all would be made. Hope and despair are existential attitudes that we bring to the world from within our being. Optimism and pessimism are rational expectations about the probable course of events. Therefore, it is possible to be a hopeful pessimist without contradiction.

The split in point of view between the overdeveloped and underdeveloped is in some ways new but has its roots in the old division between Marx and Malthus. The Marxian and Malthusian traditions represent the major competing explanations of poverty in Western thought (Daly, 1971). The difference between them is reflected in the two meanings of the word "proletariat," and the differing theories of poverty implicit therein. The literal Latin meaning of proletariat is "those with many offspring," and the full ancient Roman sense of the word is "the lowest class of a people, whose members, poor and exempt from taxes, were useful to the republic only for the procreation of children." The correlation between proletarian and prolific is implicit in our very language and is given explicit theoretical development in the Malthusian tradition. The second meaning of proletariat is the Marxian definition as "nonowners of the means of production, who must sell their labor power to the capitalist in order to live." By Marx's time the literal meaning of the word had been lost, and it was used as a synonym for "the laboring class, the poor, the common people." Marx's definition completed the alienation of the word from all connection with its literal meaning. Implicit in the Marxian definition, and explicitly developed in Marxian thought, is the theory that poverty results from the social relations of production not from the proliferation of the proletariat.

But are these two views really mutually exclusive or logically incompatible? If we consider that poverty means "low per-capita income of a class" and that per-capita income is the ratio of total income *(Y)* to total population *(P)* for the class, then we can say, as a first approximation, that the Malthusian tradition explains low Y/P by pointing to a large or rapidly growing denominator and its causes. In contrast, Marxians explain the poverty of a class by showing why the numerator is low or growing very slowly, or even declining. To the extent that Y and P are independent, the two explanations are complementary. Certainly there are limits to the independence of Y and P. Given Y, there is a maximum P which can subsist and a minimum P technically necessary for the production of the given Y. But within the limits set by subsistence and technology (which grow wider with time), the two terms of the fraction can vary in relative independence, and instead of Marx *versus* Malthus we have Marx *and* Malthus. Even when Y and P cannot be treated independently, there still exist complementarities between the Marxian and Malthusian views, since there is no reason that we cannot recognize two-way causation, with both Y and P capable of autonomous change.

The big conflict between Marx and Malthus does not lie in any *logical* incompatibility between their theories of poverty, but in an *ideological* incompatibility between their pet remedies. Marx's remedy calls upon worker solidarity and overthrow of the capitalist system. Since the proletarians are the grave diggers of capitalism, it will not do to restrict their numbers, at least not until after the revolution. Malthus, by contrast, took capitalism as given and urged individual prudence, restraint, and responsibility in marriage and reproduction as the way to combat poverty. The neo-Malthusians urged contraception, while Malthus favored abstinence. For Marx, overpopulation was relative to capitalist institutions. For Malthus, overpopulation was absolute, defined by the limits imposed by nature independent of human social arrangements. Once again there is no *logical* conflict between the views. We can easily recognize the existence of both absolute and relative overpopulation. To deny either in defense of the other is nonsensical, though frequently done in ideological debate. To explain poverty, which is low per-capita income, Y/P, for a class, the Marxian tradition explains class differences in the numerator (income) as resulting mainly from a class monopoly on ownership of the means of production. The Malthusian tradition explains class differences in the denominator as resulting from the practice or nonpractice of birth limitation, or ownership versus nonownership of the means of limiting reproduction. The "means of limiting reproduction" includes not only contraceptive knowledge and devices but also the minimum cultural level of education and self-discipline necessary for their effective use—just as "means of production" means not only machines, but also the technical and managerial will and ability to use them. Could not this simple union of the two historically dominant theories of poverty be made to yield a more useful and informative set of categories than we presently have?

We have defined poverty as a low Y/P for a class; but as yet we have not defined a "class." Our definition of class is not in terms of numerical size of per-capita income, so that all members of the class would be homogeneous with respect to size, but rather in terms of underlying *social* characteristics (differential property ownership and differential fertility), which largely determine the size of Y/P. Our resulting categories, homogeneous with respect to fertility and property ownership, will contain varying levels of per-capita income, but these differing per-capita income levels are not the result of differential property or fertility (except at a narrow within-category level) and are determined by chance differences in intelligence, opportunity, preference, and so on.* Hence within categories, we would expect families to be distributed much more normally about a mean per-capita income representative of that class, since the factors mainly responsible for skewness, differential property and fertility, have been held constant. By following the implications of the previous section and moving from a monistic to a dualistic conception of both Y and P, we can make a large gain in within-category homogeneity at a relatively small cost in terms of multiplying categories.

The Marxian tradition insists on distinguishing two kinds of Y—that which goes to laborers largely as wages, Y_w, and that which goes to capitalists largely as returns to property, Y_p. Hence $Y = Y_w + Y_p$. These two categories of income follow different laws of growth and embody the fundamental Marxian criterion for class division. Income to laborers and income to property owners are both functionally and ethically different and should not be indiscriminately lumped together.

The neo-Malthusian tradition distinguishes two kinds of P—those who control reproduction, P_c, and those who do not, P_n. Hence $P = P_c + P_n$. These two populations follow different laws of growth and embody the fundamental neo-Malthusian criterion for class division. That they really form two statistically distinct populations, at least at an international level, has been shown by a United Nations study (1963). A frequency distribution of countries by gross reproduction rate (GRR) is strikingly bimodal. Developed countries have a GRR of less than 2.0, while underdeveloped countries have a GRR greater than 2.0, with almost no countries falling in the dividing range around 2.0. For high-fertility countries the unweighted mean GRR was 2.94, while for the

---

*From a welfare viewpoint, the existence of effective choice is more important than the numerical level of a family's per-capita income (the family may choose high leisure or many children in preference to a high per-capita income). Possession and control of the means of production and the means of limiting reproduction are necessary to make these choices effective.

low-fertility countries it was 1.41, or less than half as large. The difference between the two means (1.53) is over twenty-one times the standard error (0.07), clearly showing that we are dealing with two distinct populations and that the line of distinction is controlled versus uncontrolled fertility.

Furthermore, the fact that, at the international level, the division of countries by fertility criteria and the division by wealth or level of development criteria tend to coincide, is highly significant. The study found a remarkably high inverse relation between income and fertility on an international level when the world was divided into two fertility blocs. Almost all countries with GRR > 2.0 are in Asia, Africa, and Latin America. Almost all countries with GRR < 2.0 are in the developed parts of the world, and practically no countries have GRRs in the neighborhood of the 2.0 dividing point. The exceptions (high-fertility Albania and low-fertility Israel, Japan, Argentina, and Uruguay) only tend to prove the rule, since for their regions they are not only demographic exceptions but also economic exceptions and still conform to the rule of inverse association of fertility and economic development. However, *within* each bloc there appears to be no association at all between fertility and level of development.

With two kinds of income, Y_w and Y_p, and two kinds of population P_c and P_n, we have four possible types of per-capita income: Y_p/P_c, Y_p/P_n, Y_w/P_c, Y_w/P_n. To each of these types corresponds a social class with its own per-capita income distribution. If we knew the size and the rates of growth, and the percentage of the population contained in each of these four per-capita income classes, we would have a vastly better picture than that obtained by lumping everything together. The first category, Y_p/P_c, combines control of production and reproduction and is characteristic of an upper class or stable bourgeoisie—stable because, with both population control and property, they are unlikely to fall into the proletariat. The last category, Y_w/P_n, is characteristic of a stable proletariat. With no property income and uncontrolled fertility, there is little chance of rising out of the proletariat. The intermediate categories represent transitional, unstable phases. The proletarians who control fertility may accumulate a small capital and rise out of the lower class. The bourgeois family that fails to control fertility may dissipate its capital and fall into the lower class.

Most growth models in the contemporary literature trace the path of aggregate Y/P (or just aggregate Y) according to various assumptions and are quite incapable of distinguishing among the infinitely many combinations of the four components that could correspond to any given aggregate per-capita GNP. The tacit assumption, if these models are to be included in the economist's tool kit rather than in his toy box, is that the average per-capita incomes of the four classes increase more or less proportionately. If not, then an important element of change is being omitted. A case in point is northeast Brazil, the largest poor area in the Western Hemisphere, which has had an annual growth rate in per-capita income of around 3.4 percent in the 1960s (Daly, 1970). But almost all of this growth has taken place in the upper-class per-capita income (Y_p/P_c) with that of the lower-class category (Y_w/P_n) remaining constant at best, perhaps even decreasing. At the same time, the percentage of the total population in the latter category has been increasing while that in former was decreasing! Conventional growth models thus leave out the most important feature of economic change in this region. The fourfold typology easily encompasses both even and uneven growth and is sensitive to the differences between them.

If we reject this fourfold disaggregation of per-capita income, we must do it on one of two grounds: 1. Disaggregation is not necessary, in which case it must be argued that equal growth of the four per-capita incomes is a realistic description of the process of economic growth for all countries. This, as just indicated, can be refuted. 2. Disaggregation is desirable, but the particular Marxian-Malthusian disaggregation here advocated is not a good one. Then, of course, we would be obliged to offer a better one. There may well be a better disaggregation, but it is argued below that the Marxian-Malthusian criteria have a very high degree of universality and deep-rootedness.

"The first principle of all human history is, of course, the existence of living human individuals," we are informed by Marx. The continued existence of living human individuals is the result of the two life-sustaining processes of production (to maintain human organisms) and reproduction (to replace human organisms). These two processes, then, are the most basic in society, and differential control over them gives us the first principles of division into social classes. The two processes are the basic force functions that generate class differences. Production provides the means for the short-term maintenance (and enjoyment) of life; reproduction provides for the long-term continuation (and enjoyment) of life. The basic social unit in the productive process is the firm and in the reproductive process, the family. In neither case is it the individual, who is a middle-run disequilibrium process; that is, he dies. But the firm and the family do not necessarily die and may be viewed as long-term equilibrium processes capable of indefinite, though not eternal, self-replacement.

Given the two fundamental life processes, let us note some ways in which they are analogous. Production is essentially reproduction of commodities by commodities. Reproduction is the production of people by people. We have two self-renewing sets, people and commodities, which are dependent on each other for their self-renewal. Both processes require specialization and division of labor, both are time consuming.

The biological term "gestation period" is widely used in economics. The first political economist, William Petty, could not resist calling land the mother and labor the father of wealth, and since earliest times the fertility of soil and the fertility of woman have been associated. The aggregate stocks of people and commodities both have birth (production) rates and death (consumption) rates, age structures, and life expectancies (durabilities). From a strictly physical point of view, the maintenance of these two stocks is accomplished by the same process: the importation of low-entropy matter-energy from the environment and the exportation of the same quantity of high-entropy matter-energy (waste) back to the environment. Both people and commodities are entropy converters, capable of mutually dependent self-renewal as long as the supply of low entropy holds out. This much is familiar from the discussion of Chapter 2, in which the SSE was defined in terms of the same stocks of people and artifacts.

The important question from a social viewpoint is: Who controls these two processes and to what purpose? Our social classes are defined on the basis of differing participation in and control over the two processes of production and reproduction. Control over production is, under capitalism, vested in capital, in the broad sense of property. He who owns the means of production by and large controls the process of production and directs it to his own purposes. Property hires, organizes, and directs labor. Our two classes are laborers and property owners—the fundamental Marxian division of classes. To what end do capitalists control the process? To the maximization of their private profit, according to the classical economists, to Marx, and to the neoclassical economists.

Control over the reproductive process has likewise been vested in the owners of the means of reproduction, that is, under capitalism in men and women, who own their own bodies. Under slavery the control over reproduction was still vested in the owner, who was, of course, the master not the slave. But the control of reproduction has, for the majority of mankind throughout history, been left to the natural consequences of the sex urge as unconsciously conditioned by social custom. Only since the middle of the nineteenth century has there been, and only for a minority, an effective rational barrier between the sex act and its natural outcome in proliferation. That the *desire* for (but not possession of) such a rational barrier, effective contraception, is a cultural and historical universal has been admirably demonstrated by Norman E. Himes in his classic *Medical History of Contraception* (1936). The attainment of this desire is relatively recent and still limited to a minority of the world's people. The incompleteness of what Himes termed the "democratization of contraception" means that the owners of the means of reproduction really do not *control* the process in any rational sense, because they do not possess effective means of limiting reproduction.

On the frontispiece of his classic study, Himes has the following quotation from Lippert: "The farther a notion reaches back into primitive times for its origin, the more universal must be its extent, and its power in history is rooted in this universality." It is to Himes' great credit to have shown that, contrary to popular opinion, the desire to control conception is a cultural and historical universal—not a recent product of birth-control propaganda. The control of *numbers* (effected by abortion and infanticide as well as by contraception) is even more universal, extending in all probability back to our prehuman ancestors. It is hardly necessary to argue the universality of property. Both individual and collective property holding have been traced back through human history and into the animal kingdom in the instinct of territoriality.

In sum, the deep-rootedness and universality of the two criteria is apparent. Can we imagine more basic lines of division for defining social classes than differential control over the two basic life processes? Is it at all surprising that in the history of economic thought, each of the two great traditions of explaining poverty should have seized upon one of these criteria as providing the key to understanding and combating poverty? That the two traditions should have been seen as mutually exclusive substitutes rather than as complements is an unfortunate historical circumstance that economists must now strive to put right.

To show how, in spite of severe data limitations, these categories might be usefully applied, let us consider the case of northeast Brazil in the 1960s, which in terms of conventional development criteria has been a great success (Daly, 1970). Total GNP for the region has grown at between 6 and 7 percent (say, 6.5) annually, with population growing at around 3.1 percent annually and per-capita income thus growing at around 3.4 percent—well above the hemispheric goal of 2.5 percent expressed at the Punta del Este conference. Add the fact of sparse density and there appears to be no population problem at all.

But let us apply the concepts just considered in order to go behind the misleading average and ask what is happening to each type of per-capita income and the corresponding social class. As a first approximation, let us take Y_w/P_c and Y_p/P_n to be empty categories; that is, there is a high inverse correlation between wealth and fertility. In other words, by our definition there is no middle class—only a stable bourgeoisie (Y_p/P_c) and a stable proletariat (Y_w/P_n). If we consider that a typical completed bourgeois family has four surviving children, while a typical completed proletarian family has eight surviving children, then over one generation (say 25 years) the bourgeois family doubles (4 children ÷ 2 parents) and the proletarian family quadruples (8 children ÷ 2 parents). If over the same 25-year period the total income of each class grows at the same 6.5-percent rate at which the total income of both classes taken together has been growing, then the total income of each class will have increased by a factor of $(1.065)^{25} = 4.8$. Therefore, the per-capita income of the bourgeois family will have increased, over one generation, by a factor of $4.8/2 = 2.4$; that of the proletarian family will have increased by a factor of only $4.8/4 = 1.2$.

Even this meager increase of 20 percent over 25 years for the proletarians disappears when we recall our very optimistic assumption of equal growth rates for the total incomes of the two classes. Total income of the proletariat surely grows at less than the average 6.5 percent, while total income of the bourgeoisie surely grows more rapidly. This is because the proletariat lacks bargaining power due to nonownership of property, lack of labor unions, and lack of education; and because inflation tends to benefit property income at the expense of labor income and to benefit those who have access to credit. Thus it appears extremely likely that the per-capita income of the proletariat has not increased at all, while that of the bourgeoisie has increased very rapidly indeed. The bourgeoisie becomes richer and relatively less numerous; the proletariat remains equally poor and becomes both absolutely and relatively more numerous. Looking at aggregate per-capita GNP, we can see only "economic growth." Looking at the fourfold disaggregation forces us to distinguish between growth in the sense of "improvement" and growth in the sense of "swelling." And we are led to recognize the key role played by differential fertility in the dynamics of swelling. The rather more important role of differential property ownership has been more generally recognized intellectually, even if avoided politically.

Finally, in a world increasingly polarized into right and left, might not the inclusion of the true insights of both the Marxian and neo-Malthusian traditions in our informational categories go at least some distance toward uniting these factions to a common development effort? The underlying moral viewpoint capable of embracing the best in both traditions is that stated in Mark 2:28: "The Sabbath was made for man, not man for the Sabbath." If this rule applies to sacred institutions, then it must apply with even greater force to secular institutions. The institutions, laws, and conventions governing the dual life-sustaining processes of production and reproduction are to serve man, not vice versa. Man was not made to serve Mammon—nor the goddess of fertility.

Let us take a further look at the specific case of Brazil as representative of the conflict between development and the environment. At international conferences Brazil has been noted for hard-line stands against any environmental constraints on economic development. Brazil also has achieved one of the highest growth rates in the world. This accomplishment can be viewed from at least three very different perspectives—the neoclassical, the neo-Marxian, and the neo-Malthusian. Old economic doctrines never die, they just add the prefix "neo" and continue their subversive or apologetic existences.

Keynes warned us that economists are more powerful than common-ly realized: "Practical men who believe themselves to be quite exempt from any intellectual influences, are usually the slaves of some defunct economist. Madmen in authority, who hear voices in the air, are distilling their frenzy from some academic scribbler of a few years back" (1936, p. 383). Prior to 1964 in Brazil, both neoclassical and neo-Marxian "voices in the air" spoke to those in authority. Since the revolution of 1964 the neo-Marxians have been placed beyond the pale. Neo-Malthusians have never been a dominant force anywhere, especially not in Brazil. Their inclusion here is based not on their past importance but on my estimate of their future importance. The neoclassical paradigm thus has, for now, a virtual monopoly on official Brazilian economic thinking. Neoclassical economics has been applied with originality and imagination and, within its own terms, has been highly successful. Let us examine the nature of the Brazilian neoclassical development strategy first in a sympathetic way and then give it a more critical look from the neo-Marxian and neo-Malthusian perspectives, especially the latter.

The current technocratic military regime in Brazil has based its development strategy overwhelmingly on its ability to maintain a very high rate of growth in real GNP, arguing that this would make unnecessary any direct confrontation with the politically divisive issues of redistribution (exit neo-Marxians) and population control (exit neo-Malthusians, if any). If GNP continues to grow at 10 percent per year, it will double every seven years, quadruple every fourteen years, and so forth. Surely, it is argued, the poor will benefit more from this rapid doubling than from any "premature" or "emotional" redistribution, which would kill incentives and lead to economic stagnation. It is considered natural that income distribution should become more unequal in the early stages of rapid growth—after all, universal poverty is highly egalitarian and any movement away from that position is bound to have nonuniform effects and therefore increase the inequality of income distribution. As for the nearly 3-percent rate of demographic growth that the "demophobes" fear, that too is "solved" by economic growth. If the 10-percent rate of GNP growth is maintained, then a 3-percent rate of demographic growth means that per-capita GNP will grow at about 7 percent and double every ten years. If, by heroic and expensive effort, the population growth rate were cut to 1 percent per year, then per-capita income would grow at 9 percent and double every eight years instead of every ten years—not a significant difference and certainly not worth the enormous effort. Besides, people are needed to colonize the Amazon, which is viewed as a great potential source of agricultural and mineral wealth and as a temptation to greedy foreigners. Furthermore, the "demographic transition thesis" holds that as incomes increase, the birth rate automatically tends to fall, so that rapid economic growth is itself the best birth-control policy.

In sum, rapid growth in aggregate GNP is the turnpike to development, and redistribution and fertility reduction are bumpy, dirt-road detours that will at best slow the journey down and at worst rattle the car to pieces. The best strategy is to stay on the turnpike and pay the relatively cheap toll.

Reality is always more complex than our descriptions of it, and I would not claim that this brief sketch does total justice to Brazilian development policy, but I believe it captures the essential strategy. There are, however, countercurrents. Everyone recognizes that income distribution became more concentrated during the intercensal period 1960–1970, and the regime has expressed concern. The literacy program (MOBRAL) and some educational and social welfare expenditures have no doubt benefitted the poor. Some influential Brazilians (Mario Simonsen and Rubens Costa, for example) have long argued for a voluntary family-planning program. Moreover, Brazil ratified the Bucharest World Plan of Action on Population. It remains to be seen whether that is an index more of the vacuity of the action plan than of Brazil's intention to worry about population growth (*"Brasil admite,"* 1974).

The successful policies undertaken to promote growth include: tax incentives for exports and for investment, especially investment in poor regions; reduction of inflation and monetary correction, or "indexing" to correct the worst distortions of the remaining inflation; adjustable exchange rates and frequent minidevaluations to discourage foreign exchange speculation; welcoming foreign capital from a diverse mix of countries; administrative enforcement of tax laws; and other measures. I will not describe these policies in detail, since it is clear enough that the goal of growth was being achieved (at least until the oil crisis of 1974). Rather, let us take a closer look at that goal itself and judge its adequacy from our other two perspectives.

We need not be Marxian to appreciate the importance of the main points of what I have called the neo-Marxian tradition. The major emphasis of that tradition is on social justice and on breaking the monopoly of economic and political power of the elite class. Brazil is governed by a military dictatorship. In recent elections most Brazilians, in spite of the benefits of economic growth, cast their somewhat meaningless ballots for the opposition party. Social justice has not been served by the worsening distribution of income. In 1960 the poorest 80 percent of the population received 46 percent of total national income, while in 1970 they received only 37 percent. Correspondingly, over the same period the share of the richest 20 percent increased from 54 percent to 63 percent, while the richest 1 percent increased its share from about 12 percent to about 18 percent (Simonsen, 1972, p. 51). To put it bluntly, the great majority of the population has, since the revolution, gotten both a reduced share of the national product and a reduced voice in national affairs. Hence the popular saying, "Brazil is doing well, but the Brazilian is doing badly."

But is the Brazilian majority getting worse off absolutely as well as relatively? Between 1960 and 1970 the *absolute* income of the lower 80 percent taken as a whole increased by 8.4 percent, while that of the richest 20 percent increased by 55.4 percent. For the richest 1 percent the increase was 103.2 percent (Simonsen, 1972, p. 53). Within the large category of the poorest 80 percent, there were no doubt many people (especially in poor areas like the northeast) whose absolute real incomes did not rise at all, or actually declined. But the data are too global to permit more than a guess at the actual numbers. However, the falling purchasing power of the real minimum wage (actual inflation has been greater than the anticipated inflation used in calculating the minimum wage adjustments) suggests that many of the poor are getting worse off absolutely.

It is sometimes argued that the pursuit of growth will eventually require a more even distribution of income in order to have a mass market in which to sell the growing output. This is not very convincing, for two reasons: First, there are export markets available. Second, the upper 20 percent of Brazil's 110 million people consists of 22 million consumers (almost equal to the entire population of Argentina), who can provide adequate markets for each other, with little need to sell much beyond rice and beans to the lower 88 million. As growth continues, the product mix shifts more to luxuries and consumer durables and away from basic necessities. The increase in luxury consumption of a minority at the expense of the basic needs of the majority is, of course, the real meaning of income inequality and the real cost of a "trickle-down" development policy.

The one thing that the poor definitely get more of than the rich is children. Completed family size differs probably by a factor of about 2 between the richest 20 percent and the poorest 80 percent. That is a crude estimate, but it is unmistakably clear, as we have already seen, that differential fertility is an important determinant of per-capita income distribution, a point generally ignored by neo-Marxians and neoclassicals alike. It seems that differential population growth in Brazil has promoted aggregate economic growth at the expense of the lower class. The high fertility of the lower class serves to perpetuate an unlimited supply of labor at a constant low wage. This helps to keep profits high, and, since most investment comes from profit earners, the result is more investment and faster growth than would be the case if labor were scarce and wages were being bid up. The cheap service of abundant labor is a key part of the Brazilian growth pattern and is of enormous benefit to the upper and middle classes, who have not only cheap labor for their factories and *fazendas* but also cheap domestic servants for their households. Jonathan Swift observed a similar condition in his time. Explaining how his rational Houyhnhnms limited their reproduction to one of each sex, Swift wrote, "But the race of inferior Houyhnhnms bred up to be servants, is not so strictly limited upon this article; these are allowed to produce three of each sex to be domestics in the noble families" (Swift, 1952, p. 166).

But what of the demographic transition thesis that fertility falls as income increases? For one thing, the real income of the masses hardly seems to be rising at all, and for another the thesis itself may be just wishful thinking. Rising per-capita income may be as much the result of lowered fertility as the cause, and the expectation that a process that took place over centuries in Europe will be repeated in the Third World in a matter of decades inspires skepticism. Death control did spread in a matter of decades, but procreating is a much more popular activity than dying, and social values that evolved during a history in which mortality was high, must, for survival, favor high fertility. A lowering of fertility will take a long time at best and may never take place if governments sit back and wait for some automatic transition to occur as a by-product of economic growth (Teitelbaum, 1975). It is a fact that illiteracy has declined with economic growth, but on the basis of that commonplace no one invents a "literacy transition thesis" and counsels Brazil not to waste money on MOBRAL because economic growth will automatically induce literacy!

The neo-Malthusian view has recently been generalized from a demographic focus to a concern for total ecological balance among population, resources, and environment. Since the Brazilian strategy is so heavily committed to rapid growth, it is a question of great interest whether and for how long a growth rate of 10 percent can be sustained by the natural ecosystem of which the Brazilian economy is a subsystem. What is politically and economically expedient may turn out to be biophysically unacceptable. Very little study has been devoted to this question, because it is considered a nonproblem. The official view is that, "in relation to the special human carrying capacity of the earth, it is obvious that it is infinitely greater than present levels" (Osorio de Alameda, 1973). Since the growth-based strategy would be rendered untenable by any imminent limits to growth in the form of steeply rising costs resulting from minerals depletion, environmental pollution, or ecological disruption, the regime simply declares by fiat that any such limits are infinitely remote. Any research that might cast doubt on this "obvious" fact is not likely to be welcomed, just as economic and demographic research on fertility is limited by a kind of taboo (Lyra Madeira, 1971, p. 42). This denial of the problem is hardly surprising, since most politicians in the United States take the same attitude and dismiss any argument that growth must be limited as "doomsaying."

Admittedly, Brazil is a large country with abundant resources and plenty of space in which to spread the inevitable pollution resulting from production and consumption. But the resource and waste-disposal demands of other countries also impinge upon Brazil and provide an important reason for the large inflow of foreign investment that has been a major factor in rapid growth. Such investments offer foreign countries an alternative to importing raw materials and further polluting home environments—a prospect that is doubly attractive to polluted and re-source-poor countries, such as Japan. Ironically, Brazil already is experiencing the environmental problems of overdevelopment before it has solved the traditional problems of underdevelopment. With the help of West Germany, the most intractable of all problems of overdevelopment, managing fission power, will soon increase Brazil's prestige while decreasing its national well-being. The enormous ecological destruction being wrought on the Amazon jungle in the name of development has been admirably documented by Goodland and Irwin (1975). Therefore, it is simplistic to argue that pollution replaces hunger and that rapid growth has substituted lesser for greater evils. The problems of underdevelopment and overdevelopment do not cancel out; instead, they add together or perhaps even multiply.

A famous formerly exiled Brazilian, Celso Furtado, is one of the few economists to have recognized the increasingly apparent contradiction of our present concept of development: that an upper-middle-class standard of per-capita resource consumption for the current world population of 4 billion is simply impossible (Furtado, 1974).

The Brazilian elite suspects that "environmentalism" is part of a plot to stifle their growth and thwart the destiny by which Brazil is "condemned to greatness." Certainly it is unreasonable to expect the poor to limit their resource consumption until after the rich have limited theirs. This applies not only between rich and poor nations but also between social classes within nations.

Perhaps the real goal of "development" in Brazil has nothing to do with individual welfare of the majority and everything to do with national power. The mercantilists proclaimed this goal openly, and perhaps the regime is really more neomercantilist than neoclassical. If the goal is to maximize the economic and military power of the "nation" (meaning the current elite), then nothing more need be said. We can assume that we know other peoples' real goals and then interpret contradictory behavior as an aberration or a mistake. Or we can assume that behavior is always rational and consistent and that the real goal, which may be secret or even unconscious, is exactly what the behavior implies. According to which view we adopt, the regime will appear either neoclassical or neomercantilist. But if the goal is to increase the welfare of the majority of Brazilians in the present and future generations, then it seems clear that Brazil will have to get off the rapid-growth turnpike and follow the slower, bumpy road of redistribution and population control. At least those two elements of the steady-state program are already relevant to Brazil, and probably to a number of other Third World countries as well.

While not referring specifically to Brazil, Raul Prebisch, head of ECLA, recently expressed to a U.S. audience a certain disenchantment with growth in Latin America:

> Reference has been made to the so-called high rates of growth that are possible in Latin America. I do not share the rejoicing over this prospect. Indeed the high rates of growth that have been attained by some countries are accompanied by a growing disparity in income distribution and by the lack of ability of the economic system to absorb with satisfactory productivity the continuous increment in the labor force.
>
> The introduction of the consumption society means that we are "benefitting" from all the "delights" of your patterns of consumption such as pollution, irresponsible use of nonrenewable resources, growing congestion in the cities, and erosion of some human values that we would like to preserve [Prebisch, 1974, p. 40].

The growth ethic will have to end sometime, and the neo-Malthusians will have their day, perhaps sooner than anyone thinks. But in the meantime it seems inevitable that the rhythmic crescendo of the GNP samba will drown out the somber Greek chorus of rational foresight. Now that the Brazilians have learned to beat us at our own game of industrial growthmanship, it seems rather ungracious to declare that game obsolete. We can sympathize with Brazilian disbelief and suspicion regarding the motives of the neo-Malthusians. But the dialectic of change has no rule against irony.

The purpose of this chapter has been not to offer a treatise on the Third World but merely to show that while the SSE has, quite appropriately, been discussed mainly in the context of overdeveloped countries, it is not at all irrelevant to underdeveloped countries. As Richard Wilkinson has noted:

> Predictions of when the resources which modern industrial technology depends on will run out are usually within the same time scale as the predictions of when many underdeveloped countries may reach industrial maturity. The industrial nations cannot avoid having to change their whole resource-base and technology for a second time, but some of the pre-industrial nations might manage to avoid making more than one change [Wilkinson, 1973, p. 216].

Hopefully, the underdeveloped are not condemned to repeat the mistakes of the overdeveloped.

REFERENCES

"Brasil Admite o Livre Planejanento Familiar," O Globo, August 5, 1974, p. 4.
Brown, Harrison. "Human Materials Production as a Process in the Biosphere," *Scientific American,* September 1970.

Daly, Herman E. "The Population Question in Northeast Brazil: Its Economic and Ideological Dimensions," *Economic Development and Cultural Change,* July 1970, 536–574.

Daly, Herman E. "A Marxian-Malthusian View of Poverty and Development," *Population Studies,* March 1971, 25–37.

Furtado, Celso. *O Mito do Desenvolvimento Economico.* Rio de Janeiro: *Editora Paz e Terra S. A.,* 1974.

Goodland, Robert J. A., and Howard S. Irwin, *Amazon Jungle: Green Hell to Red Desert.* New York: Elsevier Scientific Publishing Co., 1975.

Himes, Norman E. *A Medical History of Contraception.* Baltimore: Williams & Wilkins, 1936.

Keynes, J. M. *The General Theory of Employment, Interest, and Money.* New York: Harcourt Brace Jovanovich, 1936.

Lyra Madeira, João. *"Migraçoẽs Internas no Planejamento Econômico,"* in Manoel Costa, ed., *Migraçoẽs Internas no Brasil.* Rio de Janeiro: *Instituto de Planejamento Economico e Social,* 1971.

McCracken, Paul W. "A Way Out of the World's Slump," *Wall Street Journal,* September 17, 1975, p. 16.

Meadows, D. H. et al. *The Limits to Growth.* New York: Universe Books, 1972.

Mesarovic, Mihajlo, and Edward Pestel. *Mankind at the Turning Point.* New York: Dutton, 1974.

Osorio de Almeida. Statement of the Brazilian Representative to the 17th Session of the U.N. Population Commission, Geneva, October 3, 1973.

Prebisch, Raul. "Third World Viewpoint," in George M. Dalen and Clyde R. Tipton, Jr., eds., *The Dilemma Facing Humanity.* Columbus, Ohio: Battelle Memorial Institute, 1974.

Simonsen, Mario Henrique. *Brasil 2002.* Rio de Janeiro: *APEC Editora, S.A.,* 1972.

Swift, Jonathan. *Gulliver's Travels.* Chicago: University of Chicago Great Books Edition, 1952. Originally published in 1726.

Teitelbaum, M. S. "Relevance of the Demographic Transition Thesis to Developing Countries," *Science,* May 2, 1975, 420–425.

United Nations. *Population Bulletin of the United Nations, No. 7.* New York: United Nations, 1963.

Wilkinson, Richard. *Poverty and Progress: An Ecological Perspective on Economic Development.* New York: Praeger, 1973.

8

CONCLUSION:
ON BIOPHYSICAL
EQUILIBRIUM
AND MORAL GROWTH

The real science of political economy, which has yet to
be distinguished from the bastard science, as medicine
from witchcraft, and astronomy from astrology, is that
which teaches nations to desire and labor for the things
that lead to life: and which teaches them to scorn and
destroy the things that lead to destruction.

John Ruskin (1862)

From the preceding chapter, it is clear that the twin sacred cows of
property and fertility both must be demythologized. As was shown in
Chapter 3, both a distributist and a population-control institution are
required. For too long, the Population Establishment, financed by the
very wealthy, has been either blind or hostile to the valid criticisms aimed
at it by leftist radicals. Conversely, the Marxians, in their excessive zeal
for grand dialectics and revolution, have neglected to oppose the class
exploitation inherent in the very incomplete democratization of birth
control. The steady-state point of view gives due recognition to both
traditions. Along with the Marxians, it insists that there must be limits to
inequality, and that social justice is a precondition for ecological balance
in all but totalitarian societies. Birth control without property reform
will, at best, reduce the number of poor people but will not eliminate

poverty. With the Malthusians, the steady-state view recognizes that without population control of both human bodies *and their extentions in physical artifacts,* all other social reforms will be cancelled by the growing burden of absolute or Malthusian scarcity, discussed in Chapter 2.

Many radicals decry any call to limit population or wealth as long as enormous resources are being squandered on weapons. Their point cannot be avoided. The B-1 bomber, for example, would require between 300 million and 1 billion gallons of fuel per year. By comparison, it required only 325 million gallons to run all the buses in all the cities and towns of the United States during 1974 (Hayes, 1976, p. 14). The obvious first step toward an ecologically sane economy is to stop building up our capacity for destruction. In the face of the enormous dissipation that results from our perverse values and goals, it seems a waste of time to worry about the minor losses due to technical flaws in our economy. Why strain out the gnat if we are going to continue swallowing the camel? In addition to optimizing the arrangement of deck chairs on the Titanic, economists are too often caught up in the devil's game of suboptimization—of figuring out how better to do that which should not be done in the first place. A job that is not worth doing is not worth doing well. In economists' jargon the marginal benefit of an improvement in purpose is enormously greater than the marginal benefit of an improvement in technology. And the marginal costs are enormously lower.

The more we study the emerging world crisis, the more apparent it becomes that solutions that could work require large value changes and that solutions based on existing values will not work. Like the monkey in the South Indian monkey trap, we are held prisoners by the excessive rigidity of our conventional values. Social scientists seem to regard any appeal to changing values as an infraction of the rules of their game. They are committed to finding technological palliatives achievable by minor social engineering within the context of existing values and only slightly malleable institutions. But disarmament, ecological balance, and social justice are interrelated goals that require sound values and right purposes that can only come from moral growth.

At this point, the economist shrugs his shoulders and says, maybe so, but who knows anything about moral growth, who can define "sound values" or "right purposes"? As a minimum and often sufficient definition, we might describe "sound values" as those that do not promote the indiscriminate destruction of terrestrial life. As argued earlier, minimization of suffering is a more operational goal than maximization of pleasure. But the question itself is more revealing than any answer to it. If we believe that sound values and right purposes cannot be defined and agreed upon, that such knowledge is impossible of attainment, then we are in serious trouble indeed. If one purpose is as good as another, then the only question of interest is how to achieve the goal (any goal) efficiently.

But even efficiency loses its meaning, because it demands, at a minimum, that greater goals not be sacrificed in the achievement of lesser
goals. We must be willing to rank goals before we can speak of efficiency. To rank goals, we must have an ordering principle or an Ultimate
End. We must also rank various degrees of attainment of different
goals—although food is a more pressing need than clothing, we will
value basic clothing higher than marginal increments of food beyond an
already sufficient diet. The only time efficiency does not require a ranking of goals is when there is only one goal. Singleness of purpose may be
purity of heart on the religious plane, as Kierkegaard said, and as is
implied in the necessary concept of a single Ultimate End if goals are to
be ranked. But singleness of purpose at the more concrete and mundane
level is fanaticism. Build the biggest bomb possible and forget the
costs—indeed if there are no other goals sacrificed, then there are no
costs, and building the biggest bomb possible becomes a purely technological operation, with technological efficiency the only criterion.
But, realistically, even at the apparently technological level, multiple
goals creep in, and valuations and tradeoffs appear. For example, even
the military would not want the biggest bomb possible but the biggest
bomb that could be delivered by airplane or rocket. Now explosive power
and lightness of weight become competing goals, and economic aspects
emerge even here. What do we want from a bomb? Efficiency, even at the
lowest levels, requires that we know what we want, that the questions of
relative values have been settled. We need a higher value (potential
megadeaths inflicted) by which to measure the subvalues of explosive
power and lightness of weight. Attempts to be efficient regarding only a
single specific goal, or without any concept of a highest good by which
goals are ranked, is an enterprise suitable only for morons and fanatics.

In Chapter 1 it was argued that economics has overlooked ecological
and moral facts of life that have now come home to haunt us in the form
of increasing ecological scarcity and increasing existential scarcity. Much
of this book has been dedicated to coming to terms with ecological
scarcity, though it was frequently noted that this could not be accomplished
without moral growth, without also coming to terms with existential
scarcity. For the early economists, the important test of economic
institutions and policies was their likely effect on man's character.
Adam Smith cautioned about the stultifying effects of specialization
and wrote the *Theory of Moral Sentiments*. The mechanistic and behav-
ioristic dogmas have banished all such ghosts of subjectivity from the
chrome-plated mechanism of highly tooled analytic thought. Introspection and concern for the "withinness" of things, and even of people, has
been rejected as unscientific. But an economist is a person and knows by
the most direct experience, unmediated by the sometimes deceptive
senses, what it is to be a person. A physicist can know about atoms only

what his amplified senses tell him; he would be pleased to experience the withinness of being an atom, if only he could. To declare the knowledge attained by introspection invalid is the grossest of unscientific prejudices, indicating that many social scientists merely mimic the methods of the physical sciences while understanding nothing of the basic spirit of science.

The locus of moral values is within, and our focus exclusively on the exterior has led to a superficial view of human behavior and economic life that neglects moral values and the necessary guides, controls, and restraints that shared values provide. Of course, people can also be enslaved by false values and superstitions, but in combating false values not enough care has been given to protecting true values from the blindly wielded ax of the reductionists, behaviorists, and relativists. The political consequences of the indiscriminate gutting of interior values was foreseen by Edmund Burke:

> Men are qualified for civil liberty in exact proportion to their disposition to put moral chains upon their own appetites. Society cannot exist unless a controlling power on will and appetite be placed somewhere, and the less of it there is within, the more there must be without. It is ordained in the eternal constitution of things, that men of intemperate minds cannot be free. Their passions forge their fetters [quoted in Ophuls, 1973].

An overpopulated and overconsuming community that is pressing the carrying capacity of its local and global ecosystems must, for survival, come under the authority of a controlling power. The less of that power we find within, the more it will have to come from without. The political logic of Burke; the centralizing logic of modern large-scale, high-information, and high-energy technology; and Skinnerian behaviorist views are all pointing directly to a totalitarian state. The straightest route to such a state, as argued in Chapter 6, is via the "plutonium economy." In the words of physicist Dean E. Abrahamson:

> The decision on nuclear power will determine how our future society will look. The perceived impotence of the powerless when confronted with forces which appear to be beyond their control is one of the basic factors leading to alienation in our society. This is as true for the small, poor nation in the world community as it is for the individual in the industrialized state. Nuclear power presents to the alienated minority and the poor nation alike a means to greatly amplify their political power. What measures will be deemed necessary to cope with the constraints posed by nuclear power with its enormous quantities of highly radioactive waste materials and with the ever present dangers associated with nuclear fuels? It is obvious that society could not tolerate disruptive nuclear events. The response to nuclear power will be the garrison state [Abrahamson, 1974].

If the garrison state is to be run efficiently, then behavioral control technology will be required, and the conditioners with their ratomorphic view of man will take charge.

What is the presumed benefit that justifies these enormous costs? A continued increase in growth and consumption beyond any need, for the sake of filling an existential void with more hours of senseless employment to produce more items of senseless consumption, plus the avoidance of sharing as the true cure for poverty. The sins of present injustice are to be washed away in a sea of future abundance vouchsafed by the amazing grace of compound interest and technological razzle-dazzle. To maintain exponential growth we need fission power. If we cannot share, if we cannot even conceive of having enough, then we must grow and pay the costs of fission power. "Men of intemperate minds cannot be free. Their passions forge their fetters."

As argued in Chapter 6, the so-called cost-benefit analyses used to justify fission power on "objective" grounds are, at best, arbitrary and, at worst, conscious deceptions. One of the leading experts on cost-benefit analysis states:

> It is my belief that benefit-cost analysis cannot answer the most important policy questions associated with the desirability of developing a large-scale, fission-based economy. To expect it to do so is to ask it to bear a burden it cannot sustain. This is so because the questions are of a deep *ethical* character. Benefit-cost analyses certainly cannot solve such questions and may well obscure them [Kneese, 1973, p. 1].

Another example of the misuse of cost-benefit analysis (or even straight economic calculation) comes in the dollar comparisons of solar-energy costs with the cost of energy from fossil fuels. At the current margin, fossil fuels are cheaper for most uses. Do we then conclude that solar energy is uneconomic? Not unless a good move in checkers is also a good move in chess. Different rules of the game are involved. Living off temporary geological capital is just a different ballgame from living off permanent solar income. The latter game accepts permanence and ecological discipline as rules of the game; the former does not. Of course, it is easier to live off capital than off income, for as long as the capital lasts. That hardly need be disputed! The real issue is not economic, but ethical: should we undertake the discipline of living on income, or should we just consume capital while it lasts? The choice between oil and gas (both fossil fuels), or the choice between photovoltaic and biomass conversion (both solar) is the proper domain of economic calculation. But the choice between solar and fossil fuels is of a different order, more "heroic" or ethical in nature than "economic" in the usual sense of marginal calculation.

Why do we insist on ignoring the ethical character of so many major economic decisions? Why this compulsion to substitute mechanical calculation for responsible value judgment? Perhaps it's because our mechanistic paradigm has reduced values and ethics to mere matters of personal taste, about which it is useless to argue. Quality involves difficult judgments and imposes self-definition and responsibility. Quantity involves merely counting and arithmetical operations that give everyone the same answer and impose no responsibility. Thus university deans make promotion decisions by counting words published and number of citations rather than by attempting a qualitative judgment about the true worth of a scholar's work, which is bound to cause some disagreement. Counting is an easy way out—a retreat from the responsibility of thinking and evaluating quality.

An especially important role in the quantitative short-circuiting of responsibility is played by randomness. Randomness is, in fact, an excellent moral scapegoat. Consider that some 50,000 Americans are killed annually by the automobile. Suppose that the specific identities of these people were known in advance. To save 50,000 specific individuals, we might lower speed limits drastically and return to bicycles for local transportation. To save 50,000 unknown, randomly determined individuals, we do nothing. If a soldier kills specific women and children at close range with a rifle we are horrified; if a bomber pilot kills many more women and children, whose numbers are predictable but whose identities are unknown before the fact, we are only vaguely upset. In eighteenth-century England people who abhorred infanticide nevertheless consigned unwanted children to foundling hospitals where the death rate was known to be exceedingly high. "Thou shalt not kill thy specific identified brother, but mayest murder random persons at will, in order to achieve thy 'progress,' however shallowly defined." How much economic growth is based on this expanded version of the shorter, less sophisticated commandment? I would not argue that we should never do anything that will predictably increase deaths (since then we should not even have been born), but only that such decisions are ethical, existential, and heroic, not economic. We cannot throw responsibility for such collective existential decisions on to the moral scapegoat of randomness with its phony numerical calculations.

The way in which these phony calculations work is via "economies of ignorance and scale," as John U. G. Adams (1974) has scathingly illustrated. Consider what happens when we apply the concept of Pareto efficiency to the cost-benefit analysis of a project involving the predictable loss of life. Let V_j be the compensatory money payment to individual j to make him indifferent to the proposed project. That is, if j is to be hurt by the project, then V_j is what he must be paid to accept it, and it carries a minus sign; if j is to be benefited, V_j is what he must be paid to forgo the project, and it carries a plus sign. If the algebraic sum for all individuals (ΣV_j) is positive, then there is a potential Pareto improvement; that is, the winners could compensate the losers and still be better off.

Suppose now that individual j would be killed as a result of the project. Consistency with the Pareto criterion requires that he be compensated for the loss of life according to his own valuation. Since most people would put a very high or even infinite cash value on the remaining years of their lives, the result is that any project involving predictable loss of specific lives would fail the test of Pareto improvement and could not be justified by cost-benefit analysis. This is so even if more lives are saved than lost by the project, since there is no way for those saved to compensate those killed, and any cancelling out by the analyst of lives saved against lives lost violates the Pareto rule of no interpersonal comparisons.

It is obvious that many projects justified by cost-benefit analysis do result in the predictable loss of life. This is true for any projects that increase air or ground traffic, radiation exposure, or air pollution, for example. What allows cost-benefit analysts to "justify" such projects? It is essentially the fact that we never know in advance the identities of the specific people who will be killed. The result is that we never have to compensate *anyone* for his certain loss of life but instead we must compensate *everyone* for the additional *risk* to which *he* is exposed as a result of the project (Mishan, 1971). If the population is large, the individual risk becomes very small, perhaps below the *minimum sensible,* so that everyone is indifferent to such a negligible risk and no compensation at all is required, and the project passes with honors.

Note that *in theory* we have passed from a case requiring infinite compensation to a case requiring zero compensation, simply by *throwing away information,* that is, by remaining ignorant of the specific identities of the victims. This is odd, to say the least. In practice, of course, we never have the specific identities of victims beforehand, but that fact does not resolve the theoretical anomaly. The population subset most at risk could often be specified but usually is not, so that the risk often appears more diluted than it really is. Many economists would treat the zero-compensation case as the more rational social decision and give thanks for the veil of ignorance on which approval of the project depends. But then we must say that in this case extra information, even if freely given, would lead to a *less rational* social decision. No one can be happy living with that paradox. Nor are we comfortable with the fact that a mere increase in population size could reverse the decision by diluting the per-person risk to a negligible threshold. Adams sarcastically calls these effects "economies of ignorance and of scale" (1974).

These economies of ignorance and scale are so vexing to common sense that we are led to look for a false step in the reasoning that gave rise to them. I believe that there is a false step, which allows randomness to function as a moral scapegoat. In the change from known to unknown identities of victims, it was assumed that this *logically* implied a switch from compensating some individuals for certain death to compensating each individual for the additional risk to which *he* is exposed. But this does not logically follow from the mere introduction of randomly determined identity. What follows logically is only that we must compensate all individuals for the *certainty* that a predictable number of their community will be killed, identities yet to be determined. This is not the same as compensating each person for the increased risk that *he* will be killed. To arrive at the latter proposition, we need to make the assumption that people care about only their own skins. Only with that extra assumption is the latter proposition equivalent to the former.

If people care only about their own skins, then there can be no community in the first place; however, assuming there were, the mere introduction of randomness could be sufficient to enable a life-taking project to meet the Pareto test. But if we go to the other extreme of an assumed community of complete brotherly love, in which the first rule was "love your neighbor as yourself" and the second was "everyone is everyone else's neighbor" (not exactly novel ethical ideals), then *each* individual would have to be paid an infinite compensation to make him indifferent to the sacrificial deaths of his unidentified brothers. Instead of passing the Pareto test as a result of ignorance, the project would fail by an infinitely greater margin than it did in the first case, because now *everyone* requires infinite compensation, not just the victims. The cost-benefit analyst cannot make interpersonal comparisons, but citizens can and do in all cases. It is the differing criteria by which these comparisons are made by citizens in evaluating their own welfare that is crucial. The key issue is one of ethics, not economics, much less randomness.

In sum, it was not the random element or veil of ignorance that by some mathematical sleight of hand reduced an infinite compensatory payment to zero. Rather, it was the tacit assumption that people care only about their own skins. Admittedly, people are not saints, but they are not totally selfish either. The upshot is that random variables do not solve moral problems, at least not for anyone who is capable of feeling brotherhood for a random person. Cost-benefit analysis should be used to illuminate rather than to obscure moral responsibility.

Decisions involving predictable loss and gain in human lifetime are existentially difficult and cannot be made easy by resorting to phony calculation. No doubt such decisions are sometimes unavoidable, but when they become too frequent is it perhaps indicative of some deeper defect in our institutions and values that we should so often be faced with such impossible decisions? Maybe it is a symptom of having pursued growth too singlemindedly—of having painted ourselves into a corner from which there is no ethical way out.

The recognition of the enormous costs of economic growth is, of course, not new. The British economist A. C. Pigou quotes Dickinson's *Letters of John Chinaman:*

> In short, the attention of the German people was so concentrated on the idea of learning to *do,* that they did not care, as in former times, for learning to *be.* Nor does Germany stand alone in this charge; as witness the following description of modern England written by an Englishman from the standpoint

of an Oriental spectator. "By your works you may be known. Your triumphs in the mechanical arts are the obverse of your failure in all that calls for spiritual insight. Machines of every kind you can make and use to perfection; but you cannot build a house or write a poem, or paint a picture; still less can you worship or aspire . . . Your outer man as well as your inner is dead; you are blind and deaf. Ratiocination has taken the place of perception; and your whole life is an infinite syllogism from premises you have not examined to conclusions you have not anticipated or willed. Everywhere means, nowhere an end. Society is a huge engine and that engine itself out of gear. Such is the picture your civilization presents to my imagination." There is, of course, exaggeration in this indictment; but there is also truth. At all events it brings out vividly the point which is here at issue; that efforts devoted to the production of people who are good instruments may involve a failure to produce people who are good men [Pigou, 1932, p. 13].

If Pigou were writing about the United States in the 1970s rather than England in the 1930s, would he consider "John Chinaman's" indictment an exaggeration or an understatement? Certainly, economic theory has in fact become one infinite syllogism from unexamined premises to unrealistic conclusions. Ratiocination, preferably in the form of mathematical manipulation and electronic data processing, has taken the place of perception and understanding of basic concepts. All of this flurry of symbols and printouts lends an air of scientific respectability to unimaginative demonstrations of the obvious and painstaking documentations of the insignificant.

Arthur J. Cordell has commented perceptively on the data barrage:

> Today information can be transmitted at 240 words per minute via teletype. It is estimated that computer to computer transmission will soon be at 86,000 words per minute. Add to this the barrage of information beamed via TV and radio and consider that human beings can process only about 250 to 1,000 words per minute. In an attempt to understand ever more by generating more information we overload our capacity to integrate or assimilate what we are doing. The barrage of information has led society to a condition where it is "data rich but perceptually poor." We have all the numbers but can't seem to make sense out of them.
>

> The quest for information appears to lead to a condition which could be described as "information neurosis." We can't get enough primarily because we don't know what we are looking for or why we want it. We just have a vague feeling that more information is better than less information [Cordell, 1972].

What is true for information is true for other economic goods—namely, we cannot get enough primarily because we do not know what we are looking for or why we want it. As argued in Chapter 2, ultimate means have been treated as if they were limitless, and the Ultimate End as if it were unreal. Or as "John Chinaman" said, "Everywhere means, nowhere an end." The economy is still a "huge engine and that engine itself out of gear." What is new is that the engine has become so power-ful that it now can destroy the biosphere wholesale, rather than just piecemeal, as in Pigou's time. Hypertrophied power is in search of atrophied purpose, and the power is sufficient for self-destruction. It is utterly insane to go on increasing power while denying the claims of right purpose.

The steady-state paradigm is far from a sufficient answer to the question of right purpose. It is merely a strategy to correct some past mistakes before we are destroyed by their cumulative effects. It recognizes the error of omission in our past treatment of ultimate means and of the Ultimate End. It attempts to establish institutions that do not depend on continual growth. It recognizes that ultimate means are scarce in an absolute sense, and that the Ultimate End is such that, beyond a certain level, it is not served by further physical production.

Whenever life denies us the good we had expected, it seems to present us with an alternative good we did not expect. If we think only of the unfulfilled expectation, then we will overlook and waste the unexpected possibility of fulfillment. Although we are being denied the rather shallow expected good of continuing economic growth, life is offering us the unexpected alternative of stability on the material plane, which will free our freshest energies for growth in those infinite moral and spiritual dimensions that intersect our finite lifespan and its finite material base. To stubbornly persist in chasing the expected good at the expense of the offered good would be the greatest possible folly—a folly that the Prophet Isaiah warned about some three millennia ago: "Why do you spend your money for that which is not bread, and your labor for that which does not satisfy? . . . Incline your ear and come to me; hear, that your soul may live" (Isa. 55:2). Sufficient wealth efficiently maintained and allocated, and equitably distributed—not maximum production—is the proper economic aim.

REFERENCES

Abrahamson, Dean E. Statement to the Minnesota Pollution Control Agency, Hearing on Proposed Nuclear Moratorium Legislation, December 12, 1974 (mimeographed).

Adams, John U. G. ". . . And How Much for Your Grandmother?" *Environment and Planning*, Vol. 6, 1974.

Cordell, Arthur J. "The Socio-Economics of Technological Progress." Paper presented to the Faculty of Science Lecture Series on Human Environment: Problems and Prospects, Carleton University, February 23, 1973, mimeographed.

Hayes, Denis. *Energy: The Case for Conservation*. Washington, D.C.: World-watch Institute, 1976.

Kneese, Allen V. "The Faustian Bargain," *Resources,* September 1973, 1–5.

Mishan, E. J. "Evaluation of Life and Limb: A Theoretical Approach," *Journal of Political Economy,* July/August 1971.

Ophuls, William. "Locke's Paradigm Lost: The Environmental Crisis and Collapse of Laissez Faire Politics." Paper delivered at the 1973 Annual Meeting of the American Political Science Association, New Orleans, September 1973, mimeographed.

Pigou, A. C. *The Economics of Welfare,* 4th ed. London: Macmillan, 1932; reprinted in 1962.

Ruskin, John. "Unto This Last," in Lloyd J. Hubenka, ed., *Four Essays on the First Principles of Political Economy.* Lincoln: University of Nebraska Press, 1967. Originally published in 1860.

INDEX